Domesticity with a Difference

DOMESTICITY
with a DIFFERENCE

The Nonfiction of
Catharine Beecher, Sarah J.Hale,
Fanny Fern, and Margaret Fuller

Nicole Tonkovich

University Press of Mississippi / *Jackson*

The paper in this book meets the guidelines for permanence
and durability of the Committee on Production Guidelines
for Book Longevity of the Council on Library Resources.

Library of Congress Cataloging-in-Publication Data
Tonkovich, Nicole.
    Domesticity with a difference : the nonfiction of Catharine Beecher,
Sarah J. Hale, Fanny Fern, and Margaret Fuller / Nicole
Tonkovich.
        p.   cm.
    Includes bibliographical references (p.) and index.
        ISBN: 978-1-60473-848-3
    1. American prose literature—Women authors—History and
criticism.   2. American prose literature—19th century—History and
criticism.   3. Women—United States—History—19th century—
Historiography.   4. Women and journalism—United States—
History—19th century.   5. Hale, Sarah Josepha Buell, 1788–1879—
Prose.   6. Beecher, Catharine Esther, 1800–1878.   7. Fuller,
Margaret, 1810–1850—Prose.   8. Fern, Fanny, 1811–1872—Prose.
9. Sex role in literature.   10. Marriage in literature.   11. Family
in literature.   12. Home in literature.   I. Title.
PS152.T66   1997
814'.3099287—dc21   96-53363
                                                                   CIP
    British Library Cataloging-in-Publication data available

In memory of my parents:
Ila Jensen Tonkovich (1923–1994)
Vincent N. Tonkovich (1917–1995)

Contents

Acknowledgments

For their support to me as I worked on this book, my most sincere thanks go to my colleagues in the Department of Literature at the University of California, San Diego. I cannot imagine a friendlier, more accommodating, and more comfortable intellectual environment in which to work. Roy Harvey Pearce gave this project his encouragement even before I joined the department and has continued to be a mentor and friend. Colleagues who were members of my writing group—Beth Holmgren, Stephanie Jed, and Pasquale Verdicchio—gave incisive critique and support. Other colleagues listened to ideas, offered their own, and read chapters and complete drafts, including Frances Foster, Kathryn Shevelow, Michael Davidson, and Susan Kirkpatrick. Rosaura Sánchez has been a marvelously supportive chair. My particular regard and thanks go to two of my first graduate students, Carolyn Haynes and Shawn Smith, for support, close readings, relevant sources, and editorial advice. More recently, Ed Cutler and Christina Accomando have joined me in stimulating tutorial discussions. My research assistants included Matt Worcester, Madeleine Jacot, Amy Hoffman, Ashley Hoffman, Jennifer Hoffman, and Fraser Pilkington.

The preparation of this manuscript has introduced me to many good friends in the scholarly community whose support I am delighted to acknowledge as well. Greg Clark and Michael Halloran helped me see how my *Godey's* research fit a larger rhetorical history; Catherine Hobbs became a valuable discussant about women's education; Barbara White offered archival sources on Sarah Josepha Hale; Sherbrooke Rogers generously directed me to Hale sources; audience members and respondents at American Studies Association, Modern Language Association, the Conference on College Composition and Communication, and the Stowe-Day Society helped me refine insights. Staff members and colleagues at the American Antiquarian Society's Summer Seminar in the History of the Book offered early and invaluable direction.

I have had substantial financial support toward the research involved in this book from the University of Utah and from the University of California, San Diego. This support has included fellowships, travel grants, and sabbatical leave time.

My intellectual debts began accumulating at the University of Utah, where a much earlier version of this book began as a dissertation under the direction of Stephen Tatum. Professors Susan Miller, Christine Oravec, Karen Lawrence, and William Mulder offered substantial encouragement and help. The dissertation benefited most substantially from the friendship and theoretical sophistication—as well as the irreverence—of Marianne Barnett.

I am most grateful to archivists and librarians whose interest in this project and professional expertise helped immensely. Guiseppe Bisacchia and Roberta Zhongi of the Boston Public Library made working with their sources a pleasure. Gary Wait of the Connecticut Historical Society generously shared sources and insights about Nancy Johnson. Lynne Templeton Brickley also graciously responded to my questions with valuable information about Sarah Pierce; Litchfield, Connecticut; and Litchfield-Cincinnati connections. I especially thank the staff of the Stowe-Day Foundation, including Jo Blatti, Diana Royce, and particularly Suzanne Zack for their good humor, friendship, and help.

For permissions to quote archival material I thank the Boston Public Library, the Cincinnati Historical Society, the Connecticut Historical Society, the Newport Richards Free Library, the Arthur and Elizabeth Schlesinger Library on the History of Women in America, Smith College, the Stowe-Day Foundation, Vassar College, and the Watkinson Library of Trinity College. Portions of several chapters of this book have been published in slightly different forms. I am grateful to the editors of *Legacy* and to Southern Illinois University Press and the University Press of Virginia for permission to use these materials.

Seetha A-Srinivasan has been a most helpful and encouraging editor.

Friends and family deserve the most thanks for their making sure this project became a reality. I could not have finished the project without the kind counsel of Miriam Iosupovici, who believed in me. Freddie Fenster and Richard Watson of the Wildwood Inn were ideal hosts. My husband, Gary Hoffman, was an invaluable reader and computer guru; my daughters, Jennifer, Ashley, and Amy were patient, sympathetic, and interested. This project has been part of their lives for so long that they grew old enough to help with editorial matters and research. My brother and sister-in-law, Kevin and Pamela Tonkovich, offered refuge and love in the darkest times.

I completed this manuscript during a period when both my parents were seriously ill and died. They taught me to love learning, to read, and to write, and to persist. This book is dedicated to their memory.

ECCENTRIC
DOMESTICITY

Writing for the *New York Ledger* in 1867, Fanny Fern, that newspaper's most popular columnist, declared, "[A] woman who wrote, used to be considered a sort of monster—At this day it is difficult to find one who does not write, or has not written, or who has not, at least, a strong desire to do so. Grid-irons and darning-needles are getting monotonous. A part of their time the women of to-day are content to devote to their consideration when necessary; but you will rarely find one—at least among women who *think*—who does not silently rebel against allowing them a monopoly" (*Ledger* 10 Aug. 1867). Here Fern has written a miniature history of women's literacy in the first half of the nineteenth century. She refers briefly to an era in which writing for public consumption was held to "unsex" a woman, making her into a kind of monster. Yet by 1867, Fern is able to claim a significant change in attitude toward writing women. Using overtly economic terms, she insists that domestic concerns do not monopolize the mind of a thinking woman. The very tools employed in the domestic tasks of sewing and cooking have come to suggest writing and typesetting, as well. Fern's assertion that domesticity no longer monopolizes the time of thinking women thus does not imply the overthrow of domesticity, but a different way of dividing its tasks. That *thinking* women may selectively practice domesticity implies that nonthinking women attend to its daily details. In thus naming the different approach of literate women to domesticity, Fern implies a hierarchy of women, with those who *think* at the apex.

By entitling this book *Domesticity with a Difference*, I follow Fern's implication that writing women in the mid-nineteenth-century United States are not contained within a "domestic sphere," as it has conventionally been understood. Rather, I argue that they move among a number of subject positions constituted in the interplay among family, school, and community. Within these three locations, the writing woman held an ambiguous status, initially construed as an aberration, then given the literacy that fueled her desire to write, and finally accorded a different status both as a domestic subject and as a willful and desirous writer who redefined what domesticity might mean for "a woman who wrote."

Whereas Fern leaves the reasons for this change unspecified, I trace how this different attitude toward domesticity and writing developed. Seeking a more detailed understanding of women who wrote in the nineteenth century, I have focused on nonfictional texts written by four of the century's most prolific and successful professional authors—Sarah Josepha Hale, Catharine Beecher, Fanny Fern (Sarah Willis Parton), and Margaret Fuller—whose purpose it was to prescribe, to categorize, and to (re)define domestic behaviors. Building on important foundational studies that have demonstrated a major political effect of women's fiction writing to be the inscription of a democracy of women whose similarity as domestic subjects overrode their political differences,[1] I will emphasize the differences—based primarily on class entitlement—these writers inscribed *among* women in their nonfiction, differences often articulated along the axis of domestic behavior.

Those differences suggest several other paradoxes that characterize these women's lives and writings. Their domestic writings described nuclear, suburban, and self-sufficient families while their own domestic arrangements were corporate, urban, and impermanent. They articulated procedures for housework and homemaking, yet their writing was made possible by salaried domestics. To married white women these writers prescribed domestic stability and reticence; but they, like their servants, were peripatetic and loquacious. Advocates of women's education, they urged other women to become teachers, while they abandoned teaching for more lucrative pursuits. Thus, I will argue, because these women were important constructors of domesticity, their differences from the life they prescribed demand attention.

Such paradoxes point to another group of texts foundational to this study—life writing. Although this study is biographically based, its major purpose is not to construct definitive biography. Rather, by reading multiple and often contradictory (auto)biographical accounts, and by trying to discover the implications of their differences from each other and from the more public urgings of their writers, I have intentionally refused to inscribe coherence on sometimes unruly subjects. Rather, I have used (auto)biography to explore these writers' class privilege and to measure the difference between their own textual representation of family background and the domesticity they prescribed for other women.

By studying a group of women who were contemporary with each other, who promoted, critiqued, publicized, and interfered with each other's agendas, I delineate a variety of domestic practice in an era whose women writers were once thought to have inscribed "woman" as "hostage in the home" (Welter 151). Attending to the biographies of four women has allowed me to consider a spectrum of privilege among families loosely classified as middle-class; to trace the changes in the theory and practice of women's education over three generations; to show how family, class, and educational privilege are intertwined; and to consider how writing women are also the product of their larger communities. These writers' texts on domesticity address community norms, both honoring and modifying them to yield larger spaces for different practices and configurations of domesticity.

The relations of these women go beyond historical concurrence, however, to demonstrate the relation of teacher to student, of mentor to mentee, of reviewer to author, biographer to subject, and friend to friend. Catharine Beecher and Sarah Josepha Hale, the older of the four, were among the nineteenth century's earliest domestic theorists and proponents of higher education for women. Although Beecher never married, her *Treatise on Domestic Economy* became a best-seller and was used as a textbook in women's seminaries. It outlined a rationalized system of domestic management designed to elevate housework to the status of a profession, establishing the seminary-educated domestic woman as the manager of subordinate and illiterate domestic underlings. Hale, a widow left with the responsibility of supporting her five children, turned to writing as a means of earning a living. Her efforts earned her an editorial position with the century's most successful women's magazine, *Godey's Lady's Book*. Here her major goal was to publicize institutions of women's education nationwide; as part of this agenda, she supported the educational efforts of her friend and associate, Catharine Beecher. Hale currently has notoriety as the woman whose magazine institutionalized and publicized the "piety, purity, submissiveness, and domesticity" taken to constitute an ideology of True Womanhood (Welter 152). However, the entirety of Hale's journalism published over her forty-year career as the magazine's literary editress establishes her as a major, if conservative, advocate of (white, literate, and middle-class) women's increasing legal rights, their involvement in national political issues, and their identity as a national constituency with distinctly feminine agendas.

The careers of Fanny Fern and Margaret Fuller, a generation younger, overlapped with those of Hale and Beecher from about 1835 to 1870. Fern was a student at Hartford Female Seminary, where she was taught to write by Catharine Beecher and her sister Harriet. Following her husband's death and a disastrous second marriage, Fern turned to journalism as a means of self-support, quickly becoming the nation's most popular newspaper columnist. As such, she molded public opinion about public and private educational enterprises while describing and justifying a range of behaviors eccentric to the domestic sphere. Finally, to this group of women whose writing has conventionally been classified as domestic or sentimental, I add a woman usually not included under this rubric, Margaret Fuller, who remained unmarried and childless until late in her life. Known primarily for her association with the transcendental circle in Boston and Cambridge, Fuller wrote the United States' first feminist manifesto, *Woman in the Nineteenth Century.* Although that book has emerged as her most important, attending solely to it gives a skewed picture of Fuller as a protofeminist that is significantly modified in her autobiographical writings and in her journalism regarding education and domesticity. By including her in this group, I will demonstrate that any woman who wrote at this period was considered, as Fern's paragraph demonstrates, to be always already domestic.

How writing women exceeded these textually constructed domestic spheres while maintaining the illusion of their containment within them is the central issue of this book. The figure of separate spheres has recently come under close literary and historical scrutiny best exemplified by the work of Linda Kerber, who has argued that although nineteenth-century writers invoked the notion of separate public and private spheres, the force of this construction was primarily as a trope, an ideological construct taken too literally by twentieth-century scholars. Such uncritical acceptance has obscured the overlapping ideas and interdependence of these "spheres" in theory, practice, and text. Thus, I intend to show the extent of the contradictory behaviors made possible under this trope. Specifically, this book considers the economic benefits that accrued to domestic theorists as a result of inventing women as a reading audience and analyzes the structures of class and ethnic/racial privilege that make ideal domesticity possible. Thus, I posit the existence of a number of active counterdiscourses to True Womanhood, political positions that were not necessarily aligned with suffragism or with other organized women's movements, positions advanced by some of the same women credited with (or blamed for) promulgating the notion of separate spheres.

I have relied in the main on nonfictional texts because of their announced intent to be direct, objective, partisan, scientific, and/or prescriptive. However, I do not see these texts as transparent. I consider nonfiction to be as carefully crafted as fiction, although in the nineteenth century the trajectories of novels and nonfiction differ. While novels were often proscribed as appropriate reading for women, journalism, self-improvement books, devotional literature—the kinds of texts these women wrote—enjoyed cultural sanction. These writers bolstered the already-privileged status of nonfiction by soliciting and displaying social and institutional support of their agendas. They presented themselves as the representatives of community opinion by appending to their books testimonials and endorsements from clergy, socialites, educators, and legislators, and by aligning themselves with the political and community groups represented by the journals for which they wrote.

Hale, Beecher, Fern, and Fuller, although women of different generations, nevertheless share significant similarities that yield a distinctive profile of some of the nation's earliest professional women writers.[2] Daughters of families who already claimed a social identity founded in literate privilege, they were prepared by fathers or by paternal figures to assume socially significant roles as writers. Their fathers represent a spectrum of professional entitlement that ranges from clergy and legislators to merchants and publishers. All four writers lived in loosely configured corporate families closely affiliated with their surrounding communities. Each woman's family benefited from the labor of domestic workers. As adults none of these women wrote and kept a traditional domestic establishment concurrently. Two did not marry; two became writers after their husbands had died and their children were otherwise cared for. All four, therefore, enjoyed significant physical, psychic, and financial independence.

This book begins by delineating the domestic, educational, and community matrix within which these women learned to write. It then outlines the differences of class encoded in Beecher's and Fuller's, Hale's and Fern's prescriptions for the identity of the domestic woman—her name (and thus her family identification) and her community standing. Although these writers advocated education for women, they also sought to limit the class mobility such schooling afforded. Particularly they deplored the ability of an increasing number of self-taught women to imitate the dress, behavior, and speech appropriate to ladies. These chapters demonstrate that although these domestic behaviors are claimed as self-evident, they are presented in class-coded terms that exempt a few highly literate women from domestic norms and grant them the right to practice domesticity with a difference.

In the book's final chapters, I demonstrate how these writers sought community sanction for their revisions of school, the domestic establishment, and the composition of the nuclear family, at once separating and delineating the functions of women within them according to their ability to *think*, to use Fern's term. They removed schools from the strictures of normative domesticity while allowing for educational and child-rearing functions to be contained within a family unit not dominated by a patriarch and independent of the gender-encoded economies that delimited heterosexual marriage.

This book thus uses literacy and social class to articulate the differences among the (white, upper-class) women who defined and practiced ideal domesticity. As a literary and cultural studies scholar, I bring to this work several assumptions. I assume that the texts these women wrote, although they claim to be nonfictional and transparent, are as carefully crafted and as deserving of close textual scrutiny as are their fictions. Therefore, I bring into conversation with each other a multitude of canonical and noncanonical, fictional and nonfictional, publicly circulated and privately circumscribed texts, endeavoring to understand how and why each of their stories about domestic women differs from the others. Like Joan W. Scott, I presume that "identities and experiences are variable phenomena . . . discursively organized in particular contexts or configurations" (*Gender* 5). Thus I seek to understand the texts written by Beecher, Hale, Fuller and Fern in terms of the gendered identities they prescribe for a variety of domestic women. I have found immensely suggestive, as well, the work of feminist philosopher Judith Butler, whose work demonstrates that gender is a discursively mediated performance. Hence, I have sought to discover how these four women scripted, costumed, and wrote the stage directions for the performance of gendered behaviors comprising domesticity in the mid-nineteenth-century United States. This study thus reinserts issues of sex and gender into political history, showing the connection of the gendered body to the body politic by arguing that while politics determine domestic configurations, domestic writing can and does resist political constructions of home, school, and family. Beecher and Hale, Fern and Fuller show those configurations might be honored at the same time they are revised to accommodate a different domestic practice.

Domesticity with a Difference

Chapter One

HER FATHER'S
BEST BOY

Catharine Beecher and Margaret Fuller

On 30 September 1845, Margaret Fuller reviewed Catharine Beecher's *Duty of American Women to Their Country* for the *New-York Daily Tribune*. In this review, she notes especially that Beecher had proposed a reasonable solution to the problem of how single, orphaned, and widowed women might support themselves economically. According to Fuller, while critics have objected that her own *Woman in the Nineteenth Century*, published two years earlier, "exhibit[ed] ills without specifying any practical means for their remedy," Beecher's book offered "not only such a principle, but an external method for immediate use" (*Woman in the Nineteenth Century* 1855, 226–27). Fuller's generous review suggests that she and Beecher shared domestic concerns. However, their similarities in this regard have, in the intervening 150 years, been obscured as a result of the vagaries of literary history and canonicity. In fact, their interest in the economic plight of single (white, upper-class) women is only one of many issues on which their views coincide. Without a doubt, the similarities of their family backgrounds and education undergirded their adult concerns with women's place in their families, in the schools dedicated to their education, and as educated professionals in their communities.

Catharine Beecher (1800–1878)

When Catharine Beecher was about five years old, Lyman Beecher opened a small school in his home, taught by his wife, Roxana, who was assisted by her sister Mary. The curriculum included courses in "the higher English branches, besides French, drawing, painting, and embroidery"; Lyman himself "took great interest in the school, and used to help about subjects for composition" (*Autobiography* 1:98). The school prospered, enabling Beecher to meet the expenses of his rapidly multiplying family. Catharine supplemented her father's "official" account in a separate and privately circulated manuscript entitled "My Autobiography for the Entertainment of Family Friends," which includes the telling detail that "while teaching school mother hired an old lady called by us 'Aunty Jones' for a housekeeper. She was a black, easy, old soul liking snuff abundantly" (4; Katharine S. Day Collection, Stowe-Day).

Catharine Beecher's life, as it can be reconstructed from published autobiographical reminiscences, was from early childhood associated with education. Family, school, and community overlapped as sites of instruction offered as a part of capital exchange. Family needs—in this case, financial pressure—called forth an educational enterprise, which, in turn, drew its support from many segments of the community: relatives, Lyman's congregation, families from the surrounding towns, and a hired woman of color. The surviving accounts of this school are the result of a similar collaboration. The chapter of Lyman Beecher's *Autobiography* in which the school is recalled is a textual pastiche, a print colloquy among Lyman's first-person narration, his daughters' written recollections figured as a dramatic dialogue, and two letters written by his wife's sisters. Catharine's contributions to her father's autobiography, in turn, are colored by her concurrent work at revising her phenomenally successful *Treatise on Domestic Economy.* Thus, an attempt to reconstruct the familial influences on Catharine Beecher's literacy needs to account for the public nature of Lyman Beecher's ministerial family and the intertextual agendas of the sources that constitute that family's history.

Regardless of the textual source it is apparent that although the Beecher family was never wealthy, its members enjoyed unusual advantages. Lyman Beecher had taken his degree at Yale in 1797, at a time when less than 1 percent of the population attended college (Vinovskis and Bernard 859). Roxana Foote had also received a remarkably complete informal education that included instruction in French. All the Beecher children who contributed memoirs to their father's *Autobiography* attested to the cultural richness of their home environment. According to Catharine, "some of the most vivid of my early recollections are of the discussions between father and mother and Aunt Mary at table. They read the Christian Observer . . . and such works noticed in it as they could procure. An Encyclopedia, presented to Aunt Mary by an English gentleman whose two daughters boarded with us was mother's constant resource" (*Autobiography* 1:100). The family also received books from Roxana's seafaring brother Samuel, who, whenever he visited, brought with him "a stock of new books, which he and Aunt Mary read aloud . . . in the family circle" (*Autobiography* 1:161). The Beecher parents exemplified intellectual attitudes for their children, their household functioning as a node in a network of actively curious associates who mutually enriched each other in the Beecher parlor. Lyman, Roxana, and their children shared their home with any number of permanent or semipermanent boarders, including servants, students from the neighboring Litchfield Female Academy and Litchfield Law School, and visiting relatives. Among these numerous adults, Catharine's reminiscences make clear, her father dominated her childhood. Perhaps to compensate for his disappointment that his firstborn child was a girl, perhaps because he had fewer preconceptions about how to raise this first child, Lyman Beecher had high expectations of his daughter and encouraged her to identify with him. She recalls, "my father never in his life praised me, although he used to say I was the best boy he had" (Rugoff 314). Lyman Beecher gave his first child his exclusive attention, taking her with him on pastoral visits and encouraging her to emulate him. She recalls, "I was his constant companion" (Sklar, *Catharine Beecher* 3).

The structure of Catharine Beecher's childhood memoirs is as significant as the biographical facts they document. Here she presents her family as exemplars of the domesticity she prescribed in her professional life. Her contributions to Lyman's *Autobiography,* for example, emphasize his public administrative skills, while diminishing Roxana's intellectual activity, often by figuring it as a component of her domestic pursuits. Lyman Beecher recalls that Roxana taught the "higher English branches" in the family school; Catharine's private account, however, has it that she "taught only the primary branches" (*Autobiography* 1:98; "My Autobiography" 3). Catharine repeatedly presents Roxana as a reader, a consumer of intellectual information, whereas Roxana's own writings suggest that her intellectual activity did not always relate to household concerns. Indeed, she complained to her sister-in-law Esther that her reading and study had been reduced by her increasing maternal duties, including in the same letter the decidedly unmaternal observation that "the fixed alkalies are metallic oxyds. I first saw the notice in the 'Christian Observer.' I have since seen it in an 'Edinburgh Review.' The former mentioned that the metals have been obtained by means of the galvanic battery; the latter mentions another, and, they say, better mode. I think this is all the knowledge I have obtained in the whole circle of arts and sciences of late; if you have been more fortunate, pray let me reap the benefit" (*Autobiography* 1:168–69). This letter is included in a section of the *Autobiography* not written by Catharine.

Significantly, Roxana does not relate her reading either to her school or to her domestic responsibilities. Although it is quite likely that Roxana's intellectual life became increasingly circumscribed by the demands of her increasing family, such documents argue that it was not altogether lost. It is significant, however, that Catharine mentions her mother's interest in chemistry only as a component of her teaching: "I remember how mother and Aunt Mary studied Lavoisier's Chemistry together. Chemistry was a new science then, and a constant subject of discussion. They tried a great many experiments too, and sometimes with most ludicrous results" (*Autobiography* 1:98). Not only does she implicitly devalue Roxana's study by the remark that chemistry was a subject of general intellectual interest, but she also judges her mother's and aunt's experiments as amateur and slightly silly.

Catharine figures all the feminine members of this household as objects of Lyman's activity, for Lyman's part in her memoirs is that of the active educator, producer of knowledge, overseer, and manager. The hagiographic tone in which his activities are presented, it might be argued, is defensible in the context of an autobiographical project. Yet Catharine's portions of the *Autobiography* seem to exceed simple praise; as I will explain more fully below, they are part of her larger attempt to establish her family as the exemplars for her *Treatise*. Catharine recalls, for example, that her father was never "satisfied with his writings till he had read them over to mother and Aunt Mary or Aunt Esther. By this intellectual companionship our house became *in reality a school* of the highest kind, in which he was all the while exerting a powerful influence upon the mind and character of his children" (*Autobiography* 1:104; emphasis added). Catharine's interpretation of Lyman's action does not emphasize her mother's and aunt's importance as the critics of his work. Instead it establishes a contrast between the "family school" led by Roxana and Mary and the more authentic education that happened as a result of Lyman's powerful intellect. The notion of intellectual parity and respect for the opinions of his wife and sister-in-law, strongly implied by Lyman's actions, become by Catharine's interpretation a demonstration of his dominant "influence" on his children.

Despite Roxana Beecher's indisputable qualifications to offer instruction beyond the usual basic reading and mathematics associated with dame schools, in Catharine's accounts, Lyman Beecher dominates the home school. While she briefly dismisses Roxana's and Mary's chemistry experiments, she provides this most vivid and detailed memory of her father: "Sometimes, in school-hours, when he had got tired writing, he would come out of his study and go into the sitting-room under the schoolroom, and begin to play the violin as loud as he could. Pretty soon he would hear the schoolroom door open. . . . Mother would come into the room, quietly walk up to him—not a word said by either of them, only a funny twinkle of the eye—and would take the violin out of his hands, . . . and lay it on her table in the schoolroom" (*Autobiography* 1:102).

Although this incident can be read as establishing Roxana's womanly authority, its silences are gendered. The right of disruption is a masculine imperative: Lyman's silences are those of writing, and of his choice to cease disrupting the school. Roxana's silence, by contrast, is that of a wife who does not reprimand her husband's boyish pranks. It is as likely the result of her daughter's retrospective account. At the time this incident took place, Catharine was only about six years old and presumably sitting in the schoolroom. The adult Catharine focalizes this passage through Lyman Beecher ("he would hear"), who allows his wife to remove the violin and who authorizes the transaction as jovial and understanding with a "twinkle of the eye."

As well, such a textual representation of a home run by two parents whose intellectual and literary pursuits complement but do not overlap obscures the essential function of other domestic adjuncts. Certainly a share of the household work was assumed by visiting relatives and boarders. Nor would the animated conversations, teaching, reading, painting, experimenting, sermonizing, and letter writing have been possible without the presence of servants who carried out much of the work that otherwise would have been given to the children and would have occupied even more of Roxana's time. In addition to "Aunty Jones," at least two other bound servants assisted the Beecher women. Although Catharine recalls that these servants were treated like family members, and even instructed in some basic literacy, the fact should not be overlooked that they freed other members of the family, women in particular, to pursue "higher" interests.

In a large family such as Lyman Beecher's,[1] servants and relatives also functioned as surrogate parents. Although Roxana figures in her daughter's reminiscences as a domestic paragon, she is not associated with warm maternal love. Catharine's affection is reserved for Roxana's sister Mary, who lived with the family. This aunt Catharine describes as "the poetry of my childhood" and a "sympathetic" observer of her earliest literary pursuits. She recalls: "I remember my imagination had been fired by hearing her read, in some poem, of the curls of some fair heroine dropping on her book; and so, one day, with great labor, I coaxed my hair into curl, and placed myself conspicuously before her, with the curls dropping on the page of an open book. She saw the artifice, and said, in her sweetest tones, 'Oh mother, come here and see these beautiful ringlets!' Even to this late hour of life the memory of those kind tones has endeared her to my recollection" (*Autobiography* 1:101). Here Mary introduces her young charge to a textual model for gendered behavior, which Catharine imitates. Her resemblance to the text depends, however, on Mary's recognition; Mary, in turn, calls Roxana's attention to her daughter's skill at reproducing the signifiers of femininity. Rather than call Roxana by name, Mary uses her title—mother—to remind the presumably intelligent and literate mother of her maternal duty to "[intuit] . . . the little wants and feelings of others" (*Autobiography* 1:101). In this, as in others of Catharine's contributions to the autobiography, she has constructed versions of herself and her family as textual ideals. Catharine's textual artifice was recognized by Mary; these family stories, by contrast, have achieved the status of autobiographical fact; the traces of their fabrication are almost entirely erased.

Catharine's early skills in invention were further nurtured in Miss Sarah Pierce's Litchfield Female Academy. Begun in 1797, this school was, by the time Catharine enrolled in 1810, "one of the most celebrated in the United States" (Sklar, *Catharine Beecher* 16). An extraordinarily cosmopolitan school, the academy enjoyed the support of prominent Litchfield men, who "utilized complex family, social, economic, political, educational, and professional ties" to promote the school (Brickley, "Sarah" 39). For Catharine Beecher, school and home were coextensive. Sarah Pierce was a parishioner of the Reverend Beecher and, according to Catharine's reminiscence, "found frequent occasions for seeking counsel and aid from her pastor. In return, she gave gratuitous schooling to as many of our children as father chose to send, for occasionally young boys found admission" to her school (*Autobiography* 1:164).

Unlike the world of home school and mother, where classes were subject to interruptions by Lyman Beecher's violin, Miss Sarah Pierce's school was strictly governed. Its structure replicated that of the patriarchal and authoritarian family with a difference: the father/lawgiver position was occupied by a woman. The pupils were subject to a list of twelve "Rules for the *School and Family*" (Vanderpoel, *Chronicles* 146; emphasis added), a dodecalogue whose burden was regularity, schedule, and chronic responsibility. These rules, whose immediate purpose was to order and regulate the school, had multiple effects. As Horowitz has pointed out, an emphasis on measured time signified a girl's physical separation from the unstructured and natural rhythms of "domestic enclosure" and her entrance into a cultural order that privileged the life of the mind (16–17). Further, the rules suggested that even the most traditional and seemingly natural actions could be systematized, prioritized, divided, and ordered, procedures that lie at the root of Beecher's subsequent professionalizing of the "natural" "feminine" tasks of domesticity.

Sarah Pierce's pupils copied these rules into their private journals, heard them read aloud each Saturday, and reproduced them in formal examinations. The students also held the primary responsibility for their enforcement. They recorded their obedience in a public journal that documented private shortcomings—a combination learning log, attendance report, schedule, and confession. Students submitted their journals for examination by teachers; they also read them aloud to their classmates, although they could choose not to. Unlike some of her classmates, who dreaded the public confessional reading of journals, Beecher excelled at the task. In fact, in April 1814, Beecher won first prize at the school over another girl who refused to have her journal seen.

The process of self-surveillance and public confession necessitated that students become aware of themselves as objects of attention by another (Foucault, *Madness*). At Litchfield Female Academy, young women and young men alike stood before the assembled student body to read aloud their compositions and passages from their journals. Such self-assessment and self-reporting undoubtedly accomplished the effect for which it was intended—to maintain a system of institutional discipline—but it also surely taught those who wrote such journals how to write in prescribed forms and afforded them the opportunity to invent publicly acceptable personae that were linked by convention to the gendered body that voiced them.

Sarah Pierce offered her students instruction in amateur dramatics, as well. Although the practice was generally considered improper for women, the school offered a "dramatic exhibition" at the close of each term.

Moreover, these dramas were written by Pierce herself, and schoolwork suspended while the students rehearsed (*Autobiography* 1:165). Although Albert von Frank's account of Pierce's school emphasizes that Lyman Beecher exercised a significant censorship over these dramatics, Catharine's account reveals that the community participated in furnishing props for the productions, implying at least a provisional approval of such goings-on. Additionally, the less scandalous subject matter that Lyman Beecher apparently imposed seems to have done little to dampen the effect of drama on the mind of his daughter. Like her teacher/mentor, Catharine Beecher gained notoriety as a writer of dramatic pieces, among Academy and Law School students, the numerous Beecher children, and the students of Miss Pierce who boarded at their home.

The experiments in subjectivity afforded academy students by journals, self-surveillance, memorization, imitation, and amateur dramatics reached their logical culmination in the writing Miss Pierce's students produced. Oral recitation and mental composition were supplemented by a wide range of writing tasks, from letter-writing to rigorous philosophical speculation. Whereas Sarah Pierce favored assigning composition topics calculated to form desirable character, her nephew John Brace, who began teaching composition at the academy in 1814, required more academic topics. Titles of compositions written under his supervision include "On History," "View of Literature of the United States," and "What is the Disposition, Is It Innate or Acquired?" (Brickley, "Sarah" 44).

An anecdote told by Harriet Beecher Stowe demonstrates how school, community, and patriarchal family were combined in the lives of Lyman Beecher's elder daughters. When Harriet was twelve years old (approximately five years after Catharine had left Miss Pierce's school), her composition on the question "Can the immortality of the soul be proved by the light of nature?" was honored at the school's annual exhibition. She recalls that many of her classmates had taken the affirmative response to the question, while "Mr. Brace himself had written in the negative." Like Brace, she, too, "adopt[ed] the negative." She continues, "the hall was crowded with all the literati of Litchfield. Before them all our compositions were read aloud. When mine was read, I noticed that father, who was sitting on high by Mr. Brace, brightened and looked interested, and at the close I heard him say, 'Who wrote that composition?' '*Your daughter, sir!*' was the answer. It was the proudest moment of my life" (*Autobiography* 1:399). As this anecdote suggests, although school training was coextensive with family governance, it served to remove its pupils irrevocably from any fiction of "privacy" and trained them as publicly competent writers. Their public exposure was carefully monitored, however, by fathers and other paternal affiliates and effected by the practice of having their texts read in public by bodies that were acceptably gendered male.

Moreover, Catharine Beecher's familial and formal education was authorized by community support. Formally educating daughters, a practice not widely followed, seemed less dangerous when it was done under the Beecher name, with its allied connotations of community and ministerial sanction. Additionally, in the town of Litchfield, which housed both the Pierce Academy and the Litchfield Law School,² the education of women, as well as of young men, was considered the norm. Lyman Beecher was closely allied with the town's educational elite in a network of cultural interchange with other families of similar means and tastes. Beecher's closest friend was Tapping Reeve, founder of the Law School, author of the *Law of Baron and Femme* (1816), and a pioneer theorist of women's legal rights. Reeve, Beecher, and their wives met weekly; while the men discussed religion and politics, the women "read aloud to each other" (*Autobiography* 1:163). These community leaders joined the students and faculty of the Pierce Academy and the Litchfield Law School in informal coteries for amateur dramatics and literary discussions. Family connections to both schools ensured that Beecher children would be central to these groups. Harriet Beecher Stowe recalls that even Catharine's mock epic poems about domestic events, presumably written for reading by members of the family circle only, would be "passed round among the social visiting circles which were frequently at our house," along with "compositions of a graver cast, romantic or poetic," written by Catharine and others (*Autobiography* 1:396, 397).

Catharine Beecher's writing for community literary societies continued into her adult life. At Hartford Female Seminary she instituted regular levées, which brought together townspeople, seminary faculty, and students. Later, in Cincinnati, where Lyman Beecher had assumed the presidency of Lane Theological Seminary, she continued her involvement in dramatics. Indeed, Cincinnati's remarkable literary culture soon absorbed Beecher's attention. A number of transplanted Litchfield friends now lived in Cincinnati and associated in the Semi-Colon Club, a salon that had been founded by her uncle, Samuel Foote. Its members included James Hall, the editor of the *Western Monthly Magazine*; novelist Caroline Lee Hentz and her husband; Salmon P. Chase; Elizabeth, Emily, and Anna Blackwell; and Calvin and Harriet

Beecher Stowe. The meetings of this group combined social and intellectual intercourse. Following the reading of selected anonymous compositions by an appointed male moderator, members critiqued and discussed the writings. Substantive interchange was more than balanced, however, by flirtation and courtship among the group's single members. A Semi-Colon hostess/writer emphasized that she took care to invite equal numbers of "young and tender lawyers or other young men about town and the same number or more according to taste of pretty young girls" (Cincinnati Historical Society). A male member suggested that the group meet in other venues than stuffy city parlors: "cannot we laugh and sentimentalize—and get in love with each other—in the country?" he asked (Cincinnati Historical Society).

It seems apparent that the club membership duplicated in small the outside affiliative connections of author and publisher, and may have allowed publishers to solicit a variety of new material for their pages. Tradition has it that Harriet Beecher's first journalistic publication, "An Essay on Languages," reached the pages of the *Western Monthly Magazine* because James Hall first heard it read at a Semi-Colon Club gathering. Such a happy coincidence seems to be an exception, however, since the group's members favored writing on topics that were domestic rather than philosophical or political. Essays and poems bearing titles such as "The Babe on My Knee" and "New England Snow," apparently written by women and men alike, suggest that although the club furnished a forum for budding women writers, the relative homeliness of its discussions ensured that they did not exceed womanly propriety.

The combined effects of sustained fatherly encouragement, formal instruction, exposure to women who presumed and enacted privileges coded as masculine, and the continued public acceptance of her work by members of the communities in which she lived and worked produced in Beecher a remarkable multidiscursive facility. Her textual production included a range of genres: "private" texts that translated everyday occurrences and common language into poetic flights of fancy, cautionary homiletic fiction, domestic handbooks, theological treatises, biography and autobiography, public argumentation and polemic. Many of these texts depend on her facility in adapting raw "experience" to conventional forms, whether that "public" be immediate family, friends, students, members of literary clubs, or an anonymous national readership.

This simultaneous attention to cultural expectations and private agendas describes the writing Beecher did throughout her life, particularly of family stories. When Beecher was forty-four, her brother George, who had suffered a series of mental breakdowns, committed suicide. Almost immediately thereafter, she began to sort through his papers and the next year published *The Biographical Remains of Rev. George Beecher,* presenting his life not as a failure to come to terms with the pressures placed on him by his father's expectations but as a series of "heroic efforts to overcome his self-doubts and dedicate himself to his small congregation" (Sklar, *Catharine Beecher* 147– 48). This overt attempt to frame a positive interpretation of a family crisis suggests that we read the other autobiographical sources critically, as well. The documentary value of Lyman Beecher's autobiography, for example, is compromised by the vagaries of memory as well as by his children's filial respect and their need to "come to terms with the meaning of their personal and intellectual independence" in light of the failing health and declining rationality of the man who had dominated their lives (Sklar, *Catharine Beecher* 230). His eldest daughter's reminiscences, as I have suggested, trace a particular agenda in support of her revisions of her *Treatise on Domestic Economy.* The *Treatise*'s argument for professional domesticity depends in large part on Beecher's claim that traditional methods of household management were inefficient and needed to be replaced by regular routines and standard procedures. Thus in writing for the autobiography, Beecher recollects her early home life in terms that support the argument of the *Treatise.* As she recalls her mother's death, she emphasizes not so much the emotional turmoil this bereavement caused but the chaotic methods of housekeeping that resulted from her mother's absence. This condition, the story strongly implies, would never have resulted had Roxana had a system of orderly management whereby the children and husband would have been able to continue in her absence.

Yet Roxana emerges as the prototype for the ideal domestic woman Catharine Beecher invented and enshrined in the American woman's home. Her textual incarnation bears the traces of the family, school, and community expectations within which Beecher learned to write. Literate, responsible for the education of her children and servants, intelligent, curious, always bringing intellectual inquiry to bear on domestic circumstance, this textual Roxana resides in a biographical memoir that constructs the Beecher family as a model for all white, middle-class, New England patriarchal families, with its separation of spheres that ensured a smoothly run household. In this textual construct, Beecher ignored the permeable boundaries of her own family, erasing the boarders who swelled its ranks, the relatives who boarded in and assisted with the less onerous domestic chores, and the numerous and often anonymous domestic helpers who undertook the sweat-labor of laundry, cooking, water hauling, wood chopping and hauling, and nursery care.

Beecher's interpretations and recollections of her early family life have predisposed scholars to emphasize her domestic concerns as the natural focus for a woman writer, and have determined how generations of scholars have understood the Beecher family myth. Yet the *Treatise*'s model of domestic stability bears little resemblance to the nomadic life Beecher herself lived, for she modeled her own practice on her father, not on her mother. The Roxana version of domesticity in the *Treatise* must be modified by attention to Catharine's more covert agendas that interrupt its text just as Lyman's violin distracted his wife's schoolroom, covering and justifying her life of travel and finally offering a radical alternative to the patriarchal family.

Margaret Fuller (Ossoli) (1810–1850)

In his 1884 biography of Margaret Fuller, reprinted fifteen years later in the Riverside Press's American Men of Letters series, Thomas Wentworth Higginson recounts her brilliance as an adolescent. He names some of her illustrious fellow students at the Cambridge Port Private Grammar School— Oliver Wendell Holmes, John Holmes, and Richard Henry Dana—and reports their memories of their classmate. According to Higginson, the young women who attended C. P. P. G. S. did not have the "impression that [Fuller] neglected her home duties for the sake of knowledge; such was her conceded ability that she was supposed equal to doing everything at once. It was currently reported that she could rock a cradle, read a book, eat an apple, and knit a stocking, all at the same time" (25). Higginson's biography—and the series of which it was a part—exemplifies the degree to which Fuller has been measured against her contemporaries' expectations for women. Her male peers evaluated Fuller's appearance as well as her intellect; her female associates measured how her intellect intersected with her domestic abilities. Yet the inclusion of her biography in the American Men of Letters series implies that as an adult she transcended the domestic concerns usually held to preoccupy women writers such as her contemporary Catharine Beecher.

Yet Fuller's background of family privilege, formal schooling, and en-riched community affiliations is strikingly similar to Beecher's. Like Beecher, she was the eldest daughter of a man whose community authority was undisputed and who encouraged her to identify with his masculine entitlements. Timothy Fuller had graduated from Harvard (1801), as had his father before him. A prominent Boston lawyer, Fuller served during Margaret's childhood as a Massachusetts state senator and a four-term congressional representative. Less is known about the details of her mother's education, although Margarett Crane taught school while still a teenager and continued to read "amply" after her marriage (Capper, *Margaret Fuller* 18–19). By most accounts, she was only a shadowy figure in her daughter's upbringing, while Timothy Fuller dominated her childhood. Like Roxana Foote, Margarett Crane devoted her attention to managing her household and garden. Nor does there seem to have been a great emotional attachment between her and her daughter.

From her early years, Margaret enjoyed access to books, intellectual conversation, and the life of the mind. Her father, like Lyman Beecher, had hoped that "his first child would be a son who could be reared in his pattern as his heir" (Wade 6). At the birth of his second child, also a girl, Fuller determined to educate Margaret as he would a boy. That resolve was only intensified by the untimely death of his second daughter. Thus for the first five years of her life, Margaret was her father's only child and received his full attention. Unlike Lyman Beecher, however, Timothy Fuller was less inclined to acknowledge his daughter's need for childish pursuits. When she was three, he began to teach her to read. At age six, under his direction, she began to learn Latin grammar and soon progressed to daily readings in Roman history, Ovid, and Horace. Later she learned to read Greek. So intent was Fuller on overseeing his daughter's education that when he was away from home attending to legislative duties he left lesson plans for his wife to carry out in his absence. As well, he arranged for his brother, then a Harvard student, to continue his daughter's instruction in Greek and Latin, topics his wife could not supervise.

From the beginning, Timothy Fuller made his expressions of affection to his eldest daughter contingent on her intellectual performance. When she was only three years old, for example, he sent his "love to the little Sarah Margarett. I love her if she is a good girl & learns to read" (Capper, *Margaret Fuller* 30). At other moments, he apparently withheld messages and letters to her as a means of discipline. During his frequent and extended legislative absences, he treated his daughter's letters as schoolroom assignments, correcting grammar, spelling, and punctuation in his replies, as his own father had done to his childhood letters, and as Margaret would later do, after Timothy's death, to her brother Richard's letters. At age eight she wrote him: "Papa I do not suppose you think it a good excuse to say that I could not write. No Papa nor do I either for I could have done it. But I have been like Basil in the 'Tomorrow' and have determined to be so no longer. I am resolved to write you every week. . . . Now I will tell you what I study Latin twice a week and Arithmetick when Aunt Elizabeth is here. If you have spies they will certainly inform you that we are not very dissipated" (*Letters* 1:84).

From this letter it is clear that the young Margaret was continually aware of her father's presence, even in his absence. She anticipates his responses to her work and is aware that the other adult figures in her life, "spies" as she figures them, function as agents of her father's supervision. In this letter she identifies herself with a male literary figure as a means of making herself agreeable to her father. Another letter, written at age ten, Margaret closes with a paragraph in Latin, asking her father to correct it for her. His reply is characteristic. After criticizing her translation, he writes, "I would not discourage you, my girl, by being too critical and yet I am anxious to have you admit to one *fault*, which you will remember I have often mentioned, as the source, the very fountain of others—carelessness" (*Letters* 1:97, n. 7).

Such an intense family preoccupation with conversing and composing, writing and reading, teaching and learning suggests a class-based and ample leisure in which to pursue such activities. Fuller's routine at age fifteen, for example, is noteworthy for its ambitiousness, but also denominates a richness of intellectual and cultural capital—books, musical instruments, access to materials associated with literate practices, as well as an apparent absence of household responsibility:

> I rise a little before five, walk an hour, and then practise on the piano, till seven, when we breakfast. Next I read French,—Sismondi's Literature of the South of Europe,—till eight, then two or three lectures in Brown's Philosophy. About half-past nine I go to Mr. Perkins's school and study Greek till twelve, when, the school being dismissed, I recite, go home, and practise again till dinner, at two. Sometimes, if the conversation is very agreeable, I lounge for half an hour over the dessert, though rarely so lavish of time. Then when I can, I read two hours in Italian, but I am often interrupted. At six, I walk, or take a drive. Before going to bed, I play or sing, for half an hour or so, to make all sleepy, and, about eleven, retire to write a little while in my journal, exercises on what I have read, or a series of characteristics which I am filling up according to advice. Thus, you see, I am learning Greek,

and making acquaintance with metaphysics, and French and Italian
literature. (*Letters* 1:151)

Such a regimen would be possible only if Fuller were responsible for almost
no other labor than physical and mental self-culture. Ironically, Fuller
composed this passage at approximately the same time as her peers at
C. P. P. G. S. perceived that she was able to balance her studies with more
domestic pursuits. However, cooking, cleaning, and general maintenance
in the Fuller household was carried out by several servants whose place,
Margarett Crane Fuller instructed her daughter, was "under us" (Capper,
Margaret Fuller 18). Even when the family moved to Groton and the number
of servants was reduced, it is clear that Fuller escaped much of the household
drudgery that would have interfered with her mental culture. She traveled
frequently and regularly to Boston, kept up a voluminous correspondence,
and maintained a rigorous program of study. In Fuller's writings these
household adjuncts function as they did in the family's life, never attracting
notice unless they became obstreperous enough to interrupt intellectual
pursuits. Margarett Crane Fuller, for example, did not approve of servants'
endorsing "ultra Republican principles" (Capper, *Margaret Fuller* 43); her
daughter reproduced the sentiment, writing of one of Emerson's servants:
"I had a good talk with Louisa Snow—she is a fine girl though made coarse
by her democracy" (Myerson, "1842" 339).

Within this family, where fatherly approval was contingent on devotion
to study, and where her mother was an adjunct to her father's pedagogical
plans, it is not surprising that Margaret Fuller sought affection outside the
family. At age eight she formed an intense attachment to Ellen Kilshaw,
an adult family friend. According to Blanchard, Fuller's parents "strongly
encouraged the attachment, seeing in Ellen a model of feminine accomplishment" (27). Illustrating the central importance of Kilshaw to her childhood,
Fuller recalls a scene whose details parallel Beecher's recollection of her Aunt
Mary, in which emotion does not depend on intellectual performance but
upon the interpersonal emotional identification that reading may effect.
She recalls that she had come into a room where Kilshaw had left her
novel, Scott's *Guy Mannering,* and began to read "merely with the feeling
of continuing our mutual existence by passing my eyes over the same page
where hers had been. . . . Just then she entered with light step, and full-
beaming eye. When she saw me thus, a soft cloud stole over her face, and
clothed every feature with a lovelier tenderness than I had seen there before.
She did not question, but fixed on me inquiring looks of beautiful love.

I laid my head against her shoulder and wept" (*Memoirs* 1:35–36). As does Beecher, Fuller emphasizes the ideal of womanly fusion, of affirming a "mutual existence" by sharing a textual understanding. The older woman recognizes the significance of the child's action, rewarding her precocity with an outpouring of unconditional sympathy and love.

Fuller wrote the "autobiographical romance" that contains this reminiscence when she was thirty years old (*Memoirs* 1:11). In this document she argues that her father's dominance of her childhood caused her serious and permanent physical and emotional damage. She recalls "as he was subject to many interruptions, I was often kept up till very late; and as he was a severe teacher, both from his habits of mind and his ambition for me, my feelings were kept on the stretch till the recitations were over." This early discipline affected her subsequent intellectual and emotional development, "prevent[ing] the harmonious development of my bodily powers and check[ing] my growth, while, later, they induced continual headache, weakness and nervous affections, of all kinds" (*Memoirs* 1:15). Yet Timothy Fuller's intellectual requirements of his daughter were not exceptional; indeed, they typify the requirements made of most boys of similar age and similar social and intellectual class who were her contemporaries.

The disjunction of these accounts suggests that Fuller's autobiographical recollections of her childhood, like Beecher's, are written in relation to larger, gender-coded agendas. This memoir, penned at the height of an emotional crisis, has at its heart Fuller's struggle to escape her dead father's dominance of her literary production. In it Timothy Fuller functions as the paradigmatic guardian of "culture, civilization and language" (Lemaire 85). By this time, however, Fuller had begun to consider that women might make a claim to cultural guardianship as well. As she wrote this memoir, she was leading the second series of her Conversations with upper-class intellectual women of Boston. These Conversations combined the social ambiance of a salon with the formal rigor of classroom instruction and increased her respect for women's intellectual abilities. As well, she could see how, in this setting, feminine intellect, often curtailed in its application by masculine demands for "accuracy and clearness in everything," blossomed under the effects of her own nonlinear, associative, "subtle and indirect motions of imagination and feeling" (*Memoirs* 1:18).

Thus in the autobiographical romance Fuller characterizes her own facility at linear, logical thinking and writing as masculine artifice, while assuming her conversational facility to be natural and feminine. According to Fuller, her father taught her that "you must not speak, unless you can make your meaning perfectly intelligible to the person addressed; must not express a thought, unless you can give a reason for it, if required; must not make a statement, unless sure of all particulars—such were his rules. 'But,' 'if,' 'unless,' 'I am mistaken,' and 'it may be so,' were words and phrases excluded from the province where he held sway. Trained to great dexterity in artificial methods, accurate, ready, with entire command of his resources, he had no belief in minds that listen, wait, and receive" (*Memoirs* 1:17).

As this passage suggests, at this point in her life, Fuller believed that there was an essential womanly way of thinking and writing that she associates here with receptivity and a kind of passivity. Yet as this passage also demonstrates, fluency and rigorous control, whether of writing or of speech, may be taught and learned. In Fuller's day (as in our own) they marked a perceived difference in approach to language thought to be linked to gender; in Fuller's day (as in our own) this difference was the result of access to educational institutions that taught these skills. This passage finally demonstrates, then, the opposite of what Fuller apparently argues. Feminine receptivity and masculine rigor are less the result of essential traits than of instruction, imitation, and practice. As Fuller's own publications subsequently demonstrated, a woman could acquire facility in both modes.

As did Catharine Beecher's, Margaret Fuller's education overlapped with her home environment. However, although Lyman Beecher had effected and even supervised a home school, he left its execution to his wife. Catharine learned public and formal academic behaviors—scientific appropriation of time, monitorial writing, argumentation, parody and imitation of culturally honored forms—at Litchfield Female Academy under the direction of Miss Sarah Pierce. By contrast, Fuller learned these coded behaviors from her father, who dominated her home education. In the main, Margaret Fuller was sent to school to learn behavior appropriate to her gender. Even so, she was still under her father's watchful domination.

In her first forays into public schools, she went unaware of the consequences of displaying a competitiveness that was deemed appropriate only to young men. At age nine she entered Cambridge Port Private Grammar School, one of two area schools that prepared boys to enter Harvard. Although the school admitted a few precocious girls, none of its students was ready for a classmate as unconscious of gendered proprieties as was Fuller. Oliver Wendell Holmes's recollection suggests the stir caused by her

behavior: "Sitting on the girls' benches, conspicuous . . . by that look which
rarely fails to betray hereditary and congenital culture, was a young person
very nearly of my own age. . . . This was Margaret Fuller, the only one
among us who, like Jean Paul, like the Duke, like Bettina, has slipped the
cable of the more distinctive name to which she was anchored, and floats on
the waves of speech as Margaret. . . . Her talk was affluent, magisterial, . . .
some would say euphuistic, but surpassing the talk of women in breadth
and audacity" (116). Holmes's account, written long after he and Fuller
had achieved their adult reputations, suggests his continuing struggle to
reconcile Fuller's gender with her obvious intellectual abilities. Although she
sat with other "girls," he calls her a *person,* a terminology that anticipates
her later inclusion in Riverside's Men of Letters biographies, and echoes
others' mystification at Fuller's apparent resistance to classification simply
by gender, best exemplified by Poe's dictum that "humanity is divided
into three classes: men, women, and Margaret Fuller" (Miller, *Margaret
Fuller* 192). Holmes does not retain the generic, however, but immediately
returns to an apparent guarantor of gendered identity—her first name.
This ploy, however, is also fraught with danger since even at this early point
"Margaret" could be identified without the accompanying authority of her
patronymic—the more distinctive name—an act that is underscored by
Holmes's averring to other "schoolgirls of *unlettered origin.*" Even Holmes's
final classification is ambiguous: although Fuller talks like a woman, she
surpasses her peers in "breadth and audacity." Such difficulty in classifying
Fuller, to the point of inventing a third, generic category to contain her,
suggests the extent to which her intellectual abilities challenged the qualities
thought to describe womanly ability in her day. Fuller learned to look and act
like a woman; she learned, as well, to display those behaviors in appropriate
contexts. And she spent a good deal of her adult life trying to understand
the culture that made such dissimulation necessary.

Fuller's competitiveness as a student quickly earned her a reputation for
being difficult. Hoping to compensate for what he perceived as his daughter's
lack of social skills, Timothy Fuller enrolled her in the Young Ladies'
Seminary at Groton, conducted by Susan and Mary Prescott, the daughters
of a lawyer friend. Fuller informed his daughter that he expected her to learn
to manifest a "discreet, modest, unassuming deportment. These qualities are
indispensable to endear any one, especially a young lady to her friends, & to
obtain the 'world's good word'—than which few things are more desirable,
this side of Heaven." He concluded his instructions to her with his usual

conditional encouragement: "Depend upon my undiminished affection as long as you continue dutiful" (Capper, *Margaret Fuller* 74).

In May 1824, Margaret reluctantly commenced her studies with the Misses Prescott, even though it meant a much less intellectually challenging experience. She wrote her father of the Prescott curriculum, "I feel myself rather degraded from Cicero's Oratory to One and two are how many[.] It *is* rather a change is it not?" (*Letters* 1:139). Prescott students rose at 6:30 to pray, attended to studies from 8:30 until noon and from 2 until 4:30, and adhered to many detailed rules of behavior intended to inculcate normative gender behaviors. Fuller's sketch, "Mariana," demonstrates how these behaviors, rehearsed and monitored within the context of the school's offerings in amateur dramatics, were taught. According to this text, Mariana's "ardent . . . nature . . . was constantly increased by the restraints and narrow routine of the boarding school. She was always devising means to break in upon it," among which was her affectation of "costume and fancy dresses" and inappropriate use of heavy rouge. The amateur dramatics of the seminary offered her a "vent" for these predilections. "The principal parts, as a matter of course, fell to her lot; most of the good suggestions and arrangements came from her; . . . she ruled mostly, and shone triumphant" (*Summer on the Lakes* 83).

Dramatic imitation proves, however, to be the means whereby she is finally disciplined for her inability to dress and behave in appropriately feminine ways. Coming to the dining hall one day, Mariana discovers that "every schoolmate" had heavily rouged her own face. "The teachers strove to be grave, but she saw they enjoyed the joke. The servants could not suppress a titter" (85). The lessons—formal and extracurricular—in appropriate public demonstrations of gender that Fuller learned at the Prescott Seminary suggested to her that behaviors deemed appropriate to gender and location could—and should—be fabricated as needed. By the time she was twenty, Fuller had become skillful in summoning the requisite gendered behavior to meet a variety of situational demands. She wrote Amelia Greenwood in 1830: "I have escaped from the parlour where Ive been sitting the livelong eveg playing auditor to Judge Weston[.] . . . I fairly ache sitting three hours *in a boarding-school attitude hemming a ruffle and saying never a word.* Pa—always thinks my presence gives a finish to the scene" (*Letters* 1:163–64; emphasis added). Fuller's uncharacteristic use of the term "Pa" suggests the wry tone in which this letter was composed. This domestic moment is a "scene" in a drama of her father's design. Like Beecher she clearly had become facile at public masquerade. But while Beecher devoted her efforts to integrating masculine rigor into pursuits she and others recognized as appropriately feminine, Fuller spent her next years seeking ways in which women could honor their femininity without being obliged to hide their intellect.

The Misses Prescott's School was effectively Fuller's last formal education. Although she briefly continued her study of Greek at the Cambridge Port Private Grammar School, her subsequent education took place in the enriched public environment of Cambridge. During Fuller's teen years, the city was, like Litchfield, the site of "intellectual ferment" (Blanchard 49). Many Harvard College faculty members and students socialized with the Fullers: Edward Everett (professor of Greek), Edward Tyrell Channing (professor of English), Joseph Story (head of the law school), George Ticknor (responsible for founding the department of modern languages), and George Bancroft (a tutor), all Fuller intimates, had been trained in the new and revolutionary methods of German scholarship. Fuller found that these scholars welcomed but were puzzled by a young woman whose intellectual ability threatened to limit her prospects for normal socialization and marriage.

On the one hand, Fuller enjoyed the fullest intellectual benefit from her associations with Harvard's "renowned class of 1829" (Blanchard 49). These young men nurtured the sense of intellectual entitlement planted in her by her father; often, in fact, they acted as his simulacra. Although women had not yet gained admission to Harvard's precincts, Fuller's associations with its students regularized, validated, and gave new direction to her individual study. She met frequently with Harvard men to read, converse, study languages, translate, and write. As an aid to her study, Fuller kept a reading journal and built a large circle of correspondents to whom she reported her reflections upon her reading. This journal was not an exclusively private document but was written for circulation among friends, serving as a record of and spur to their verbal interchange.

On the other hand, however, Fuller's community associates monitored and ensured her womanly socialization. Eliza Farrar, the wife of a Harvard professor, seems to have figured as a later version of Ellen Kilshaw. Capper reports that Fuller wrote of Farrar, "At 17 I elected a mother" (*Margaret Fuller* 97). Farrar, who later wrote a conduct book, *The Young Lady's Friend* (1836), tutored Fuller in the grammar of personal appearance and gesture, codes as foundational to femininity as skill in linear argument and classical rhetoric were to elite masculine privilege. She offered Fuller more than feminine advice, however, since she also led an active intellectual life. This balance of qualities she later propounded in her advice book, where, according to Capper, she stressed that "academic learning . . . was valuable itself and not something that ended with school or marriage" (*Margaret Fuller* 96). At this same time, Fuller also made the acquaintance of Lydia Maria Francis (later Child), who, although only seven years older, had already published two books and was editing a magazine for children. These women offered Fuller models that suggested that intellectual excellence and femininity were not mutually exclusive.

Fuller's involvement with these various groups in Cambridge earned her a reputation for the ability to form sympathetic friendships. Emerson, for instance, remarked that "she could not make a journey, or go to an evening party, without meeting an new person, who wished presently to impart his history to her" (*Memoirs* 1:286). Although this facility at friendship is generally attributed to Fuller's talent as a listener, it must also be connected with Fuller's emerging skills at adaptive behavior. A child who had been trained to read, study, write, and recite as a son, but who later was also taught to reproduce behaviors appropriate to a well-bred young woman, she was able to adapt herself to any social encounter.

Her father's emphases on regularity and rigor, an enriched community and home environment, and her wide-ranging formal education combined to produce Fuller as a writing woman who did not confine herself to conventionally feminine topics. This much is clear by the fact that literary scholars have, almost from the beginning of their attempts to codify an "American" "literature," been willing to include her among its Transcendentalist founders. Such a classification, however, does not recognize the limits of Fuller's identification with masculine norms. The several versions of her autobiography suggest that she spent a good deal of energy trying to sort out the sources and effects of her gender-coded *Bildung* and that, rather than settle on a consistent account of the process, she found a certain satisfaction in producing ambiguous and contradictory narratives of her intellectual development, figuring her father alternately as central or absent, cruel or enabling.

That she was entirely aware of the inconsistencies in these versions of her "self" is confirmed by a letter she wrote to William H. Channing upon the occasion of the publication of *Summer on the Lakes*, a book that contained one such autobiographical narrative: "it is amusing to see how elderly routine gentlemen, such as Dr Francis and Mr Farrar, are charmed with the little story of Mariana. They admire, at poetic distance, that powerful nature that would alarm them so in real life. . . . Nobody dreams of its being like me; they all thought Miranda was, in the Great Lawsuit. People seem to think that not more than one phase of character can be shown in one life" (*Letters* 3:198–99).

Both Mariana and Miranda, as well as other unnamed personae, addressed different cultural expectations and audiences. For example, in the *Memoirs,* Fuller condemns her father for pressuring her too greatly and robbing her of a normal childhood. That account was written after she had taught under the direction of Bronson Alcott in his Temple School. Alcott and Elizabeth Peabody, his assistant, whom Fuller succeeded, are generally credited with offering the first kindergarten education, a practice that assumed that children should be educated differently than adults because of their innocence. Clearly this thinking led Fuller retrospectively to evaluate her own childhood and to discover that it had not conformed to such an ideal. By contrast, a second account of her relationship with her father, removed to the level of myth or hagiography, is crafted to demonstrate to readers of "The Great Lawsuit" that enlightened masculine attention could benefit women. Here she tells the story of Miranda, whose father raised "his eldest child" as an intellectual equal. "He respected his child . . . too much to be an indulgent parent. He called on her for clear judgment, for courage, for honor and fidelity; in short, for such virtues as he knew" (*Woman in the Nineteenth Century* 1971, 38–39).

The extent to which "elderly routine gentlemen," Holmes and Higginson among them, were determined to routinize Fuller's celebration of ambiguity and to unify her character is best demonstrated by the posthumous *Memoirs.* As any scholar who has worked with the purple-penciled documentary sources can attest, to construct a unified version of Margaret Fuller required monumental excision and revision. The efforts of the not-so-elderly but certainly "routine" Emerson, Channing, and Clarke to bring a consistent and respectable order to her papers—an order her father would have applauded—has impacted the work of all subsequent Fuller scholars. Much of that work, in turn, has been an effort to inscribe a similarly unified biographical "truth" and/or to (re)affirm Fuller's position as an American Woman of Letters. In some sense, they recapitulate, as I have here, the measure of Fuller offered by her earliest peers, establishing her both as a competent woman and as a writer of stature. The cradle, the reading, the apple (reminiscent of Eve), and the knitting—these tropes measure the capacity of peers, community, and subsequent scholars to absorb and naturalize an intellect that exceeded gendered boundaries.

While the differences between Beecher and Fuller are certainly important, they have been too long honored: such intellectual splits have obscured the similarities of these women. Each prescribed and inscribed versions of womanly subjectivity in their writings, behaviors that were coded as to social class, racial entitlement, and geographic location. Each wrote extensive and complex revisionary plans to address what they perceived as difficulties facing literate white women. They revised not only individual feminine subjectivity but also the areas in which it was most often formed: the patriarchal family, the public and private school, and the communities that contained them.

Chapter Two

FATHERLESS DAUGHTERS
Sarah Josepha Hale and Fanny Fern

In her "Literary Notices" column of *Godey's Lady's Book and Magazine* for February 1855, Sarah Josepha Hale noted the publication of Fanny Fern's *Ruth Hall: A Domestic Tale of the Present Times.* By that time *Ruth* had been extensively promoted by its publishers, who had claimed that the book was in its third edition only four days after its initial appearance (Geary 388). Hale, who had herself profited from such publicity only three years earlier, was a reviewer whose notices of books she liked were glowing and lengthy. She gave *Ruth Hall* only two sentences: "As a writer, the author of this volume has been very successful and very popular. Her success and popularity may be increased by this 'domestic tale;' but, as we never interfere in family affairs, we must leave readers to judge for themselves" (50: 176).

Hale's dismissal of Fern's novel is certainly not surprising, since *Godey's* public reputation dictated that it promote only novels suitable for ladies' and family reading. *Ruth* was a racy novel. The book was already notorious as an autobiographical exposé of strained family relations between two of the popular press's star columnists. In the novel, it was reported, Fanny Fern, a popular writer for the *True Flag,* the *Olive Branch,* and the *Musical World and Times,* had effectively accused her brother N.P. Willis, one of New York's leading editors, of refusing to aid her financially after her husband's death. Hence Hale's punningly dismissive phrase "we never interfere in family affairs" refers both to the book's subtitle and to the public controversy then raging around the book.

Hale's review seems to suggest a great difference between these two women. As the oldest woman and the youngest woman treated here, they represent two generations of writing women. Hale, one of the first women in the United States to pursue a career in journalism, assumed the editorship of the *Ladies' Magazine* in 1828. The magazine was the first in the United States published expressly for women. Only a quarter century later, Fern was able to publish a best-selling collection of newspaper columns addressed specifically to women's concerns, *Fern Leaves* ("40,000 SOLD IN FOUR MONTHS" [Geary 382]). Hale was educated at home; Fern attended several of the country's finest women's schools, including Catharine Beecher's Hartford Female Seminary. Pairing these two women demonstrates the range of training, topics, and approaches used by two women who wrote contemporaneously for more than twenty years (from approximately 1850 to 1870). Indeed, the contrasts between Hale and Fern, especially when they are compared with Beecher and Fuller, as well, serve to delineate a spectrum of family privilege, venues for education, and kinds of community support woman writers in this time period might receive.

Sarah Josepha Buell Hale (1788–1879)

The details of Hale's educational background are sparse and ill-documented. They credit her mother with teaching her reading and her brother and husband with her mastery of the "higher branches" of writing, Latin, mathematics, and philosophy. In her earliest autobiographical account, Hale recalls that she had access to "few, very few [books] in comparison with the number given children now-a-days," and that her mother, who "had enjoyed uncommon advantages of education for a female of her times," presided over her earliest education. "She had read many of the old black letter chronicles and romances of the days of chivalry; and innumerable were the ballads, songs and stories with which she amused and instructed her children. . . . We did not need the 'Infant School' to make us love learning" (*Wreath* 384). This autobiographical sketch was addressed to a readership that, in 1837, believed that "it requires, usually, a powerful pressure of outward circumstances" to make a woman an author (383). Hale thus emphasized how accidental was her assumption of authorship and offers comfort to readers who may thus "find, in their 'halcyon lot' the reason that their talents have never been directed to literary pursuits" (383). She figures her mother's intellectual skills as natural, aligning her mother's reading with simple, folk forms free of the artifice associated with manly forms of writing—Martha Whittlesey Buell read chronicles, not history; ballads, not poetry.

Hale's father had received no formal education and thus did not dominate his daughter's home education. As is established by later autobiographical accounts whose purpose is to authorize Hale's literary reputation, Gordon
Buell's position as his daughter's primary educator was supplemented by his
eldest son and his son-in-law. While Beecher and Fuller were sent to public
or private schools that extended the family's function, Sarah Buell was taught
at home by her brother, who regretted "that [she] could not, like himself,
have the privilege of a college education." During recesses from Dartmouth,
Horatio Buell, a law student, supervised his sister's progress in a course
of study paralleling his own and which included "Latin, and the higher
branches of mathematics, and of mental philosophy" (*Woman's* 687). The
details of this relationship are sparsely documented, and the entire episode
has taken on dimensions of folklore as biographers have embellished the
story from their imaginations. Olive Burt's biography, written for children,
assumes that Sarah read her brother's school texts and that Horatio corrected
her writing and "required her to keep regular school hours and to prepare
her lessons meticulously" (22). Burt also writes that upon his graduation
from Dartmouth, Horatio Buell brought his sister a diploma, a near replica
of his own, but embellished with a drawing of the Buell home instead of
Dartmouth Hall.[1] Whether or not this is a "fact," the figure of such a diploma
captures the overlapping functions of home and school in this woman's
formative years, and challenges the artificial distinction between public and
private spheres that later scholars have credited Hale with promulgating.

While her brother was at Dartmouth, Sarah Buell taught a primary
school for boys and girls to supplement her father's small income as a farmer
and unsuccessful innkeeper. Unlike many dame schools of the period, in
her classes "the girls were not taught sewing, but to write well and read
intelligently for their own leisure and profit, and each was made mistress
of more mathematics than was known by all their fathers and mothers put
together" (Finley 30). Biographers repeat the story that Buell exposed her
pupils not only to the "higher branches" but also to at least a little Latin.
(Her innovation was reportedly not enthusiastically received by at least some
portion of her students' parents and by her supervisors.) She continued to
teach until her marriage at the relatively late age of twenty-five.

Although Gordon and Martha Buell were not among Newport, New
Hampshire's social or intellectual elite, their home life was rich in intellectual
stimulation. The details of Sarah's childhood reading and the fact that her
brother Horatio met Dartmouth's admission requirements, suggest, that

her family was well read. Hale claims, "Next to the Bible and The Pilgrim's Progress, my earliest reading was Milton, Addison, Pope, Johnson, Cowper, Burns, and a portion of Shakespeare" (*Woman's* 686). She also read Radcliffe's *Mysteries of Udolpho* when she was seven (*Wreath* 384) and Ramsey's *History of the American Revolution* when she was ten (Rogers 12).

If Horatio Buell supervised his sister's home education as a father surrogate, it is clear from her reminiscences that her facility in writing came from other sources. Although Buell did not attend a formal educational institution, she seems to have internalized the gendered codes associated with public writing at the hand of her husband, David Hale, whom she married in 1813. Hale describes her husband as "a number of years my senior, and far more my superior in learning" (*Woman's* 687). This sentence argues tellingly that the husband also functioned as a father figure to his adoring wife. During their marriage, the Hales together studied "French, Botany . . . Mineralogy, [and] Geology; besides pursuing a long and instructive course of reading" (*Wreath* 386–87). Their studies were conducted in hours freed from household duties, arguably enabled by domestic "help," although Hale's biographers and her own accounts scarcely mention the presence of servants. Finley's undocumented observation that "there was always one servant, at least, to save the busy mother from fatigue too great for enjoyment of the famous evenings" (37) seems to be the basis for subsequent biographers' notice of these necessary but silent household adjuncts.

Hale recalls that "in all our mental pursuits, it seemed the aim of my husband to enlighten my reason,—strengthen my judgment, and give me confidence in my own powers of mind, which he estimated much higher than I" (*Woman's* 687). Characteristically, she does not directly claim to possess, nor even to recognize, her own intellectual powers but gives responsibility to David Hale for making her into a creature of reason, judgment, and confidence. This carefully worded narrative demonstrates how Hale crafted a gendered version of her intellectual pursuits that has been honored by most scholars who have since studied her.[2] Within the family circle, emphatically encoded by Hale as a domestic private space, words generally understood to characterize masculine intellectual accomplishments— "reason," "judgment," "powers of mind"—may describe women's "mental pursuits" as well.

However, when Hale describes her more "public" intellectual activities, she insists that her own intent was appropriately circumscribed. Elaborating on her husband's role in forming her as a writer, she continues, "Under his instruction and example, my prose style of writing, which the critics generally allow to be 'pure idiomatic English,' was formed. I acknowledge that my early predilection was for the pompous words and sounding periods of Johnson; and I had greatly admired the sublime flights and glittering fancies of Counsellor Phillips, the Irish orator, then in the meridian of his fame; but my husband convinced me, by analyzing his sentences, that these were, as he had called them, 'sublime nonsense' " (386). Latinate diction and oratorical syntax, although apparently within his wife's imitative abilities, David Hale deemed inappropriate to a woman. The plain style Hale affected (an approach later perfected by Fanny Fern) was probably to her advantage. By the time she entered editorial work in 1830, a "middling" style increasingly characterized publicly circulated periodicals. Hale's writing was emphatically personal and approximated conversation caught in print. This combination made her writing accessible to the readers, men and women alike, who enthusiastically responded to the magazines she edited. Ultimately, then, Hale makes her husband responsible for teaching her the literary skills (echoes of his own) that made her success possible. The extended logic is that, just as her textual persona approximated her husband's, so, too, she might assume his place as provider for their children upon his death. To the end of her life, Sarah Hale asserted that she had become a writer only to "support my young family of five children and educate them as their father would have done" (*Godey's* 95 [Dec. 1877]: 522).

Newport, New Hampshire, does not figure on the literary map of the early nineteenth-century United States as an intellectual center equivalent to Cambridge, or even to Litchfield or Cincinnati. Yet its residents were highly literate, and used their literacy as markers of their social position. A remarkably complete account of an informal literary club that Hale organized has been preserved in Joseph W. Parmelee's "History of Newport." In this group, Hale and other women were able to experiment with public performances and writings with the sanction of the social elite of their community. The Coterie's membership speaks to the difficulty of classifying it as either a public or private phenomenon. It included women as well as men,[3] family members (David Hale and his sister Hannah) as well as other men of substance in the community, such as Cyrus Barton, editor of the *New Hampshire Spectator*. Its membership bespeaks class privilege, or so one must conclude from the rather florid account of the group, which notes the members' "well-sustained complacence at their advanced social position" (267). This, in turn, suggests both a freedom of publicly and socially sanctioned experimentation by people secure in their social identities. This coterie met regularly to "[give] audience to dramatic performances, recitations and readings from books and magazines, or the productions of some of their leading spirits. In addition to the more dignified exercises, free scope was given to conversation, songs, merriment, wit and repartee" (267). If, as Parmelee's account suggests, the Coterie afforded its members some exposure to drama, Hale and other members, women especially, might have found in it a forum wherein they could experiment, with the sanction of its members, with alternate public identities, as did Margaret Fuller and Catharine Beecher in similar situations.

As in Cincinnati's Semi-Colon Club, submissions to the Coterie were tendered anonymously and read aloud to the assembled members. And as in the Semi-Colon Club, the anonymity seems to have served as a spur to flirtation among the "single [members] in all the incipient stages of the tender passion leading up to the connubial state," (Parmelee 267): "A most interesting episode in the routine of the afternoon was the withdrawal and investigation of the contents of a sly pocket, or covert place in or about the venerable tree which had become the receptacle of all manner of anonymous contributions" (267–68). Parmelee likens the Coterie's festivities to "character and scenes in 'As You Like It,'" referring directly to the "love-making and philosophizing in the forest glades of Ardennes." The comparison to *As You Like It* is particularly apt, not only for the Coterie, which met outdoors, but for the Semi-Colon Club as well, where the practice of anonymity seems to have sparked an interest in a kind of textual "drag" performance, wherein women assumed men's personae, and men women's, a practice that only heightened the sexual atmosphere of the meetings.

It is likely that the retrospective accounts of such incidents use the trope of anonymous writing as flirtation to ensure that the writing and dramatic performances of women members did not "unsex" them. The trope holds in other situations, as well. For example, Alexander Fisher sought Catharine Beecher's acquaintance after reading some of her anonymous verses published in a journal edited by her father, and Margaret Fuller exchanged her private journal with several men for whom she felt more than intellectual attraction. Aligning the disclosure of private or anonymous writings with heterosexual courtship ensures that writing by women will always be done with reference to and in accordance with womanly behavior and will lead to domestic enclosure and a reinscription of women's writing as private.

Finally, as did the Semi-Colon Club, the Coterie provided a site wherein local publishers could gather material for their periodicals. Several club members subsequently published their writing in the *New Hampshire Spectator*, whose editor was a member of the group. Parmelee's memoir thus accords with accounts of how such literary groups functioned both to encourage and to normalize the idea of women's writing and public performances. Coupled with Hale's autobiographical sketches, it also suggests that elements of her formative experiences echo Beecher's and Fuller's: an exposure to books, reading, and the gender-coded split in literary praxis they encoded; the encouraging attention of male family members and her close identification with a paternal figure; an acquaintance with amateur dramatics; public and semipublic exposure in literary groups and at least implicit acceptance of her work by men, men of public and community stature who offered both criticism and support and who received their thanks by these women's acknowledgment that men enabled their textual productions.

It is tempting to assert that without a model of strong women such as Sarah Pierce, who assumed the masculine prerogatives of educational administration, Hale maintained a lifelong commitment to a conservative position regarding women's public roles.[4] Yet as Michelle Zimbalist Rosaldo suggests, "women's place in human social life is not in any direct sense a product of the things she does, but of the meaning her activities acquire through concrete social interaction" (400). Hale did much to ensure that her activities were understood to epitomize properly private womanhood. She maintained the appearance of deference to masculine power throughout her long life, a fiction that masked her own intervention in and manipulation of public opinion.

That deferential stance has made it difficult to separate the (auto)bio-graphical "facts" of Hale's life from retrospective textual representation. As she became prominent, Hale maintained an especially tight control over how her early life was represented. She wrote three autobiographical accounts—one early in her career as a preface to her poetry in her anthology, *The Ladies' Wreath* (1837); one mid-career in *Woman's Record* (1853), an account that depends heavily on Louis Godey's biographical sketch published in 1850, which, in turn, draws from the *Ladies' Wreath* account; and one when she retired from her editorship of *Godey's* only months before her death (1877). These texts are remarkably similar and vary primarily in emphasis. Most biographies depend on these sources, scattered letters, her brief prefaces, and public records for their information.

Of her early reading Hale recalls that Anne Radcliffe's *Mysteries of Udolpho* was a favorite. Rather than explain or justify reading a Gothic novel, a practice considered improper for women—not to mention seven-year-old girls—in the early 1800s, Hale links the incident to a larger agenda in the development of a patriotic but always private woman: "I name it on account of the influence it exercised over my mind. I had remarked, that of all the books I saw, few were written by Americans, and none by *women*. But here was a work, the most fascinating I had ever read, always excepting 'Pilgrim's Progress,' written by a *woman*. How happy it made me!—The wish to promote the reputation of my own sex, and my own country, were among the earliest mental emotions I can recollect" (*Wreath* 384–85).

Fifteen years later, Hale reprinted this paragraph, altering only the punctuation, in her *Woman's Record,* but added, "These feelings have had a salutary influence by directing my thoughts to a definite object; my literary pursuits have had an aim beyond self-seeking of any kind. The mental influence of woman over her own sex, which was so important in my case, has been strongly operative in inclining me to undertake this my latest work, 'Woman's Record' &c. I have sought to make it an assistant in home education; hoping the examples shown and characters portrayed, might have an inspiration and a power in advancing the moral progress of society" (687). Hale first disarms the potential threat of women writing, in this case subsuming *Udolpho* to more respectable works, those deemed especially appropriate for women's reading, such as *The Pilgrim's Progress.* She then links women's writing with the feminine obligation to "advance the moral progress of society," an activity she claims is to be accomplished privately. That is to say, women may influence women, and perhaps even men, at home. Hale next excuses her own obvious nonconformity to this pattern as the result of an excess of patriotic feeling. The obstreperousness of a woman's pointing out the dearth of books by American men is defused by the fact that the insight is attributed to a seven-year-old child. Such a strategy argues implicitly that the omissions are obvious even to a child; it likewise removes the potential threat such accusations would carry if articulated by an adult woman. Simultaneously, the potential critique entailed in her noting the lack of women writers becomes deflected onto the larger issue of America's need for writers generally. Omnipresent here is the father's gaze— apparent in Hale's invocation of God (in the text of *Pilgrim's Progress*), the Anglo-Saxon male canon, and the Founding Fathers. In a final rhetorical move, she links the fate of national literature to improved opportunities

for women's education. Understanding that this aim could only be realized
with the approval and assistance of men, Hale, in this passage, as in all of her
writing, in fact addresses a reader whose gender is male. Most significantly,
this expanded passage is included in a volume whose dedicatory page reads
in part: "Inscribed to the Men of America; Who show, in their laws and
customs, respecting Women, Ideas more just and feelings more noble than
were ever evinced by men of any other nation."

In the process of addressing this masculine readership, Hale demonstrates respect for and mastery of its discursive forms. The autobiographical
passage, ostensibly addressed to women, affects the reminiscent tone of
conversation. Hale's other writings follow this same general agenda. Even
though in one autobiographical fragment she had credited her mother with
much of her childhood learning, in later texts, she emphasized the importance of fathers. The biographical sketches of *Woman's Record* exemplify the
pattern. Hale's entry about Margaret Fuller begins with a paragraph detailing
the life and contributions of Timothy Fuller before introducing "Margaret"
as "the oldest child of the family, [who] at an early age evinced remarkable
aptitude for study; it became her father's pride and pleasure to cultivate her
intellect to the utmost degree" (665). This structure syntactically links the
daughter's aptitudes with the assertion that her father's patronage was the
key to their cultivation. Nowhere in the lengthy biographical sketch does
Hale mention Margarett Crane Fuller.

Even in cases where biographical fact is undifferentiated from myth,
Hale employs the same structure. Her introduction to the entry on Cornelia,
whose name she frequently used as a pseudonym, is subtitled: "The mother
of the Gracchi"; the first section of the essay paints "in forcible colours the
vast influence of mothers in the education of youth." But mid-entry Hale
asserts that "the whole life of Cornelia presents a beautiful character; and
from the facts which have come down to us we may [infer that] Cornelia
must have been educated in a very superior manner by *her father.* For in no
other manner can we account for her knowledge and love of literature" (33).
In the sentence crediting Cornelia's father with her "superior" education
and "love of literature" Hale could as well have left the agent of Cornelia's
education unspecified, since it is the result of purest speculation. But in
Sarah Josepha Hale's time, literary training was understood to be exclusively
a male preserve. Hence, although she credited her own mother with her
"predilection for literary pursuits," Hale did not see her as an exemplar.
Her mother's uses of literacy were confined to oral instruction, and did not

enter the realm of public discourse. Even after fifty years of public life, Hale continued to assert the importance of her brother's and husband's patronage and to credit them entirely for her success. In the entry she wrote about herself in *Woman's Record,* Hale concludes, "Yet I cannot close without adverting to the ready and kind aid I have always met with from those men with whom I have been most nearly connected. . . . To my husband I was . . . deeply indebted. . . . And if there is any just praise due to the works I have prepared, the sweetest thought is—that *his* name bears the celebrity" (687). Here Hale does not name her father as one of the men who furthered her career, giving his place to her husband. Lacking specific autobiographical information, we can only speculate why this is so: Perhaps her father's attention was reserved for his eldest child, a son; or perhaps because her father did not enjoy the same advantages of education and heightened social position as did David Hale, she omitted him from her narrative.

Nevertheless, Hale's training resembles that of her contemporaries: she became literate, credited men for her professional success, and championed the right of other women to seek advanced learning. The difference in her training marks a difference in her subsequent approaches to writing, self-representation, and educational policy and delimits another dimension of how, through manipulating codes of gender, women writers assumed the right to redefine and restructure cultural institutions.

Fanny Fern (1811–1872)

Grata Sara(h) Payson Willis Eldredge Farrington Parton (who also used the pseudonyms "Tabitha," "Olivia," and "Fanny Fern") is a figure whose multiplicity of names marks the difficulty of positing a stable (auto)biographical subject.[5] A writer who capitalized on the ambiguity of her identity, Fern demonstrates how the relation of writing women to home, school, and community changed as formal education for women became more generally available. As fifth child and third daughter in her family, Sara Willis was distanced from her father's scrutiny and patronage; moreover, from a very early age she boarded away from her family in schools headed by several of New England's most illustrious pioneer educators of women. These schools, in turn, mediated her connection with a wide community of readers and writers and facilitated her abilities at self-fashioning in various genres—including autobiography, fiction, personal essays, and periodical journalism.

In the Willis family, as in the Beechers, Fullers, and Buells, literate practices were central to the family's identity. Nathaniel Willis's father had edited
Boston's *Independent Chronicle*, a Whig newspaper, during the Revolution.
Although Willis himself had not received a college degree, he daily associated
with literate and discerning fellow citizens. A journalist and printer, he
edited the *Eastern Argus* and founded two other papers—the *Recorder*, the
first religious newspaper in the United States, and the *Youth's Companion*,
the first newspaper for juveniles (McGinnis 3). Almost no biographical
information is available about Hannah Parker, although she apparently had
some degree of advanced literacy. Like the Beechers, the Willis family unit
often expanded to include visitors and boarders. As Nathaniel Willis and
his wife were extremely devout, their home was a crossroads for itinerant
clergymen. According to James Parton, Fern's third husband, biographer,
and memoirist, Fern's recollections of her "grandfather's house" in her sketch
"The Prophet's Chamber" are autobiographical and refer to "her father's"
house. Of this home, Fern says that it "was to all intents and purposes
a ministerial tavern;—lacking the sign. . . . almost every steamboat, stage
and railroad car brought . . . a visitor. They dropped their carpet-bags in
the hall with the most perfect certainty of a welcome" ("Memoir" 28).

Biographers agree that the Willis children absorbed much of the elevated
atmosphere of political, journalistic, and theological debate that surrounded
them. As James Parton's memoir of his wife's childhood establishes, they
"learned, at a very early age, to employ, in their familiar letters, the phraseology which used to abound in religious newspapers and biographies" (26).
This ventriloquized religious discourse had its outlet in the papers Nathaniel
Willis published, for which his daughter Sara (and presumably her other
siblings, as well) read proof and wrote fillers, and in which she eventually
published essays.

Like the Beechers, many of the nine Willis children followed their
father's occupation. As Parton recalled, "Facility in composition was too
common among them to be remarked, and they took to pen and ink as
to a native element. They were brought up among newspapers and books"
("Memoir" 32). Sara Willis and three of her siblings became professional
journalists. Her elder brother Nathaniel Parker Willis, a popular poet and
model for Fern's infamous Apollo Hyacinth and his later reincarnation,
Hyacinth Ellet, also wrote as a foreign correspondent for the *New York
Mirror*, cofounded and edited the *New York Home Journal*, and edited
the *Atlantic Monthly*. An elder sister, Julia Dean Willis, became a linguist,

teacher, and correspondent for the *Home Journal*; and a younger brother, Richard Storrs Willis, a composer and poet, edited the *New York Musical World and Times*.

Beyond these documented facts, it is difficult to establish biographical "truth" for Sara Willis, since Fanny Fern's phenomenally popular novel *Ruth Hall*, widely accepted as a roman à clef, determined (and continues to determine) the structure of subsequent biographical interpretations. *Ruth Hall* insists that its heroine is a self-made woman writer who succeeded without paternal assistance and in spite of active opposition from her already notorious elder brother. Other sketches purporting to be autobiographical emphasize her mother's literary promise, linking motherhood with writing as well as with reading. Of her mother, Fern wrote to a juvenile readership: "Had [her] time not been so constantly engrossed by a fast-increasing family, . . . I am confident she would have distinguished herself. Her hurried letters, written with one foot upon the cradle, give ample evidence of this. She *talked poetry unconsciously!* The many gifted men to whom her hospitality was extended, and who were her warm personal friends, know this" (*New* 12–13).

In its conflation of images of writing with child care, the similarity of this representation to Fuller's schoolmates' estimation of her early intellectual gifts is striking. Although Fern is the only one of these four women actually to portray her mother as a writer, she also immediately brings her mother's genius under a masculine supervisory gaze that approves even incipient writing by women as long as maternal duties are not slighted. The balance of Fern's writing on behalf of women's authorship does not stray from this pattern. She insists that women may write and that it does not detract from their maternal functions. *Ruth Hall* demonstrates, Hale-fashion, that a woman may turn to writing as the highest expression of maternal duty in the support of her fatherless children. Columns such as "A Practical Blue Stocking" guarantee that the labor of writing will never interfere with domestic duty, since the order and regularity engendered by writing can only enhance the practice of good housekeeping. Like good prose, "windows [are] transparently clean"; like columns of print, "the hearth-rug [is] longitudinally and mathematically laid down; the pictures hung 'plumb' upon the wall." Even in other columns, which make the reverse argument, showing that the literary text erases its domestic context, domestic containment and masculine supervision are still at issue. In "Writing Under Difficulties," Fern asserts: "I see parentheses in Uncle Tom's Cabin and Jane Eyre and Shirley, where the authors stated, that here they stopped to wash the ink spots from their fingers: or to make bread or put kindling in the oven preparatory to it, while the celestial spark stood in abeyance. Sometimes 'stopped to wash baby' might have been inserted on the margin opposite some interrupted pathetic passage" (*Ledger* 8 May 1869). Although writing and domesticity mutually efface each other, they are for Fern inseparable. Women writers cannot be separated from their maternal function; that maternal function, she emphasizes, differentiates their practice of literacy from men's.

Fern echoes, as well, the association of women with reading aloud that is so central to Beecher's, Hale's, and Fuller's childhood reminiscences. However, she moves it from home to school, replacing mother with teacher. Nor should this transformation come as a surprise in an autobiography structured as a progression from a mother-centered childhood to a youth spent in female seminaries. "When I Was Young," an essay written long after common school instruction routinely taught writing to girls, fictionalizes school "as it used to be," before a standard course of study replaced embroidery with writing:

> in my school-days proper attention was given to rivers, bays, capes, islands, and cities in the forenoon—interspersed with, "I love, thou lovest, he, she, or it loves;" then, at the child's hungry hour—(twelve)—were dismissed to roast beef and apple dumplings. At three we marched back with a comfortable dinner under our aprons—with cool heads, rosy cheeks, and a thimble in our pockets; and never a book did we see all the blessed afternoon. I see her—the schoolma'am . . . with her benevolent face, and ample bosom—your flat-chested woman never should keep school, she has no room for the milk of human kindness; . . . when we were all seated, she drew from her pocket some interesting book and read it aloud to us—not disdaining to laugh at the funny places, and allowing us to do the same—hearing, well pleased, all our childish remarks, and answering patiently all our questions concerning the story, or travels, or poetry she was reading, while our willing fingers grew still more nimble; and every child uttered an involuntary "Oh!" when the sun slanted into the west window, telling us that afternoon school was over.
> Ah, those were the days! (*New* 283–84)

In this passage the mother/teacher presides over a rosy prelapsarian and feminine world where even masculine pursuits such as conjugating Latin verbs are conducted in the mother tongue. In this world, desire is satiated by ample and timely nourishment. The nourishment is both literal—the roast beef and apple dumplings, dispensed presumably by nurturing mothers (and cooked by competent servants)—and, more notably, figurative, provided by the "ample-bosomed" schoolmistress. Afternoon school is the site of feminine community. The book, birthed from the teacher's womblike pocket, is a natural part of the woman-teacher. She stops for interruptions, resisting the relentless onward pressure of formal instruction in reading and writing. This passage stands in stark contrast to Margaret Fuller's recollection of how her father's rigor interrupted her childhood development. As well, it marks an implicit contrast to the strictly-disciplined public schools, now under the direction of writing-*masters*. Here every child is included as a willing participant in the reading and schooling experience. On the simplest level sewing and reading are compatible and appropriately feminine activities. The girls can sew while listening to what is read to them. If, however, one reads this text emphasizing the freedom extended the children to ask questions, the phrase "our willing fingers grew more nimble" suggests that engagement with the text, when mediated by womanly intuition, results in both increased production and enhanced intellectual engagement. If we read the girls' sewing as a metaphorical writing, the scene figures a utopia wherein women both read and write, sew and think, question and consume texts in an enclosed world safe from masculine intrusion, and the motherly schoolteacher becomes yet another embodiment of Ellen Kilshaw and Mary Foote.

Fanny Fern's autobiographical representation, then, places women at the center of her childhood education, as ideal readers, teachers, and writers. Unlike her peers, however, she says nothing of her father, brothers, or husband. Only in a fictional text, which has been taken for autobiographical fact, do these figures directly enter. The claims that Ruth Hall's brothers and father did nothing to advance her literary career are undoubtedly Fanny Fern's greatest notoriety and are generally taken as the biographical facts of Sara Willis's life. Other texts suggest, however, that Sara Willis's father and brothers held an important place in her literary training. Her home training as compositor, editor, and feature writer certainly enabled her start as a writer, as she implies in a column addressed "To Literary Aspirants." Although the column is intended to emphasize the difficulty of beginning a literary career, it establishes, as well, the importance of her early entitlements: "Many a weary tramp I had; much pride I put in my pocket, and few pennies, even with the advantage of a good education and a properly prepared ms. and the initiation of 'reading proof'—for my father, who was an editor, when I was not more than twelve years old—before I succeeded" (*Ledger* 28

Mar. 1868). Like Beecher, Willis/Hall/Fern benefited from family name and connections. James Parton remarks that N.P. Willis's "rising fame as a poet made his sister Sara, at the various schools that she attended, a person of note from the beginning" ("Memoir" 35). (Admittedly, this passage also suggests a difficult sibling rivalry.) Nor is it commonly noted that the publicity resulting from Fern's obvious caricature of N.P. Willis in *Ruth Hall* accomplished the same ends that his promotion of her would have effected.

It is difficult to determine whether any of Fern's encounters with institutional education were as rosy as the dame school experience recounted above. It is clear, however, that as the child of a "father and mother [who] shared the universal ambition of New England parents to give their children the best advantages of education" (Parton, "Memoir" 32), she enjoyed the broadest exposure to the spectrum of educational experiences available to a young girl of her generation. Like Lyman Beecher and Timothy Fuller, Nathaniel Willis was the primary agent in moving his daughter out of the home circle and into the more public world of formal women's education. Concerned that she lacked an appropriately feminine piety, he placed her in a series of schools whose listing encapsulates the historical development of the women's seminary: in early childhood, she was enrolled in two Boston grammar schools, the first for girls and the second coeducational; at age eleven she entered the Reverend Joseph Emerson's Ladies Seminary in Saugus, Massachusetts; in her midteens, she spent several years at the Adams Female Academy in Derry, New Hampshire, headed by Zilpah Polly Grant and Mary Lyon; finally she transferred to Catharine Beecher's Hartford Female Seminary in 1828. This succession of schools all failed to develop in Sara Willis the sanctity her parents had hoped for.

Sara Willis's years at Hartford Female Seminary, which she attended from May 1828 through April 1831, demonstrate how Catharine Beecher had adapted her educational methods from those of Litchfield Female Academy and show how Willis's separation from her family and her exposure to a series of strong women engaged in institutional, theological, and educational revision and administration produced in this woman writer an exquisite and finely honed sense of a mobile identity, able to assume whatever textual manifestation the rhetorical situation demanded.

When Zilpah Grant left the Adams Academy in 1828 to found Ipswich Female Seminary, Sara Willis returned home briefly while her father looked for another school that would continue the Adams emphasis on moral rectitude. The Willis family's minister, Edward Beecher, recommended that Sara be educated under the supervision of "Miss Catharine Beecher, whose orthodoxy combined with a practical application in domestic life, was unexceptionable. Sara was, therefore, enrolled in The Ladies' Seminary in Hartford, Connecticut, where Miss Beecher presided as headmistress, assisted by Miss Harriet Beecher as pupil-teacher" (Adams 4).

At Hartford Female Seminary, Catharine Beecher, a product of the self-reporting system of Litchfield Female Academy and a devotee of Zilpah Grant's preceptorship model, sought to duplicate both those methods, possibly even in a more intense manner. Like Sarah Pierce's students, the young women who attended Hartford Female Seminary boarded with local families or lived at home. However, their boarding-out was closely monitored by the school. Beecher ensured that her teachers lived in the same boardinghouses as her students; she charged them to supervise students after school hours and outside school spaces. Thus Hartford Female Seminary and its attendant facilities functioned as a family writ large: the students were children; teachers assumed the function of mothers; and the redoubtable Miss Beecher assumed the position of father/administrator.

Within the school family, each teacher was personally responsible to monitor the behavior of specific students. Catharine Beecher herself supervised Sara Willis, reporting to her parents on every aspect of her behavior, from expenditures on a "Spring bonnet" and "corsettes" to the state of her soul (27 May 1829; Sophia Smith Collection). Beecher apparently had as little success inculcating piety in the high-spirited Sara as did her predecessors. Fern recalled Hartford Female Seminary as a place where she was sent for "algebra and safe-keeping, both of which I hated" (*Caper-Sauce* 108), while Catharine Beecher's report to the Willis parents concluded: "I do not feel much confidence in Sarah's *piety* but I *do* think that religious influence has greatly improved her character. . . . tho' her faults are not all eradicated, & tho' I still fear the world has the *first* place, yet I think religion occupies much of her thoughts. She now rooms alone, & has much time for reading & reflection" (27 May 1829; Sophia Smith Collection).

While Sara Willis might have chafed at Hartford Female Seminary's regimen she never hesitated to assert that, while the school's formal writing instruction may have caused classmates despair, for her " 'Composition day' . . . was only a delight" (*Ledger* 15 July 1871). The Beecher method of instruction, under which she thrived, included "Latin and English compositions—versified translations from Virgil's Eclogues and Ovid's

Metamorphoses—[forms which] astonished those who had not been in the habit of expecting such things in a female school" (Stowe, "Catharine" 87). At such exercises, Fern apparently excelled. Among the "various methods" of teaching the composition—including oral declamation, vocabulary building, prescriptive stylistics, outlining, abstracting, and analysis (*1831 Catalog* 14)—parody or imitation of others' texts stands out as an exercise Sara Willis must have excelled in. In fact, the only one of her surviving compositions is a parody, not of a "classical" writer but of her own headmistress. Entitled "Suggestions on Arithmetic," it invokes both Catharine Beecher's efforts to revise textbooks used by the seminary and her *Suggestions Respecting Improvements in Education, Presented to the Trustees*, published the year after Willis entered the seminary. Its irreverent approach to seminary pieties accurately foreshadows the style and tone of Fanny Fern's columns.

Like Beecher, Fuller, and Hale, Sara Willis was also introduced as a writer at a comparatively early age to a larger community—parents, friends, trustees, local businessmen, newspaper publishers—who were occasionally invited to observe Hartford Female Seminary's activities. At terms' end, outsiders were invited to witness the examinations and the following "Exhibition, at which time a gentleman [would] read selections from the compositions of the pupils" (*1831 Catalog* 20). Less formal occasions brought the students' social skills under similar scrutiny, as Catharine Beecher arranged "weekly levees at which gentlemen were present" as well as local celebrities the likes of "Mrs. Sigourney." The purpose of these socials, according to Willis's granddaughter, was to prepare the "young ladies to enter society" (Ethel Parton, "Fanny Fern, An Informal Biography," 64; Sophia Smith Collection, Smith College). One of the two student newspapers produced at the seminary, the *Levee Gazette*, may have been intended to circulate to seminary friends and patrons at these gatherings.[6]

Seminary students were charged with sustaining the illusion of equitable interchange between community and seminary. If Willis's memoirs are to be believed, this was not always a duty they embraced enthusiastically. "Suggestions on Arithmetic," for example, includes a scene in which the narrator, whose "overseers" fear she is "growing pale and thin from too close application" to her mathematics, is "dragged perforce into what they styled *a levée*," where she spends the evening in the company of various "square-toed" gentlemen, "the question, 'Have you formed a favorable opinion of Hartford?' having been answered, as well as the rest of the levée catechism, in monosyllables" (Parton, "Memoir" 40).

Despite this rather laconic account, biographers of Fanny Fern have identified these exhibitions and socials as arenas in which the young Sara Willis's writings encountered a broader readership. The infamous "Suggestions," for example, was read at the end-of-term Exhibition in 1829. Biographers Ethel Parton and Joyce Warren both repeat the story that at the levées Willis met the editor of the local newspaper. Significantly, Ethel Parton begins her account of this relationship by emphasizing that Sara Willis was "first noticed as a sister of the poet, N.P. Willis," but that she quickly became "a personality in her own right. Her sayings were quoted in social circles, her compositions copied and passed from hand to hand, paragraphs from them published in a leading local newspaper. The editor had made her acquaintance at a levee. Sometimes, wanting to fill a too-short column or sprinkle in a bit of spice, he came direct to the school, to ask for Miss Willis's latest. When she had nothing available he is known to have sat beside her in the school-room with paper and pencil at one desk, while she at the next one dictated as fast as he could write" ("Informal" 70).

That three of these writers may have been brought into publication through socializing with editors at literary groups may be coincidental; but the frequency with which the story appears suggests that it may be as much a trope as biographical fact, especially in the account of Willis dictating bon mots to the editor of a Hartford newspaper. The account carefully maintains a gender coding that seems to belie the facts: Willis was a skillful writer and editor as well as talker. Nevertheless, in Ethel Parton's telling of the anecdote, the woman talks and the man writes. When she writes, he edits, choosing "paragraphs" from them to add "spice" to his publication.

In establishing the usefulness of these levées to Fern's later success as a writer, scholars have given less attention to how such occasions served to further Beecher's career. Always aware that her projects would best succeed if she could claim broad bases of support, Beecher was careful to include parents, friends of students, and town fathers who were potential donors. These social occasions served to demonstrate to a masculine scrutiny that that gender-specific education was useful, circumspect, and deferential. For example, in the *1831 Catalog,* Beecher concluded her paragraph describing the Annual Exhibitions in this fashion: "On these occasions, at first, the audience was small and select. But as the popularity of the school increased, the assembly increased, until it has become a question with many friends of the institution, whether these occasions will not be better dispensed with entirely, as involving too great publicity for those whose sphere is

retirement. Such questions are best settled by the judgment of the judicious
and refined in the vicinity, who can best learn all the circumstances of
the case" (20). Characteristically, Beecher claims no responsibility for the
schools' increasing "popularity," nor does she align herself with those "friends
of the institution" who would cancel the Exhibitions. Their concerns are
indirectly quoted but not underwritten by Beecher. Nor does she promise
any action either to continue or suspend the activities. The primary function
of this passage is to claim the school's increasing visibility and success.

The details of Hartford Female Seminary's connection with Willis,
Beecher, and their community demonstrate how difficult and misleading
is the attempt to separate home from school from community—and by
extension emphasize how misleading it is to invoke metaphors of public
and private spheres to describe the conditions under which gendered behaviors were taught, performed, and parodied. Fanny Fern is a transitional
figure, marking both the fictions of womanly retirement she and her peers
honored and the simultaneous acknowledgment that many, if not most,
of these behaviors were indeed fictions. Fern's autobiographical statements,
more than Beecher's or Hale's or Fuller's, proclaim their fictive structure
even as they invite cooperative readers to believe them as literal truth.
Students of Fern have interpreted her various and contradictory statements
of autobiography as the strategy whereby the woman who felt a "lifelong
dread of *publicity*" (Ellen Parton, 28 Feb. 1899, Sophia Smith Collection)
avoided public scrutiny. Such readings neatly fit the explanatory pattern so
long predominant in structuring our understandings of nineteenth-century
womanhood, but do not account for Fern's radicalism (certainly not the
stance of a woman determined to avoid notoriety), nor for her determined
playing on this willingness of readers to read her texts as transparent in the
service of selling more books, nor for her glee in maintaining an ambiguous
identity. If *Ruth Hall* is a sentimental novel about a devoted wife and
mother who succeeds in supporting her children despite the machinations
of evil male family members, it is also a text that refuses the conventions
of private retirement. If Fanny Fern, as her daughter claimed, "said the
public had a right to know an author only as such, and should seek to
know nothing of the woman" (Ellen Parton, 28 Feb. 1899, Sophia Smith
Collection), she nevertheless exploited the public's curiosity. Fern's "How
I Look" articulates the difficulty of establishing whether her performed
identities resulted from her avoidance of publicity, or whether the illusory
nature of her "true identity" resulted as much from readers' determination

to fix her as it did from her wish to avoid publicity. To the request of "a correspondent" to describe herself, Fern replies "I should be very happy to answer these questions, did I know myself. I proceed to explain why I cannot tell whether 'I be I.'" She then narrates a series of occasions upon which readers claim to have identified or described her. At the opera, a "strange gentleman" announces that he knows her "*intimately*"; in a picture gallery, a portrait "labelled 'Fanny Fern'" was to be sold; in California, another image "taken smiling" is "peddled round." The essay concludes with the words of "a man who got into my parlor under cover of 'New-Year's calls,'" who exclaims, "'Well, now, I *am* agreeably disappointed! I thought from the way you *writ*, that you were a great six-footer of a woman, with snapping black eyes and a big waist, and I *am* pleased to find you looking so soft and so femi-*nine*!'" (*Ledger* 9 Apr. 1870).

Ultimately, we might conclude that Fanny Fern stands as the best exemplar of multiple identities and performed gender, and use her insistence on fictive identity as a lens through which to read her contemporaries. But it is equally important to account for the degree to which she identified herself with masculine norms. Like Beecher's and Hale's, her writing addresses an omnipresent but invisible male gaze. She demonstrates her awareness of the expectations of public discourse especially in her early work. "The Model Husband," her first column, adeptly articulated cultural and behavioral expectations; many more essays of the same stripe followed. "The Model Wife" gently laughs at but does not seriously challenge conventional wisdom about the notion of "separate spheres." The humor of "The Model Minister" and of "Deacons' Daughters and Ministers' Sons" is premised on the tension between "reality" and the pressure of ideal stereotypes. Other columns exploit the notion that women writers and readers could be interested only in the sentimental. In these early columns, instrumental in establishing Fern as a writer who could be trusted, women are portrayed as light-minded gossips, dutiful daughters, and nurturing wives.

Yet like Beecher, Fern used the feminine stereotype to pave the way for more daring work. On the same *Ledger* page as a reprint of one of her most sentimental pieces, "Little Benny," appears her outspoken and positive review of Whitman's *Leaves of Grass* (*Ruth* xxxii). Fern devoted many of her early columns to demonstrating that women writers did not practice their craft at the expense of their housewifely and motherly duties, always concluding that no self-respecting woman would become a writer if it meant that she would neglect the duties men expected of her. As Ruth Hall avers,

"No happy woman ever writes" (175). Only in her final columns, written after her reputation was firmly established, did Fern publicly advance the notion that women need not marry, that they might be able to maintain themselves by their independent earnings.

Unlike Beecher and Fuller, Hale and Fern seem to share few similarities. Separated by a generation, their lives demonstrate quite different means by which women learned to write and the different ways they applied those skills. Thus they delimit the outer ranges of how family, school, and community intersected with women's writing. In other ways, however, their similarities are striking. Like their differences, these similarities mark ranges of differentiation from the pattern that is common to Beecher and Fuller. The (auto)biographies of Catharine Beecher, Fanny Fern, and Margaret Fuller seem to confirm Joan Wallach Scott's contention that "identities and experiences are variable phenomena . . . discursively organized in particular contexts or configurations" (*Feminists Theorize* 35), while Sarah Josepha Hale's life writings test the limits of that assertion. Beecher and Fuller, for example, both published several different versions of their autobiographies, varying the facts they included and drawing different interpretations of their meaning. Sara Willis, who later in life claimed legal title to her pseudonym, Fanny Fern, utterly refused the fiction of a coherent authorial identity, leaving biographers and scholars to speculate on the degree to which *Ruth Hall* and the scattered first-person reminiscences that appeared in her weekly newspaper columns represented her life. Hale promulgated an unvaryingly consistent version of her life, always insisting that she was a reluctant writer who undertook her career only to support her fatherless children. Even after those children were grown, Hale maintained this narrative; nor did she alter her dress, her hairstyle, or her public image. Yet common sense, coupled with a few tantalizing hints in her letters suggest that her protestations of invariability masked behaviors as potentially transgressive as those performed by Fanny Fern.

Chapter Three

PATRONYMICS, PROPERTY, AND PROPER NAMING

In July 1856 "James Parton and Sarah P. Parton, his wife" brought suit against William Fleming to halt him from "printing, publishing and circulating a 'Cook Book' purporting to be prepared and published by 'Fanny Fern.'" To the court "Mrs. Parton allege[d] that she is *the* 'Fanny Fern;' that all her writings are published under that name, and that she has acquired a special and the only right to use it; . . . that the [Cook Book's] preface is an attempted imitation of her style; that it is ungrammatical, vulgar, and somewhat obscene; and that the said 'Cook Book' will injure the character of the complainant, (Mrs. Parton,) will lessen the value of her title, ('Fanny Fern,') and will inflict great pecuniary loss upon her" (*Ledger* 2 Aug. 1856). At issue in this suit was not only Fern's right to own the name under which she had published much of her work but also the temporal, textual, and subjective mobility entailed in any name. Fern's suit, brought under the name of her third husband, established that regardless of how many versions of Fanny Fern people believed they had identified, those versions always were to be unified by the implicit link to one woman's body. Yet that body need not necessarily bear the "title" under dispute in the lawsuit. The multiplicity of names and titles at play in this suit suggests one of the strategies used by Fern and other writing women to maintain a uniformity of textual character (as "True Women"), to exploit a variety of personae (whereby they often exceeded the bounds of "True Womanhood"), and to retain legal right to their written work.

The court's decision, which established the legal connection of the "complainant's" name, title, body, and intellectual progeny/property, was necessary because of the inherently arbitrary and unstable connection of signifier and signified at the point of personal identity. The court's attempt to clarify the issue by separating the identity of "the complainant, (Mrs. Parton)" from "her title, ('Fanny Fern')," seems only temporarily effective, since this woman "was" no more Mrs. Parton or Fanny Fern than she "had been" at earlier stages in her life Grata Sarah Payson Willis, Sal Volatile, Sara Willis, Sarah P. Eldredge, Mrs. Samuel P. Farrington, Tabitha, Olivia, or Olivia Branch.

In establishing that Mrs. Parton might also and simultaneously be Fanny Fern, the court implied that she could legally choose her name according to situational demands. As Fern puts it: "Listen! All you who wear (blue) bonnets, and down on your grateful knees to me, for unfurling the banner of Women's (scribblers) Rights. Know, henceforth, that Violet Velvet is as much your name, (for purposes of copyright and other rights,) as Julia Parker, if you choose to make it so" (*Ledger* 2 Aug. 1856). Fern's suit suggests that she and her sister-writers exploited the anonymity of written text, invoking their names to guarantee authorial identity as a means of owning and circulating property, and extending the right of self-naming to others who shared their racial and class entitlements. By extension, it also suggests that literacy, race, and class determine who might name whom, since Fern's suit stemmed not only from Fleming's attempt to usurp her lucrative trademark name but also from his linking it to a text that was "ungrammatical, vulgar, and . . . obscene." In other words, Fleming had implied, through his inept use of language, that Fern was a woman of lower class.

These issues of class status become even clearer as Fern advances her objections against Fleming's having produced a cook book, a genre intended for a class of persons Fern did not stoop to write for. "A Cook Book! including, proverbially, ingredients out of reach, pecuniarily and latitudinally, of the very persons for whom cook books are intended; and useless . . . to those who . . . can also afford to hire cooks, who know more than any cook book can teach them" (*Ledger* 2 Aug. 1856). Cook books, in Fern's opinion, are bought only by social pretenders, those who can afford book and ingredients, but whose monetary reach exceeds their social grasp. Such fears about class status plagued Fern, a woman who wished to be thought respectable, but who was often castigated as déclassé because of her choice of topics, her impossibly breezy style, and, most of all, because she was a woman who worked—in public—for her living.

Fern's lawsuit, then, brings to the fore questions central to the connection of a name to feminine authorship: Under what circumstances might a

woman adopt a pseudonym? Use her patronym? Her married name? Are
the results of this "choice" related to her identity? To issues of domestic
containment? To her circulation as an author in the marketplace? That the
issues entailed in naming are closely tied to gender becomes clear when
they are examined against the implications of publishing without a name,
an option Fern, Beecher, and Fuller rarely employed. Nor did they often
use the conventional gendered version of anonymity, the attribution "By
a Lady." Anonymity implies the total dissociation of text and body; such
generic authorship was, by nineteenth-century grammatical convention,
masculine. Feminized anonymity offers no surer guarantee, since there
is no reason a man could not sign a text "by a Lady" (or vice versa, for
that matter).

These writers intentionally signed their texts as a way of claiming their
property. For example, Catharine Beecher rarely published without an overt
and even duplicate signature. Her *Treatise on Domestic Economy* (1843)
identifies her both by name and by reputation as "late Principal of the
Hartford Female Seminary." When Beecher chose anonymity, she did so
for a purpose. Two years later she published *Duty of American Women to
Their Country* anonymously, saying that she wished to avoid the implication
that the text came "from a mere individual" (qtd. in L.B. Stowe 123). By
1845, Beecher's name and reputation were well established. The anonymity
she elected in this case broadened the address of her book and invoked a
broader constituency—of men as well as women—who were interested in
issues of western education. Not to tie the book's authorship to a "mere
[read feminine] individual" gave her text, by extension, generic [masculine]
authority, an interpretation supported by Beecher's appending "extracts
from letters received from gentlemen of high standing in various parts of
our nation, [which] will serve to corroborate the views expressed in the
preceding pages" (131).

The equation of generic with masculine is established even more clearly
by Margaret Fuller's use of anonymity. Her first published essay, "In Defense
of Brutus," was written as a rejoinder to a speech given by George Bancroft.
As the details of the interchange make clear, Fuller's anonymity was not an
act of feminine reticence, but a gender-laden rhetorical strategy appropriate
to the encounter. Bancroft's speech, published in the *North American Review,*
had asserted that Brutus's reputation as a hero was a result simply of his
notoriety as an assassin. Fuller's anonymous response in the Boston *Daily
Advertiser* emphasized Plutarch's more favorable assessment of Brutus. In

turn, Fuller was answered by "a correspondent from Salem who signed himself 'H.' 'H' took issue with her by pointing to Gibbon's and Cicero's accounts of Brutus' moral defects" (Fuller, *Letters* 1:228).[1]

Fuller recalls, "He ['H'] detected some ignorance in me nevertheless as he marked that I wrote with 'ability' and seemed to *consider me* as an elderly gentleman *I considered* the affair as highly flattering" (*Letters* 1:226). Thus Fuller entered the world of publication not anonymously but in drag, as it were, fully engaging in the hom(m)o-social commerce of elevated literary debate. I use a variant of Luce Irigaray's terms (*ho[m]mo-sexual,* implying an immediate practice, and *hom[m]o-sexual,* implying a socially-mediated practice [171]) to mark the fact that this interchange took place within a network of "masculine . . . speculations, mirror games, identifications, and more or less rivalrous appropriations, . . . the smooth workings . . . of relations among men" (172). The terms of this debate resembled nothing so much as the topics fixed for a Harvard class in rhetoric. Fuller responded to a public speech about a classic author delivered in a set mode. Bancroft's, Fuller's, and "H" 's arguments were not new ideas but new combinations of conventional sentiments. Originality, and, by extension, authorship, was less at issue than the participants' skills in manipulating generic arguments. Hence, anonymity, for Fuller as well as for "H," was tantamount to a generic—that is, masculine—response.

Fuller later explored another variant of anonymity by signing many of the European dispatches she wrote for the *New-York Tribune* with a star. This device gave her generic authority of anonymity but allowed her to claim a group of texts that otherwise might have been attributed to multiple authors. These essays, centering on European literary and political issues, could not properly have been signed by a woman. Although the authorship of the columns was not secret, the device of signing with a star allowed the *Tribune* to gloss the issue of its correspondent's gender. At the same time, because it was standard practice for newspapers to print unsigned columns, because it was highly unusual for a woman to serve as a general essayist in a major newspaper, and because Fuller's writing style was not conventionally "feminine," such a device distinguished her writings.

If an anonymous text implied the generic male, it becomes important to ask why a woman would sign her text with a feminine signifier. The proper name has a multiple signification: The given name signifies feminine identity; the patronym, masculine filiation. The proper name (given+patronym) marks the woman as property of her father or husband—

in the mid-nineteenth century, a commodity that was his to exchange. In an age when a woman's literary production was scrutinized as if she and her text were one, the proper name also signified a woman's permission to write as an exemplar of her sex. Thus the initial act of womanly propriety was to enter literary production by presenting credentials, endorsements, affidavits, or letters of introduction from men. As Fern's heroine Ruth Hall learns to her dismay, "It were useless to apply to a long-established leading paper for employment, unless endorsed by some influential name" (121). That name would, of course, be masculine—and probably that of a relative.

Thus aside from occasional forays into anonymity, each of these women published her work under a name that identified her as feminine and equated her with father or husband, an act that, according to Irigaray, characterizes the organization of "so-called patriarchal societies." Such societies employ "a symbolic system whose instrument and representative is the proper name: the name of the father, the name of God . . . characteristic of a capitalist regime: . . . the division of labor among private producer-owners who exchange their women-commodities among themselves" (172–73). Initially Beecher, Hale, Fern, and Fuller used their patronyms as a way of signaling their affiliation with an influential family. That name could also imply the endorsement of the institutional affiliations of their fathers—the church, the school, the government. Finally, such implicit paternal approval also suggested the approbation of broader community interests—members of a church congregation, faculty and boards of trustees of educational institutions, even legal sanction.

Fathers' approval of their daughters' public work was literal as well as symbolic. After the death of Catharine Beecher's fiancé, Alexander Fisher, Lyman Beecher announced to his daughter that he had received "providential indications" that she need not marry, but might devote her life to her "establishment at Hartford" (16 Dec. 1825; Beecher-Stowe Collection, Schlesinger). Thus directly released, she turned her energies toward her professional life. Lyman Beecher used his associates ("the smooth workings . . . of relations among men") to seal her success. Sklar notes that "within a month [he] had canvassed the . . . community, obtained definite commitments from scholars" to attend Hartford Female Seminary, and "arranged for it to open within six weeks" (*Catharine Beecher* 53). Beecher also profited from her brother Edward's reputation as "Master of the Hartford Grammar School." According to Harveson, "the prestige of Edward's position as head of a very old and highly respected classical school . . . together with the esteem extended to any children of Lyman Beecher, would create a favorable attitude toward the new school" (34).

Later, after Catharine Beecher's reputation as an educator and writer was established, she, in turn, used the Beecher name to promote her sister Harriet's work. Her act extends the network of equivalences according to proper names. More important, it implies that the hom(m)o-social exchange Irigaray attributes to "men" can function among bodies gendered feminine as well. In fact, "hom(m)o-social exchange" may be undertaken by any entitled cultural producer. For example, Stowe, when not yet a recognized author, allowed James Hall to "ascribe" her "Essay on Languages" to her sister, a means of invoking Catharine's authorial reputation (Stowe, *Life* 69). Several years later, Harriet collected a group of similar essays into a volume entitled *The Mayflower* (1844). This, her first published book, was introduced by Catharine, who by that time had begun to establish herself as a moral and cultural arbiter of print fiction.

Catharine also called upon her networks of affiliation to circulate Harriet's writing. To Lydia Sigourney, a Hartford associate, she wrote from Cincinnati: "Since I have been collecting Harriets [sic] pieces it has occurred to me that as every body who wants such sort of articles comes to you, that you might dispose of these pieces *more profitably* (for it is a money making effort) than she or I could do at this distance from the head quarters of literature. Trusting to your kind interest in a young & literary mother, I commend them to your care & discretion to dispose of as you shall deem best for her interests. I wish to have her name 'Mrs Harriet Beecher Stowe' put to them—for I have taken the credit of much that she has written & entirely against my will" (24 Apr. 1838; Hoadly Collection, Connecticut Historical Society). Here Catharine, now an authorized cultural producer, (re)names her sister, signaling Harriet's move from anonymous or erroneously attributed authorship into a new arena of exchange, women's authorship, presided over by "Mrs. Sigourney," a broker for "such sort of articles." In this paragraph, names function in a complex fashion. Catharine first identifies Harriet as a "mother," but a mother with a difference—she is "literary." Next, she specifies the name under which her sister's essays are to be published, a doubled patronymic that identifies Harriet first as a married woman; second as a Beecher; and finally as the wife of a man who, for that brief moment, enjoyed a literary reputation that exceeded her own.[2] Four years later, Calvin Stowe granted his wife "permission" to write professionally and renamed her. He wrote her in 1842, "You must be a *literary woman*. It

is so written in the book of fate. Make all your calculations accordingly, . . .
drop the E out of your name, which only encumbers it and stops the flow
and euphony, and write yourself only and always, *Harriet Beecher Stowe,*
which is a name euphonous [sic], flowing, and full of meaning" (qtd. in
Hedrick, *Harriet Beecher Stowe* 138). Significantly, Calvin Stowe's "new"
name for his wife is that given her four years earlier by her broker/sister.

By contrast, Sarah Josepha Buell Hale, whose father did not wield the
cultural weight of a Lyman Beecher, did not use her family name to identify
herself as a writer. Rather she capitalized on her married name to bring
herself into public circulation, always reminding readers that she wrote
from necessity. Her career as a writer was the literal result of her husband's
hom(m)o-social relationships. After David Hale's death, members of his
Masonic lodge subsidized the publication of her first volume of poetry,
The Genius of Oblivion and Other Original Poems. Published anonymously
"by a lady of New Hampshire," the book's authorship was an open secret.
According to Olive Burt, the Masons promised that she would be able
to sell a copy to every lodge member in New England (43). With that
guarantee, her book would need no more specific identification of author
than the descriptive phrase she used, which does not so much obscure her
authorship as emphasize the image of womanly reticence appropriate to a
new and impoverished but still socially prominent widow. Lest the potential
readers of *Oblivion* forget that it was written with David Hale's permission,
Hale chided readers in a "Dedicatory Poem, Inscribed to Friends and Patrons
of the Author": "And lives there *one,* who, with ungen'rous part, / Will spurn
this offering of the broken heart!" and assures her husband's friends, "Still,
still your patronage shall be my boast— / You kindly gave it, when 'twas
needed most" (*Genius* vii, viii).

Long after her children were grown Hale remained true to that promise,
reminding readers that she wrote as her husband's surrogate. When she was
sixty-four years old, she prefaced the second edition of *Northwood* in these
words: "TWENTY-FIVE years ago the book you are about to read was written;
and thus commenced my literary life. To those who know me, it is also
known that this was not entered upon to win fame, but a support for
my little children. Northwood was written literally with my baby in my
arms—the 'youngling of the flock,' whose eyes did not open on the world
till his father's were closed in death!" Here Hale marks a division between
her former life as a wife and her new "literary life," as a widowed mother.
She does not directly claim masculine authority as a writer but establishes

herself as functionally equivalent to her husband in her ability to exchange text for money and money for education, providing for her children "as their father would have done" (iii). Thus as writers, Beecher and Hale first establish their equivalence as daughter/wife with father/husband (Catharine Beecher=Lyman Beecher).

Given the assurance of respectability and the lucrative possibilities that could result from such hom(m)o-social patronage, why did Fanny Fern adopt a pseudonym? She could have traded on the name of her father and brothers,[3] or, after her marriage to James Parton, a well-known biographer, used his name to endorse her work. Yet Fern insisted that she was a self-made, self-named woman writer who had succeeded without—indeed, in spite of—men. As she triumphantly wrote after the court ruled in her favor, " 'FANNY FERN is not my name, is it?' Let me tell you, that if I originated it, as a *nom de plume,* I have as much right to the sole possession of it, as I have to the one I was baptised by" (*Ledger* 2 Aug. 1856).

Fern's pseudonym signaled her separation from her father and her identification with women. She explains that she chose the name "Fern" as a matronym "because, when a child, and walking with my mother in the country, she always used to pluck a leaf of it, to place in her bosom" (*New* 7–8). Both *Fanny* and *Fern* are feminized terms. Together they insist that her work be read as if written by a woman and as addressed primarily to other women. The success of that claim to an overtly gendered identity as a writer is attested to by the Virginia editor who declared, "It makes not one iota of difference whether Fanny Fern is a *he* or a *she* . . . (we call her *she* in virtue of her *nom de plume*)" (qtd. in Warren, *Fanny Fern* 100).

Simply choosing to identify herself as a woman writing for women did not set Fern outside the systems of hom(m)o-social exchange. But her insistence on her feminine gender suggests, as did Catharine Beecher's marketing of Harriet Beecher Stowe's texts, that these women used their gender to drive market transactions. In turn, their actions call for a more textured interpretation of Irigaray's insistence that "men make commerce *of* [women], but they do not enter into any exchanges *with* them" (172). Irigaray bases this dictum on a binary essentialism that overlooks the fact that gender identity is established through "discursively constrained performative acts that produce the body through and within the categories of sex" (Butler viii). Fern marketed her books by undermining the conventions of True Womanhood, which assumed that women did not stoop to trifle in marketplace exchanges. *Ruth Hall* demonstrates that men *did* exchange women and *should* barter with them. It begins by rewarding its eponymous heroine with a marriage in which her every economic want is met by her financially successful husband. Yet almost immediately Harry, Ruth's husband, loses his money and then dies. The remainder of the book shows how men violate the very heterosocial contract of exchange they promote. Ruth's father and brothers abandon her financially to make her own way in the world. This she does, becoming a successful writer.

Violations of gendered behavior appeared not only in the book's plot but in the way the book was marketed as well. The Mason Brothers in partnership with Fern promoted the book not through the traditional hom(m)o-social methods of puffery among brother-publishers but by direct appeal to the reading public's sense of scandal and willingness to equate name with pseudonym, autobiography with fiction. In her study of how *Ruth Hall* was marketed, Susan Geary claims that "there is no way to know for sure whether 'Fanny Fern' deliberately set out at the urging of her publishers to sell her birthright for a mess of pottage, but she did claim in later life that *Ruth Hall* was written at their insistence and against her better judgment" (389). Geary's assertion, however, is based on third-hand information filtered through family members invested in protecting the womanly reputation of their literary forebear, and honors the image of Fern as a private woman reluctantly hustled into the harsh spotlight of publicity. Mason's contract with Fern did not dictate the content of her novel. It can be argued that Fern wrote it fully aware that her trademark pseudonym would sell the initial run of the novel and that public curiosity about the plot would fuel even more sales. The revelation of Fern's "true" identity (and thus, of the identities of the men she had allegedly slandered) was promised through teasing ads declaring that "it is not true that Fanny Fern intends to bring libel suits against those newspapers which have pronounced 'Ruth Hall' an autobiography. . . . Whether those persons, respecting whom it has been said, by various critics, that certain unamiable characters in Ruth Hall were their exact portraits, and who have been designated by name, might not bring successful libel suits against these critics . . . we are not informed" (qtd. in Geary 388–89). The resulting public scandal made *Ruth Hall* a best-seller.

Sara P. Eldredge signed the contract for *Ruth Hall*; "Fanny Fern" wrote the book, giving her heroine Ruth Hall the pseudonym of "Floy." Sara P. Parton brought suit for the "special and only right" to the results of that and other acts of authorship. *Ruth Hall,* the advertising hinted, was a roman à clef. Thus, Floy=Ruth=Fanny=Sarah P. Eldredge. If the public sense of moral outrage was sparked by the book's plot, it was fueled by this equation, for by the implicit terms of heterosexual exchange, fathers and brothers should not abandon their widowed female relatives, nor do those women publicly slander their male relatives.

Ruth Hall fictionally replicates the narrative Sarah Hale promoted as biographical "fact," connecting public authorship with widowhood, asserting that authorship is the last resort of financially desperate women. When Ruth's daughter Nettie asks, "When I get to be a woman, shall I write books, mamma?" Ruth replies, "God forbid . . . no happy woman ever writes. From Harry's grave sprang 'Floy' " (175). Thus (dead) Harry=Floy=Ruth= Fanny Fern=Sara P. Eldredge=(dead) Charles Eldredge, (absent) Nathaniel Willis, and (absent) N.P. Willis. Like Hale, Fern continues to remind her readers of her widowhood even after she has achieved financial success, although her way of maintaining it underscores how she has exploited the gendered stereotypes of the widowed writer to her financial advantage. (It suggests, as well, that we reread Hale's biographical statements as a form of fiction.)

In an apostrophe to "My Old Inkstand" published after Fanny Fern had married James Parton and after her children were far too old for hoops, sticks, and dolls, she writes: "You know, very well, that [before my success] every rough word aimed at my quivering ears, was an extra dollar in my purse; every rude touch of my little Nell, strength and sinew to my unstrung nerves and flagging muscles. I say, old Ink-stand, look at Nell now! . . . Didn't you yourself buy her that hoop and stick, and those dolls, and that globe of gold-fish? Don't you feed and clothe her, every day of her sunshiny life? Haven't you agreed to do it, long years to come?" (*Ledger* 19 July 1856).

This column is introduced by an editorial gloss written by Robert Bonner that assures readers that "Fanny Fern" is no fiction, but a real woman, a "gifted contributor" who, by dint of her success as a writer, has "purchased a beautiful and elaborately finished residence on Long Island. . . . It seems to us that no one can read Fanny's apostrophe to her 'old inkstand,' and reflect upon her early struggle for bread, without rejoicing that her brave heart and exuberant genius have enabled her to secure an elegant home and a competency, for herself and her children" (*Ledger* 19 July 1856). Despite Bonner's direct link of "Fanny's" actions to those presumably carried out by Sara P. Parton, "Inkstand" is as patently fictional as *Ruth Hall*. It implies that the devoted, impoverished widow has finally been able to provide a home for her children. However, Fern/Parton has bought not a simple cottage but an "elegant" and "elaborately finished residence." Moreover, this woman's "competency" has been secured by a marriage contract stipulating that her assets are hers alone and, upon her death, will devolve to her children, not to James Parton. Thus "Inkstand" marks the entrance of "women" into exchange, not among themselves, but with, and sometimes in spite of, men.

To summarize: the example of Fanny Fern establishes that neither patronym nor pseudonym can guarantee a writer's bodily identity. But, as the example of *Ruth Hall* demonstrates, the signifier of the author's name, whether patronymic or pseudonymous, does not become dissociated from the text. Instead, the "author's" name becomes a trademark that guarantees a particular product and in the process marks itself as suitable for a particular reading constituency. It did not matter that the authors of *Northwood* and "Inkstand" were no longer destitute widows endeavoring to provide for small children. Their texts had become associated with their names; their names, in turn, signaled a commodity with market value.

This equation of name with a guaranteed product, a second relation of equivalence, was exploited by all four of these writers. Fern titled most of her books with some variant of her name: see for example, *Fern Leaves from Fanny's Portfolio* or *Little Ferns for Fanny's Little Friends*. More indirect titles retain the distinctive alliteration, such as *Folly As It Flies*. Catharine Beecher, as well, used the titles of her books both to establish her ownership (as in *Miss Beecher's Housekeeper and Healthkeeper*) and to interpellate a gendered readership, either directly or indirectly. In texts about topics customarily assigned to women—*A **Treatise** on Domestic Economy or **Principles** of Domestic **Science***—Beecher's titles are most assertive. In political arenas, they limit the range of her authority according to gender: *An **Essay** on Slavery and Abolitionism **with Reference to the Duty of American Females***. Titles intended for a generic audience—*An **Appeal** to the **People** on Behalf of Their Rights as Authorized Interpreters of the Bible, **Letters** to the **People** on Health and Happiness,* or ***Suggestions** Respecting Improvements in Education Presented to the Trustees of the Hartford Female Seminary, and **Published at their Request***—are emphatically tentative and again limited by topics commonly assigned to women—health, Bible reading, women's education.

Like Fern, Sarah Josepha Hale promoted the equation of her name with a particular literary product appropriate to women: "the cause of sound literature and of pure morality." In her first public statement as editor of the *Ladies' Magazine* she promised men a return on their investment in

a subscription. To the husband she promised that the magazine offered
his wife "the means of agreeably beguiling the interval of his absence"; to
the father she guaranteed that "nothing shall be found to weaken parental
authority"; and to the lover she vowed that "the soft eyes of his charmer are,
for *his* sake, often employed on its pure pages" (qtd. in Martin, "Genesis"
48–49). When Hale became editor of *Godey's Lady's Book,* the significations
attached to her name made *Godey's,* too, synonymous with morally upright
content. Over the course of her forty-year tenure, in fact, *Godey's* became
popularly known as "Mrs. Hale's magazine."

Thus a name, whether a single character (Fuller's *), a patronym, a
married name, or a pseudonym, became a signal of content, propriety,
reputation, and philosophy, as well as an indication of a gendered readership.
The name did not, however, guarantee the identity of the person using it, nor
did it mean that the author necessarily led her life according to the domestic
principles that her books promulgated. The equivalence of author, text,
and content existed primarily in the mind of the reader, maintained by the
rhetorical skill of the writer. For example, neither Beecher nor Hale cooked
or kept house, although both wrote several books on domestic economy.
Beecher "wrote" a number of cookbooks and handbooks of household
management, but she did not "create" them, as an anecdote recounted at
a Hartford Female Seminary Reunion makes clear. The speaker recalls that
Beecher had "promised . . . to have the material" for one of her cookbooks
"ready for delivery to the Harpers on a specified date. The time was near,
for some reason the work was not begun, and the penalty was serious. . . .
Miss Beecher desired some ten or twelve old pupils to . . . meet her at tea
in the house of a friend; then the story was told. The slips of heading
into which a cook-book may be rightfully divided were assigned to those
present, and they were asked to round out a certain number of pages of
receipts upon fish, flesh, and fowl, cakes and dainties, and return to her
the results of their new studies. These were compiled into a book, and the
work became a reliable favorite" (*Reunion* 23). Although Beecher's prefaces
and autobiographies acknowledge the assistance of a nationwide network of
former students, now exemplary housekeepers, that attribution does little
or nothing to disestablish the equivalence of the biographical Catharine
Beecher and the works signed with her name.

As is apparent from the series of examples I have just cited, the dissociation of these women from their texts takes place within systems of
circulation and exchange. By exploiting the fictions of gendered behavior

(that is, by behaving in "unwomanly" ways while asserting their feminine gender through acts of naming), these women modified the hom(m)o-social circuits of exchange to the point that men perforce did commerce *with* them. Yet their acts of dissociation were not without dangerous consequences. Other writers could counterfeit their appearance, appropriate their names, and pirate their writings. Midpoint in her career, for example, Beecher began to warn her readers of "several well-dressed women in various parts of the country [who] have raised money on false pretenses as my agents." She assured them that "no committee, agent, or bookseller will be authorized by me or by the Association for this object except with my signature" (*Health* 191–92).

As a result of this possibility for counterfeit, all four of these writers necessarily reinvoked the hom(m)o-social workings of "mirror games, iden-tifications, and . . . appropriations" (Irigaray 172) to reassert the absolute correspondence of body, name, and text. Each of these women knew the importance of a legal title to her work; all favored the passage of a copyright law to protect their work. In order to do this, they necessarily realigned themselves, body and name, with a sponsoring masculine body. With the implicit backing of the *Dial* and Greeley's *New York Tribune,* Fuller—writing as "Margaret Fuller," not as *—argued for the establishment of American authorship as a paying profession. Hale made *Godey's* a leading patron of U.S. authors by refusing to "clip" from other publications and by paying her regular writers generously. She could not have done so, of course, had Louis Godey not been willing to endorse the reimbursement. Beecher and her sister Harriet joined James Parton in concerted actions against compilers of "gift books" who reprinted their works without sharing a fair percentage of the profits with the authors. Even Fanny Fern, the author most radically dissociated from the Name-of-the-Father, found it to her advantage to claim her legal name and—in tandem with her husband as authorizer of her right to press charges—establish that "no one has any more right to appropriate [the pseudonym she had invented] than to take the watch from my girdle" (*Ledger* 2 Aug. 1856).

Thus the proper name signals propriety and property, establishing equivalences among women so that they may be circulated among men. Those equivalences, however, are invisibly modified by equally significant differences of race and class, differences these writers codified and main-tained in the texts they wrote. As Beecher, Hale, Fuller, and Fern had discovered, the English lexicon did not register the increasing variation

among women brought about by enlarged educational opportunities, economic crisis, upward and downward class mobility, immigration, and other
social changes of the mid-nineteenth century. How, for example, would one
name a self-supporting unmarried adult woman who no longer lived with
and depended on her family? *Daughter* stipulates a relation of blood and
filiation, but implies dependency; *spinster* suggests a failure to marry. How
name a formerly married and financially independent adult woman? *Widow*
implies a continuing identification with a man now absent; *divorcée* carried
social opprobrium. Most seriously, an increasing number of literate women
who lacked the requisite social genealogy were claiming to be *ladies*. Hence
writers like Hale sought to make more precise the lexical classifications that
named women and indicated their relative social position. As a result they
sought to remap the social classifications of working women, finding more
specific and less opprobrious names for their activities. Yet they maintained
a social hierarchy by classifying women according to their race, location,
and genealogical entitlement.

The "ladies" who constituted the imagined readership of *Godey's Lady's
Book* and other similarly addressed writings were in fact a limited population: those who were literate, who had physical and economic access to the
magazine, who had the leisure to read it, and who could identify themselves
with its topics. But *Godey's* readership superseded the class coding it affected.
As the magazine pioneered the use of illustrations, a reader need not even be
literate to imagine herself[4] addressed by its needlework patterns, engravings
of domestic scenes, and fashion plates. Thus women who were not ladies—
the Lowell Mill girls or servant girls, for example—were potentially included
in its address. Nor did readers necessarily subscribe to the magazine, since
Godey's was often loaned among neighbors, available on the center table of
boardinghouses and women's schools, or shared among a group of people
who owned a single subscription. In the volatile social landscape of the
nineteenth-century United States, where fortunes could be made and lost
quickly, publications such as *Godey's*, which addressed "ladies," offered a
wide social spectrum of women a chance to learn and imitate the codes of
dress, possessions, comportment, and speech thought to be unique to ladies
but able to be imitated by upwardly mobile and ambitious women and girls.

Moreover, these texts, specifically addressed to leisured and domestically
confined ladies, were written by women who had been forced to work for
a living. With increasing frequency in the mid-nineteenth century, such
economic crises as the death of a father or husband made it necessary for

class-entitled women to support themselves and their families. Entering
the labor market, however, entailed a lowering of class status. This factor
Beecher, Hale, Fuller, and Fern sought to change. They mapped and named
the population of feminine laborers, figuring their work as necessity, and
thus making it potentially respectable. The first step in this process was to
acknowledge that not all women could approximate an ideal of domestic
confinement. *Godey's Lady's Book,* for example, which overtly addressed
women whose most strenuous activities were assumed to be reading and
parlor-table conversation, reminded these same readers that marriage did
not always guarantee a woman's ability to indulge in playful and tasteful
but private and unremunerative intellectual activity. Its own editor, after
all, had been forced out of her parlor to support her children. Hale wrote:
"Many women are . . . obliged to toil for their own support. Some mothers
have to maintain their little children, other women must provide for
parents and those who helplessly depend on them. For these reasons, it is
necessary that every young woman in our land should be qualified by some
accomplishment which she may teach, or some art or profession she can
follow, to support herself creditably, should the necessity occur" (48 [Mar.
1854]: 271). Her language here—"obliged," "have to," "must," "necessary,"
"helplessly depend"—emphasizes that Hale did not advocate a willful
exodus from home to workplace. Nor did she assume that her readers would
toil as mill operatives, seamstresses, servants, governesses, or prostitutes.
Instead, she advocated that women prepare themselves for occupations that
carried a more favorable social coding. Her lack of specificity demonstrates
precisely the limited range of "professions" for women in 1854.

Over the next decade, however, the spectrum of women's occupations
broadened as more and more women entered the workplace. *Godey's* printed
an ever-increasing number of letters from readers documenting women's
exodus from the parlor. Although these may not have been written by Hale,
they appeared in her "Editor's Table" column and thus had her implied
endorsement. By the middle of the Civil War, it became clear that the
trend was irreversible, as this letter from an anonymous correspondent
makes clear:

> This war is to make widows and orphans, sisters with no brothers
> to care for them, mothers with no sons to uphold their age and
> comfort their infirmity. The whole face of society will be changed. . . .
> Whatever the political result may be of this war, the social and domestic
> results are inevitable. . . .

> It seems to me there will gradually and imperceptibly open a way for these mothers, daughters, and sisters to maintain themselves, merely from the circumstance of their sex being in excess of the other, for a long future. Many of the occupations which have heretofore been monopolized by men, but which are suited much better to the strength and ability of women, will be open to women. Work of all sorts will be necessary and *fashionable*. (66 [Jan. 1863]: 93)

The names of the ways a woman could be impacted by war deaths are overlapping; the same woman could be simultaneously a widow, an orphan, an abandoned sister, and a childless mother. The common fact of economic deprivation unites the "sex," who will change the map of labor in the United States. By sheer force of numbers they become socially respectable.

By the early 1860s, then, *Godey's* began to notice in image, as well as in text, a broadening spectrum of occupations for women. On its 1861 cover, for example, the magazine printed an omnibus image that paired sketches of statues of such eminent and public women as Florence Nightingale and Dorothea Dix with engraved vignettes of anonymous women engaged in a variety of distinctly nondomestic (but still womanly) pursuits, including battlefield nursing and visiting prisons and tenements. That title page, according to Dominic Ricciotti, marks the beginning of *Godey's* practice of printing images of working women. Although the main focus of such images was still writing and sewing—"women involved in the publishing, textile, and clothing industries"—more and more frequently in the magazine, according to Ricciotti, "women are seen taking their places in the professions and in humanitarian work" (18). A parallel increase in textual attention to women at work mapped the new terrain. "Editor's Table" columns regularly included a paragraph headed "The Employment of Women in Cities" that noted women who worked as shopkeepers, in post offices, lighthouses, telegraph offices, restaurants, and even in the Philadelphia mint.

Such acts of representation in image and text thus made the phenomenon of women in the workplace visible and nameable. However, the ways of naming women who worked commonly entailed using the adjective *female* to modify a collective generic or masculine noun. Such a practice signaled that women were taking economic ground from those who were a family's first providers and emphasized their difference from gendered and social norms. Hale sought to revise this practice, making such workers visible as women but asserting they did not displace men; that their work was economically necessary; and that as workers they retained their respectability. She accomplished this by invoking traditional signifiers of women's domesticity, ranking working women according to how closely their occupations approximated domestic pursuits or could be figured as addressing a population limited to other women. That general mapping complete, Hale proposed to (re)name women's occupations with words that did not carry overtones of degraded class and sexual promiscuity.

Thus as *Godey's* noted the expanded number of occupations available to women it also delimited their relative respectability. These occupations descended from an ideal of remunerative but private mind-work according to the degree of bodily labor and exposure they required and their imagined congruence with the functions already assumed to be natural attributes of women:

> *Clerkship, storekeeping, type-setting, factory work*; none of these pursuits can be followed at home, therefore these branches of business do, in some degree, unfit the woman for the wife and mother. *School-keeping*, on the other hand, is one of the best professions for a young woman, because it prepares her for home duties. . . .
>
> *Needlework*, in all its branches is woman's province. . . .
>
> In short, we should like to see all pleasant, quiet *home employments* taken up and perfected by American women. Teaching . . . should be their special profession; a sufficient number qualified to act as physicians for their own sex; . . . while those gifted with talent for literary pursuits should be encouraged and rewarded. (50 [Apr. 1855]: 368)

As this passage demonstrates, Hale evaluated each occupation with reference to its presumably feminine attributes. Paradoxically, it seems, she promoted teaching, which could not be performed at home beyond the dame school level, and which was often unpleasant, physically demanding, and certainly not quiet. Supposedly, however, it required talents similar to those of mothering. She claimed medicine for women (she had begun to publicize Elizabeth Blackwell's medical studies as early as 1851) by limiting the extent of their practice to the domestic realm and to gynecology and obstetrics. Hale's list, however, is incomplete. Consistent with the address of *Godey's* **Lady's** *Book,* it does not include domestic labor performed for pay, already by midcentury a terrain ceded to racial and ethnic others. Thus a lady in straitened economic circumstances would at all costs avoid taking up employment that duplicated domestic service. Accordingly, Hale's classification is class-specific and altogether omits the domestic occupations of governess, maid, servant, or cook. Classifying sewing, because it could be performed at home, as honorable while disallowing factory work because it involved too much sweated labor and bodily exposure, Hale confines women to the notoriously underpaid out-work system and removes them from actively competing with men for better-paid positions as weavers or mill workers.

Hale's taxonomic mapping was accompanied by an emphasis on precise denomination, first seeking to advocate that women's occupations and institutions be precisely named, and not simply appropriated to women by affixing the adjective "female" to the noun (as in "female" doctor). After years of using the term "female" in her own writing, in 1855 Hale had made a public reversal, arguing that the word should be used very sparingly and always precisely. She began by advancing the opinion that the word, used either as an adjective or as a noun, was improper. She held that, while *woman* is a name "always significant of character," *female* refers "only to the animal in the sex" (53 [July 1856]: 79). Since Hale felt that the impropriety of "female" was related to its suggestions of debased class, she advised *Godey's* writers accordingly: "It would indeed be a serious mistake in the Lady's Book to use the unpleasant term, as *female never means a lady.* We request our contributors, who are mostly ladies, to bear this subject in mind" (72 [Jan. 1865]: 96).

By 1865, Hale had expanded the scope of her concern to institutions outside her immediate control. Her most sustained and successful public campaign in this regard concerned the naming of Vassar *Female* College, an institution whose establishment she followed enthusiastically in *Godey's*. As the time drew near for the college's dedication, she began to write letters to Vassar's president and trustees, urging them to drop the offending adjective. On June 6, 1864, Hale advised college president John H. Raymond that "this Queen of Colleges should not bear on its forehead the ambiguous term of *female,* which may mean an animal and never signifies a lady. It is not a pleasant word for woman; and as scholars and gentlemen will be responsible for the . . . title I do hope it will bear the definite and dignified name of Vassar College for Young Women" (Vassar College Archives). Eight months later, when Vassar's Trustees still had not acted upon her request, Hale wrote to Benson J. Lossing, a college trustee who supported her line of reasoning, entreating him to support her proposal: "I do hope the word will not be permitted to stand—a mark of the beast, on the fair forehead of the first endowed College ever erected and devoted by noble hearted benevolence to the thorough education of Young Ladies" (6 Feb. 1865; Vassar College Archives).

Hale's obsession with this issue puzzles Vassar historian Edward R. Linner, especially since she had used the term "female" so consistently in her own writing prior to 1855, and since she initially "gave no references to books or papers that she might use as authorities" in support of her argument for linguistic modification (120). Yet Hale's interference was more than the meddlings of a slightly eccentric elderly woman. At issue here is not only the college's name but also who would name it, and what the name might mean. The reasons for Hale's concern were symptomatic of women's economic and social status in the mid-nineteenth century. Her obsession with this issue is analogous to Fern's court battle for legal right to her "own" name/pseudonym. If establishing legal right to a proper name (or even a pseudonym) makes the concept of women's literary property possible, then claiming the right to name populations by gender and to differentiate them by class makes possible the concept of women's work as socially acceptable and economically significant. The Vassar issue in fact gave Hale a concrete focus for a somewhat abstract argument that might not otherwise have attracted public notice. Although she publicized and celebrated the college from the moment it was announced, she rarely mentioned Vassar without reminding readers (potential donors and students) that it bore a "vulgar" and "inferior" misnomer (73 [Aug. 1866]): 170). Hale's disavowal of *female* also signified the double-bind faced by working women. In 1855, the most common way to designate a woman's presence in an occupation heretofore understood as masculine was to use the adjective *female*. Yet *female*, in Hale's interpretation, implied a kind of prostitution—a selling of womanly talents for money—especially since she had argued that women were working at occupations that derived from their essential attributes and not making incursions into men's economic territory. Hence she proposed revisions in language that would mark working women as a special and limited case while removing the invidious overtones of *female*.

If, as Linner points out, Hale initially had no linguistic precedent for this undertaking, it may be because women had never before been so present to the public eye nor so intent on being recognized as gendered workers while maintaining a claim on class distinction and social deference. At any rate, Hale quickly found precedent and support for her argument in two sources that carried most weight with the literate population whose lexicon she sought to make more precise: Continental (particularly British) usage and the Bible. To cite British usage played on a cultural inferiority complex, while biblical precedent was, in Protestant America, an ultimate endorsement of

correctness. To Milo P. Jewett she wrote: "Is not *English* authority the highest
to which we can appeal in settling questions regarding their own language?
Are there any places of education for Girls or Young Ladies in England
that have this term of *female* incorporated in their style or title? . . . The
educated classes of Great Britain know too well the importance of a title
to allow the *lowest designation* for woman to be ingrafted with the name of
places where their daughters are educated. The term *female*, with the English
people, is applied only or chiefly to women of the lowest grade. . . . Vassar
Female College is not intended for such classes of feminine humanity"
(17 Feb. 1864; Vassar College Archives). To Vassar administrators as well
as to *Godey's* readers, she argued that "as we might expect the Word of
God" to do, the Bible uses "female" only eleven times, and "each time in
contradistinction to man as male" (53 [July 1856]: 79).

Vassar administrators initially ignored Hale, treating her cause as a
private obsession. Hoping to mollify the woman whose publicity could
benefit his institution, Matthew Vassar crossed through the offending term
on his letterhead in his correspondence with Hale. Still Hale persisted,
both in correspondence and in the magazine, refusing to let the issue
fade. Eventually she prevailed, the name was modified, and Hale, who
scrupulously avoided extraneous punctuation, announced to her readers:

> VASSAR COLLEGE ! ! ! Our first note is one of exclamations, which, fully
> interpreted, mean that, on the 25th of June last, the Trustees of Vassar
> College, at their annual meeting, voted unanimously to drop the term
> "FEMALE" from the title of that Institution ! ! !
> Therefore, in our gratitude to the Trustees for this true chivalric deed
> of honor to the NAME OF WOMAN, we give three cheers (exclamations):
> the other three express our joy that the blot of animality is removed
> from this great institution for Young Ladies, and our hope that all
> similar institutions in our country, having this blot now on their
> names, will soon follow the good example of VASSAR COLLEGE. (73
> [Sept. 1866]: 263)

It should be noted that Hale's victory was incomplete, since Vassar did not
change its name to indicate that it was a college for women but chose instead
the generic solution (probably because it was more economically feasible
simply to eliminate "Female" from signs already in place on buildings and
gates than to replace the entire title).

Having won a public victory, Hale undertook a second phase in the
project of naming women. She proposed to (re)introduce into the language
archaic gendered nouns or parallel neologisms as a means of making language indicate gender more precisely. According to Hale, "The poetry of

women is distinctive and peculiar; their acting is of wholly different parts; their manner of teaching has influences which men cannot reach; their medical practice is required for human preservation; and the language gains greatly in beauty, force, propriety, and power by conveying these differences in a single word" (75 [July 1867]: 79). Correlative terms such as *postmistress, lighthousekeeperess, telegraphess,* and *waitress* would, according to Hale, allow writers and speakers to avoid the difficulty and impropriety resulting from misusing *female,* while retaining the gendered difference. She suggested neologisms and resurrected archaic terms to prove that "our language has . . . a rich mine of words for woman and the womanly" (70 [Mar. 1865]: 279). She printed lengthy lists of "words now used by the best English writers" (75 [July 1867]: 79), including such pairs as *housewife* and *husbandman; man-milliner* and *milliner; man-midwife* and *midwife* (as parallels to *manservant* and *maidservant* or *woman-servant*); *student* and *pupil, teacher* and *teacheress.* She especially advocated the use of *Americaness* (the parallel to *Britoness,* a term favored by Spencer and Tennyson) to be admitted to general use (70 [Mar. 1865]: 280).

As Hale demonstrated how the new lexicon might be applied, she also implicitly argued that women workers posed no threat to men's existing claims on professional territory: "Is it right or proper to call a woman '*Doctor?*' she asks rhetorically, then answers, "She may have had a full Diploma from a Man's Medical College; but that does not make her a *man,* nor make it right and proper to assume the title that always signifies the masculine person and character. We think it would be more honorable and respectable for such a lady to claim her own title—'*Doctress*'—and ennoble it" (70 [Mar. 1865]: 279). By changing her professional designation, Hale implies, a woman retreats from unseemly competition and continues to endorse the feminine virtues that guarantee her respectability and elevated class.

As the territory of professional involvement continued to expand, Hale found it increasingly difficult to argue that women who worked were only extending their natural feminine endowments: "A lady having lately finished her law studies was admitted to practise, when she advertised her entrance on business as an '*attorneyess.*' We do not commend this profession for young women, but, if any one enters on it, we advise her to follow this example of retaining always the title that signifies womanhood. Thus only can she preserve her own dignity, and, if she is ambitious and successful, win fame for herself and her sex" (79 [Aug. 1869]: 176). This notice is typical of *Godey's* ambiguous stance. On the one hand, it seems conservative and reactionary; yet Hale also concedes that women in the professions must be ambitious in order to succeed. Significantly, she approves both the personal and general notoriety that would follow.

Whereas Hale's renaming sought to designate working women as separate from but equal to men, Fern and Fuller pursued strategies of naming that arranged women into "proper" hierarchies of class, using employment as only one of several indicators of social entitlement.⁵ In the frontier West, for example, Margaret Fuller undertook a similar project of specific naming, albeit less consciously than did Hale. Here immigration, rather than labor, had complicated the task of social mapping. Here the problems of social status faced by single New England women who were forced to work for a living were reversed, since many married men took their families West in an effort to solve economic difficulties. Their wives, according to Fuller, had to exert themselves to maintain the signifiers of their class in a new environment, especially if their economic status had lessened. Fuller's assertion that "the great drawback upon the lives of these settlers . . . is the unfitness of the women for their new lot" points to a class structure she, and presumably the women she writes about, imported intact from the East: "The women can rarely find any aid in domestic labor. All its various and careful tasks must often be performed, sick or well, by the mother and daughters, to whom a city education has imparted neither the strength nor skill now demanded." By specifying as "women" those who did not have such aid in the West, Fuller implies a class and sexual hierarchy. But what did she imagine to be the sex of those who aided in domestic labor? Moreover, these wives of western settlers are women, not ladies, implying a lesser social status. Perhaps their husbands have sought to escape economic hardship; perhaps they are seminary-educated social climbers. They are not, however, ladies, a term Fuller seldom uses. She continues, using words that refine the sexual hierarchy, "The wives of the poorer settlers, having more hard work to do than before, very frequently become slatterns; but the ladies, accustomed to a refined neatness, feel that they cannot degrade themselves by its absence, and struggle under every disadvantage to keep up the necessary routine of small arrangements" (61).

This section of *Summer on the Lakes* is frequently taken as evidence of Fuller's admiration for western women. Yet it also encodes a class hierarchy based on "natural" entitlement, for here Fuller implies that a *real* lady— by birth or by private (vs. "city") education—does not have to struggle to maintain her class entitlements through artificial signifiers, nor worry that her status will disappear if she must occasionally perform actual labor. "Real" "young ladies" of this sort are best exemplified by the daughters of an English gentleman, whom Fuller admiringly describes as "musicians, [who] spoke French fluently, having been educated in a convent. Here in the prairie, they had learned to take care of the milk-room, and kill the rattlesnakes that assailed their poultry yard" (38). *Summer on the Lakes*, in fact, depends on a strictly constructed and maintained hierarchy of womanhood, supported at the bottom by those who would provide the "aid in domestic labor" to "women." At a slightly higher level fall the "wives of the poorer settlers," "slatterns" who cannot afford domestic help and whose sham gentility thus quickly erodes. At the top of the hierarchy stand two ranks of ladies: those who must struggle to "keep up the necessary routine of small arrangements"; and natural aristocrats whose gentility is the product of birth and thus cannot be effaced by barnyard labor. Thus Fuller uses *lady* to designate not only monetary entitlement (demonstrated in the ability to employ servants, and which, after all, is a mutable condition), but also by privileges of birth.

Other qualities make this map of blood entitlement more precise, as Fuller imposes categories of "race" on the social mutability of the western territories. She uses "girl" and "woman" both as generic, class, and race markers, observing offhandedly, "I was the only lady, and attended in the cabin by a Dutch girl and an Indian woman" (238). In the West, immigrant women are consigned to the lower strata of social hierarchy (such as the working "girl" who operated the ferry at Kishwaukie and was not, according to Fuller, "of the most picturesque appearance" [65]). They share the terrain with women of color, including a "little Chinese girl." Fuller finds it more difficult to classify "the widow of a French trader, an Indian by birth," who also "spoke French fluently." She lingers over the encounter, puzzled. This woman, unlike the convent-educated English ladies, is of the wrong race. Thus Fuller calls her only "very lady*like* in her manners" (250; emphasis added). Although this woman enjoys great respect from her peers, who "were all the time coming to pay her homage, or to get her aid and advice; for she [was] . . . a shrewd woman of business" (250), Fuller never calls her a lady. Shrewdness in business would never characterize a lady; moreover, she is a woman of color and has cross-married. Fuller can only allow her an elevated status within her circumscribed sphere: "This lady of the tribe wanted to borrow [my companion's] sketches of the beach, with its lodges and wild groups, 'to show to the *savages*,' she said" (251). Fuller's condescension is marked by her implied italicization of "*lady* of the tribe" and by her literal italicization of *savage*. Although she is amused that this Indian woman has constructed a hierarchy against whom she has identified, Fuller engages in the same process of differentiation, assuming that only white, literate, and well-born ladies may name themselves as such and have those acts of naming be universally endorsed.

As literacy increased, and economic instability blurred the map of class, more and more women sought, as did these writers, to (re)name and (re)classify themselves in relation to others they took to be inferior. Fuller encountered the phenomenon in the cabins of Michigan and on the prairies of Illinois, while Fern noted and sought to contain similar incursions in New York City. A *Ledger* column suggests that as more women claimed increased class status, those who considered themselves still more entitled exerted a compensatory disciplinary pressure. Fern, who had fought in court to establish her "special and . . . only right" to name herself, had posited that others might profit from her suit, as well. Yet she was openly disturbed when déclassé others appropriated the privileges of constructing and naming what she considered to be counterfeit versions of themselves. Writing in response to an advertisement reading "A *genteel* girl wishes a situation as chambermaid," Fern declares that her "very soul sickens" at the use of the adjective "no matter where, or how, or to whom, or by whom it is applied. . . . It is the universal and never-failing indorser of every sham ever foisted upon disgusted human nature" (*Folly* 109–10).[6] Yet despite her disdain for whomever uses the word, Fern's discomfort is specifically with those whose pretensions to democracy muddy the clear delineations of class, as her use of the term *girl* indicates. Fern proceeds to map the territory delineated by such "sham" and to characterize its inhabitants: "the 'genteel' cabbage-scented boarding-house, where tobacco emasculated young men 'feed,' and mindless, be-flounced, cheap jewel-ried married and unmarried women smile sweetly on them, . . . The 'genteel' school-girl who, owning one greasy silk dress, imagines that she understands her geography better in that attire than in a quiet, clean, modest 'de laine' [and] the 'genteel' seminary for young ladies, who ride to school in a carriage with liveried servants, their papa having formerly been one himself" (*Folly* 110). For Fern the pretense implied by the act of naming oneself as genteel stands for other acts of sham appropriation. In each case, the term, no matter what it describes, names a fabrication that stands as a substitute for "natural" entitlements—the boardinghouse would not have to call itself genteel if it did not harbor promiscuity. The schoolgirl inappropriately links fine dress with mental capacity (a "natural talent" of entitled classes), just as her papa assumes that sending his daughter to boarding school at a "genteel" establishment can make her a "lady." Each of these pretenders, appropriating what they perceive as authentic signifiers of class, invite others to endorse their counterfeit in a charade of mutual naming and recognition. The tobacco-emasculated young man's pretensions to gentility are only encouraged by the smiles of "cheap" women; worse, the seminary's accessibility to social upstarts will only produce more of the kind. Thus naming cannot, according to Fern, signify precisely if it is done at the behest of the democratic mob. Accurate naming remains the province of professionals—barristers, judges, clergy, and authors.

Like Hale, who sought to expand a social vocabulary to endorse working women, Fern's chambermaid tried to appropriate an adjective to name herself. The chambermaid, however, is already excluded from this privilege, since her occupation stands outside of the bounds of social respectability and since she is almost certainly Irish. (The title of the chapter in *Folly* that contains this essay is "Bridget as she Was, and Is.") Hale enjoined others to endorse her project of renaming in public venues, Vassar's capitulation being only the most visible and material demonstration of her success. The chambermaid, by contrast, incurs Fern's outrage because she has attempted a feat similar to Hale's and to her own, using the same mass circulation media to advertise an act of self-naming. The other genteel pretenders who are the chambermaid's counterparts present a similar threat: their sham might succeed because they are endorsed by significant numbers of others who recognize and support their acts of naming. This column about pretense in naming thus stands as the obverse to Fern's lawsuit about claiming her pseudonym as a trademark. It demonstrates the darker side of the issues of naming and precisely summarizes the issues of who may name whom, as well as what the name may signify.

Chapter Four

DOMESTIC MASQUERADE

From its first number in July 1830, *Godey's Lady's Book* included hand-colored fashion illustrations. The earliest single-page hand-watercolored illustrations contained one or two figures amid little or no background, and pictured Continental fashions. These images became more complex as technological capabilities increased and the magazine's subscription base broadened. By 1861, the single-page illustrations had become fold-out plates, still hand-tinted by women operatives, that included as many as a half-dozen figures set in a detailed background. Its elegant fashion plates made *Godey's* the most successful of a number of magazines of the period that supported editorial content with such embellishments.

Such attention to fashion resulted from a matrix of social, economic, and technological factors, including urbanization; mechanized weaving; the home sewing machine; the availability of ready-made clothing; an increase in disposable cash; and the ease with which commodities, including clothing, dry-goods, and magazines, could be circulated nationwide. Yet despite the complexity of these material factors, it has been common to blame *Godey's* and its editors for purveying extreme fashions to a gullible readership. Ann Douglas, for example, suggests that fashion could be equated with the intellectual flabbiness of the period. Her subchapter, entitled "The Economic Value of the Euphemism: Finery to Flattery," moves seamlessly from a consideration of fashion places to "female" "alienation" to Hale's "[shrewd] exploit[ation] of this unstated dynamic" (71). Other studies equate the fashion plates with the magazine's content and the magazine with its literary editress. Ruth Finley's 1932 biography of Hale is illustrated

liberally with *Godey's* plates. Richardson Wright's biographical sketch of
Hale is entitled "Madonna in Bustles."

A similar equation of fashion, woman, and intellectual seriousness has
been made of Margaret Fuller. Her appearance and attire have been at issue
even in the most serious treatments of her life and work; occasionally they
have been invoked as reasons to doubt her intellectual seriousness. In 1963,
for example, Perry Miller read Fuller's "image" as signifier and guarantee of
the Conversations' innocuousness: "One factor in our settling a public image
of Margaret Fuller is that she cannot be dissociated from the hyperbolically
female intellectualism of the period, the slightest invocation of which invites
our laughter. Descriptions of her presiding over 'Conversations' in Boston
inevitably classify her with . . . in the phrase of Henry James, the 'glossily ringletted and monumentally breastpinned.' Yet the fact remains . . .
that she was monumentally homely. Her hair was stringy and her neck
abnormally long" (*Margaret Fuller* xvii). If the "female intellectualism"
of the American Renaissance were hyperbolic, the cause was more likely
attributable to men's negative interpretations than to women's attire. What
remains fascinating, if troubling, about Miller's passage, even at the remove
of a quarter-century, is his need to "settle" the issue of Fuller's "public image,"
as if to do so would once and for all declare that her "image" was so much
dismissable hype because of her association with other fashionably dressed
females. Douglas's and Miller's work marks a perduring double bind for
women, whose "public image" was in 1843, in 1963, in 1977—and is still—
at issue. That double bind holds women responsible for their public images
while deploring them for attending to such trivia as their appearance.

The attention Hale and Fuller, as well as Fern and Beecher, gave to the
issue of dress does not signal triviality, however; their engagement with dress
elucidated the personal, economic, and political implications of fashion. As
women who lived blatantly public professional lives, they monitored their
own attire to declare their feminine irreproachability and their elevated
class status. They did not, however, endorse the equation of fashion and
character, recognizing the mutability of both. They exploited the knowledge
that dress signifies in conjunction with other codes—name, manners, and
speech among them—to constitute identity and never signifies definitely.
In fine, they understood dress to be costume that could enhance perception
of character. Playing on the simple equation of the two, as well as addressing
others who, like themselves, read dress as mutable, they argued that costume
could underwrite a gendered national identity and guarantee the character

of feminine intellectual undertakings. They also demonstrated fashion's complicity with women's reduced economic capacity and its part in the ill health and reduced reproductive capacity of women.

In fact, Sarah Josepha Hale went to great lengths to dissociate herself from the practice of the magazines she worked for, frequently and publicly disclaiming responsibility for their fashion pages, and consistently touting dress reform. As one of the first women to be so fully in the public eye, her effort to dissociate herself from a practice that smacked of vanity and Continental decadence seems practical, if not prescient. Hale, who conceived of the *Ladies' Magazine* as an antidote to decadent European taste, refused to print fashion plates during the first three years of that magazine's run. In November 1830, however, she bowed to economic necessity, since advertising did not yet subsidize the magazine's content, and her publishers depended on fashion illustrations to increase its circulation. In September 1831 she wrote, "There is no part of our duty as editor of a ladies' Journal, which we feel so reluctant to perform, as to quote, or exhibit the fashions of dress" (qtd. in Martin, "Genesis" 53). Later, after she and *Godey's* became inseparably identified with each other, she and Louis Godey reminded readers that Mrs. Hale was not the magazine's Fashion Editress: "We must really beg of our subscribers not to address letters for the Fashion Editor to Mrs. Hale. She has nothing to do with that department" (70 [May 1865]: 469).

Yet Hale maintained a lively textual dialogue with the fashion pages. She capitulated to the publishers of the *Ladies' Magazine* over the issue of the prints but reserved the right to comment on them in her editorials, which frequently condemned "the servile imitation of European extravagances" as inimical to the "taste, and character of our intelligent, and refined, and moral community. We would do nothing to increase this mania of fashion, but much, were it in our power, to diminish it—and it is, therefore, that we endeavor to make our *plate of fashion* teach a lesson to the heart, as well as the vanity of our fair readers" (qtd. in Martin, "Genesis" 55). At *Godey's*, where fashion and dress patterns played an even more dominant role, Hale maintained her practice. Although as literary editress she had no connection with the fashion department, she periodically commented on its plates, reminding readers, for example, that "Dress . . . is something more than necessity of climate, something better than condition of comfort, something higher than elegance of civilization. It is the index of conscience; the evidence of our emotional nature; it reveals, more clearly than speech expresses, the inner life of heart and soul in a people, and the tendencies of individual character" (70 [Apr. 1865]: 370). Hale's choice of words here is crucial; she writes of dress, not of fashion, as the index to heart, soul, and character. Nor does she name dress as the only signifier of character. Here, for example, location, class, manners, and speech all combine to verify the claims of dress and to elevate it above transient fashion. This emphasis, and her determination that American women not imitate European excesses are the likely explanation for a number of midcentury plates captioned as " 'Americanized' Paris Fashions."

It is clear, however, that Hale made no simple equivalence between fashion and character. In the first place, as is immediately evident from even a surface perusal of the magazines she edited, fashions changed as quickly and as drastically in the nineteenth century as they do today. To correlate any one mode with any nameable character trait was not the point. Nor was it possible for Hale to effect such a correlation in print, since there was no guarantee that those who looked at the magazine's fashion plates read—or were able to read—the accompanying editorial comments. Ironically, it would be more accurate to claim that Hale's comments, if they were read, spurred the fashion trade among those who did not discriminate between dress and fashion.

If Hale's commentary was overlooked, the fashion illustrations were not. Their use—and misuse by unentitled "genteel pretenders" of the type Fanny Fern condemned—was debated in *Godey's* columns. Thus even as Hale justified attention to dress by trying to equate it with conscience and good character, she also emphasized that fashion could not be equated with inward qualities. Of *Godey's* fashion plates, she writes: "It seems strange that any sensible person can hold [them] to be harmful. Certainly it is the duty of all Christians to be clothed. . . . Nor is it found that one prescribed mode of dress is favorable to Christian improvement. Is the poke bonnet a sure index of humility?" (47 [Oct. 1853]: 369). The poke bonnet of Hale's example is an apt referent for her argument that fashion signified in multiple and contradictory ways. Seen from the side, its elongated and face-encircling brim protected women from the sunlight and seemed to proclaim a ladylike retirement from prying eyes. Seen from the front, however, the bonnet's lining and trim allowed a fashion-conscious woman to frame her face with enhancing colors, fabrics, ribbons, laces, and flowers. This scarcely demonstrated womanly modesty.

Thus it is more reasonable to argue that Hale understood dress as costume, a costume that signified character, to be sure, but whose significations could be manipulated by its users and, like the poke bonnet's lining, emphasize its wearer's most desirable traits. Hale depended upon the reading ability of other women to contain proliferating significations, assuming that they could both identify fashionable counterfeit by the unentitled and correctly interpret dress as the costume of their peers. Hale did not, however, consider the possibility of (willful) misreadings nor the mutability of signifiers over time, both of which led to the "Madonna in bustles" and "glossily ringletted" approaches to interpreting the intellectual activities of nineteenth-century women.

As Hale's use of the rhetorical question indicates, because poke bonnets were not sure indices of humility, she and her counterparts spent a great deal of time interpreting dress. Predictably, much of their conversation about fashion centered on fraud. A "Centre-Table Gossip" entry entitled "Fashions Below Stairs" suggests that the energy driving the worry about fashion was as much about money as it was about character: "Housemaids now wear crinoline, and whalebone, and spring petticoats, and pretend to do their work in them. . . . The wages of a servant will not enable her to obtain them honestly and also to put by a little money against sickness or misfortune" (61 [Aug. 1860]: 189). Hale's first assertion is that since restrictive foundation garments impede productive movement, high fashion should be (and is) a signal that one does not work. Hence, if one's housemaids wear excessive petticoats and restrictive corsets, they are probably not working hard enough to earn their wages. Second, since elegant dress is not affordable on servant wages, those who affect it may be earning money by other less strenuous means—gambling, prostitution, or petty thievery from their employers. By extension, although Hale does not directly address it here, if servant girls can successfully counterfeit the clothing of their mistresses, the currency of fine dress will be devalued. In fine, if a single self-supporting servant girl can pass as her mistress, sumptuary display in married women becomes meaningless.

In these meditations about counterfeits, there is little or no anxiety that a mistress might be mistaken as a servant. Such misidentification, it seems, could only be the result of full and meaningful intent on the part of an entitled woman, and frequently is taken to be humorous. What a beribboned poke bonnet might mean on a cook's head may be open for debate, but, as an incident recounted by Catharine Beecher demonstrates, bonnet-related confusion centered on the body of an entitled lady produces high comedy. In a letter to her friend, Louisa Wait, the nineteen-year-old Beecher recounts her success in "passing" as a servant girl: "our bonnets were gone & so Lucy & I borrowed the kitchen girls all trimmed with pink ribbons & we rigged ourselves like dowdy country girls . . . & so we sallied forth & such figures!! You never saw the like. I knew nobody knew me in Boston, as I felt perfectly at ease & I acted the simple country wench to perfection. . . . I kept on a simple sober face tho-I was . . . full of laugh. . . . The shopkeepers would smile at my apparent ignorance but I suspect they never would know me again & they never suspected that I was acting a part I knew by their actions" ([May] 1819; Beecher-Stowe Collection; Schlesinger).

Beecher's escapade again demonstrates that dress does not signify in a vacuum. In the absence of sumptuary codes or liveried dress for servants, dress may be counterfeitable, but when it is, other codes must be in accord. Since a servant's bonnet is inconsistent with ladylike airs, Beecher and Lucy adapt their deportment to their dress, behaving (as they imagine), soberly and simply, like "country wenches" and secure that their ruse will go undetected because "nobody knew [them] in Boston." That others might be adapting their own demeanor in response does not occur to Beecher: she does not suspect, for instance, that the shopkeepers may be enacting a parallel charade to hers by "recognizing" her as a servant. Instead, she assumes that the ability to counterfeit behavior successfully is a privilege of class. It is impossible to imagine Beecher countenancing or finding amusing a reverse charade in which the kitchen help sallied forth in public dressed in her clothing. For Beecher, cross-dressing is a privilege of the entitled; she can return the servant's bonnet to its owner and retreat upstairs. Beecher's behavior as a young woman is consistent with her lifelong obsession with how servant behavior might be differentiated from the practices of elevated and professionalized domesticity she promoted. It is, in a sense, a dress rehearsal for her advice book, *Letters to Persons Who Are Engaged in Domestic Service* (1842). Here she assumes the voice of a near-equal, concocting multiple situations prefaced with the phrase "If I were you" or "if I were in your situation." The upshot of the book, of course, is that she is not.

Beecher's slumming among the lower classes is echoed by Fanny Fern's initial forays into cross-dressing, also begun as a lark. As early as 1856, Fern and her circle had been experimenting privately with cross-dressing, but she had not written about these activities in her columns. Like Beecher's, her masquerade began with the hat. A personal friend and fellow journalist, Thomas Butler Gunn, recalled with some horror in his journal that she "told personally of her dressing up in *his* [her husband's] clothes yester evening, and *how she looked* (rather minutely), and how 'they wished *I* had come in.'

She put on my hat, too, and talked of the privilege accorded by it. It's all very innocent perhaps, . . . but I wonder *Parton* likes it" (qtd. in Warren, *Fanny Fern* 157). Gunn's discomfort with Fern's cross-dressing is clearly linked to his discomfort with her assumptions of other masculine perquisites, as well. Her open discussion of male privilege and her unmannerly appropriation of Gunn's hat suggest that her dress signals a change in her womanly deference, as does Gunn's own wonder that another man would put up with the cross-dressing, the appropriation of another man's hat, and the assumption of general masculine privileges.

This analysis is borne out by Gunn's succeeding journal entries about other women friends who cross-dressed. When the "exceedingly pretty" wife of another mutual friend, Mortimer Thomson ("Doesticks"), dressed "in male costume" at a party, Gunn's account evidences only admiration tinged with desire: "The feature of the night was 'Doesticks' ' wife—in male costume. . . . I can't describe how exceedingly pretty she looked—how *very* exceedingly pretty. Especially when the girls . . . *would* take off her coat and vest. . . . In this costume she continued all the remainder of the evening, taking part in the 'Fox and Geese,' during which her hair came down. She looked so pretty and so innocent that nobody could think it immodest for a second. *Nor was it!*" (qtd. in Warren, *Fanny Fern* 225–26). Doesticks' wife's cross-dressing only enhances her femininity. Gunn calls her attire "costume" while he accuses Fern of appropriation. His differentiation is precise. This woman—identified not by name, but only as a wife—remains passive while other women remove her coat and vest, exposing her body as the guarantee of her femininity. Her ample loose hair more than counteracts the effect of her trousers, and the combination produces an effect of innocent sexuality. Significantly, the game the friends engage in is sexual, as well, a chase of female geese by male foxes.

Fern's experiments with drag continued, becoming more and more public. With her hair "cut short,"[1] and accompanied by her daughter and husband, she ventured forth on New York City streets. She later recounted the escapade to Gunn, who recorded in his diary, "She got into a street weighing machine, to ascertain her weight, and not taking her feet from the ground, the proprietor caught hold of her leg to hold it up!" (Warren, *Fanny Fern* 184). Again, Fern's manners support the signification of her dress. Unlike Doesticks' wife, who was divested of her jacket and vest by girls, Fern was touched—on the leg—by the proprietor of the scales, a man of lower class. The touch crossed a class and sexual boundary, and infringed on her husband's right of property in her body, as well. Worst, she allowed it.

Dress used as costume thus occasioned a certain amount of humor and apparently harmless play (which also probably contributed to the assumption that women's interest in dress was an index of their attraction to trivial concerns). However, as the texts of Hale, her readers, and other women writers demonstrate, fluency in using and correctly interpreting attire—whether of dress, costume, or fashion—has significant political implications. To justify *Godey's* ever expanding and increasingly elaborate illustrations, as well as to account for the fact that the magazine's circulation could not be confined to the economically entitled, Hale invented a covering fiction that united all women, regardless of social class, as members of a community of feminine readers who understood the uses and the limits of fashion. It was a point of pride with *Godey's* and its readers to assert that the magazine united city with country and that dress was a way of effecting the unification. As Hale wrote in her "poke bonnet" editorial, "Our fashions are selected with particular care, and the plates prepared at great expense, in order to benefit that large portion of our friends who, residing in the country, naturally wish to know the style of city-made clothing. Many ladies make their own dresses. Our plates are their patterns" (47 [Oct. 1853]: 369). Here again, behavior determines how fashion will signify. Country dwellers' interest in city fashion is natural and even commendable, since these *ladies* sew for themselves. Thus they are not subject to the whim of city seamstresses interested in building business by promoting excess in fashion to their customers. Country ladies maintain control over their dress, following but not determined by the fashion.

In an era of frontier expansion, mutable fashion also linked the more civilized East with the frontier West. *Godey's* fashion plates and patterns spread the common grammar of fashion. To ensure that its far-flung readers were not excluded from owning the clothing that would prove them to be tasteful ladies, the magazine offered a shopping service that would obtain and ship to them the goods and services of eastern mercantile establishments. The sense of inclusion in a feminine community united by a current knowledge of fashion, produced by *Godey's* simultaneous invention and satisfaction of that interest, is clear in a correspondent's letter written from the frontier town of Brownsville, Texas:

> Do you know what a mail is in a country town? The arrival of a
> good handful of letters . . . interspersed with brown-wrappered papers

and stout magazines. . . . We hold up our aprons for them, white muslin, ribbon-trimmed aprons, such as "Fashion," describes, and "The Novelties" set forth. . . .

Look in my wardrobe; my dresses, even my bonnet, I made myself from "Godey!" My husband's slippers there, with dilapidated toes, are from "Godey." My table-mats, my children's clothes, my very puddings and pies are "Godey's."

Just reflect that Brownsville is one of thousands of American towns where we women-folks are similarly situated. (55 [Sept. 1855]: 286)

Godey's contribution to the sense of what Philip Fisher has termed "transparency and intelligibility" among the community of its readers is hard to overestimate (61). It is eloquently detailed in this letter, demonstrating how common possessions and common readings are central to establishing and maintaining common national identities. City and country, nation and province are united by the mails. Hale's reader specifies her possessions, perhaps similar to those of hundreds of thousands of other American women, but assuredly proper and fashionable, because guaranteed by *Godey's*. Should she or any Godey's reader return to Philadelphia, she would be immediately recognized as a lady. The magazine's assumption that all women, regardless of class or location, naturally wanted to be well (if not fashionably) dressed, and to own similar consumer goods, was endorsed by this and other enthusiastic readers. Their print conversation constituted a "vocabulary of nationalism" whose function paralleled those of custom, language, and geography (Fisher 61–62). That readers of the magazine took *Godey's* as a lexicon of womanly identity is abundantly evident in another correspondent's letter:

The absence of caste in our country and of sumptuary laws or rules, while causing some confusion in the mind of the slight observer, . . . which might well have prompted the foreigner's inquiry "Where are your poor people?" And as the LADY's BOOK penetrates to the fastnesses of the Rocky Mountains and the Pacific sands, it is not strange that a homogeneousness greater even than that produced by speaking the same language should be the result. Two ladies from opposite poles meeting each other on the plaza or boulevard of the city, recognize with lightning-like quickness the true fashionable height of the hat, the length of the plume, and the dress, with or without trail, as the case may be. Lace may be imitated, silks may be adulterated, but the general air which comes of familiarity with all the best modes, and which makes the dress and appearance what the French call *comme il faut,* can only be gained by education. (80 [Jan. 1870]: 190)

This statement emphasizes how a familiarity with fashion might unite "ladies" in a time of geographical dispersion and ethnic mixing. More remarkable, however, is its treatment of counterfeit. It argues that although materials may be imitated, the shape and general knowledge of current fashion, whether displayed by "ladies" or worn by less-entitled pretenders, bespeaks a larger knowledge that is not bound by class or language, but that comes from the common "education" each has enjoyed by subscribing to *Godey's*. Hale's figure of "two ladies from opposite poles meeting each other" suggests both class and geographical difference: mistress and servant, American and foreigner may share the ability to read and display the best modes. A woman could thus simultaneously deplore sumptuary excess and dress fashionably as a signifier of her American taste. In fact, by offering its readers exhaustive lexicons by which American ladies might be recognized, by encoding their food, their possessions, their dress, and even their physical demeanor, *Godey's* in effect invented the American woman.

This is not to argue that *Godey's* correspondents, Hale, or the other writers under study here, lost their sense of class entitlement in their common enthusiasm for new spring bonnets. However, the language of fashion, especially as it was disseminated by magazines like *Godey's*, contributed significantly to the ideology of American democratic classlessness, particularly among women. In a country where it was broadly held that any country boy could become president, the correlative, if usually unspoken, assertion was that any country girl might become his wife. If she had read *Godey's*, she would be ready to assume the proper signifiers of her station: "As there is no height to which manly talent may not attain in our happy country, so should womanly elegance and culture be ready for adaptation to any high place that may be allotted by the possible Fates. We are proud of the simple dignity and high-bred grace of our Mrs. Abigail Adams, at the English court; how much more elegant she was than the good dowdy Queen Charlotte herself. . . . These made the country-bred girl a fit companion for princes, and, what was more important, for her own superior and admirable husband" (80 [Jan. 1870]: 191). The same correspondent who noted that homogeneousness of fashion unites women separated by geography here argues that womanly elegance is an adaptable trait that should be maintained, cultivated, and demonstrated appropriately. She does not allow for the possibility that the British may have considered Abigail Adams to be overdressed. Rather, she appears as seen through patriotic eyes: both simple and fashionable, well-bred and democratic, and altogether elegantly superior to her British counterpart.

Concomitant with her equation of dress with character, Hale affected a remarkable constancy in her own dress and coiffeur as a counterpoint to the ephemeral fashions the *Ladies' Magazine* and *Godey's* promoted. Her biographers uniformly note that she never altered her hairstyle and that she affected widow's weeds for most of her adult life. This practice also put her outside the storm of controversy that the fashion plates elicited from crusaders such as Catharine Beecher, who blamed magazines such as *Godey's* for spreading expensive, frivolous, and even dangerous notions to women who, they assumed, would imitate these fashions willy-nilly. It was perhaps the ultimate demonstration of Hale's contention that if dress were to be equated with character, a wise woman would use her dress to exemplify the character she wished her public to attribute to her.

Like Hale, Margaret Fuller mimed the taken-for-granted connections of dress, gender, and character, thus emphasizing their artifice. If Hale effected a happy combination of subdued costume, subdued content, and subdued character that allowed her a significant degree of editorial latitude, it nevertheless resulted in her being misclassified as trivial and/or manipulative by subsequent readers. Fuller's approach was similar in intent and effect, although different in application. Like Hale, she saw dress as costume and exploited it as such. Unlike Hale, the costumes she affected were not subdued and muted. Thus her dress has been misread as vanity, both by her contemporaries and by several generations of scholars who have depended on their recollections.

During her adolescence, Fuller's father became increasingly concerned about her social development. For a time he even entreated his wife to keep their daughter away from social occasions, since her size, her precocity, and her appearance combined to make her an object of ridicule. Taken in hand by Eliza Farrar, however, Fuller mastered the coded behaviors of social entitlement as quickly and as thoroughly as she had learned Latin. She became known in her early adulthood for her ease in conversation, her graceful carriage, and her tasteful attire. These skills were duly noted by her contemporaries (just as her awkwardness had been). Especially during the Conversations, Fuller's attire was the subject of several admiring recollections. A friend wrote: "Margaret, beautifully dressed (don't despise that, for it made a fine picture,) presided with more dignity and grace than I had thought possible. The subject was Beauty" (*Memoirs* 1:332). Another recalled, "Margaret used to come to the conversations very well dressed, and, altogether, looked sumptuously" (*Memoirs* 1:336).

Fuller's dress elicited a disproportionate storm of response from her detractors, as well. Harriet Martineau, for example, equated dress and talk as mere surface adornments: "While Margaret Fuller and her adult pupils sat 'gorgeously dressed,' talking about Mars and Venus, Plato and Goethe, and fancying themselves the elect of the earth in intellect and refinement, the liberties of the republic were running out as fast as they could go, at a breach which another sort of elect persons were devoting themselves to repair" (qtd. in Higginson 126–27). After Fuller's death, Emerson sought to compensate for Martineau's diatribe, concluding that he found no proof that Fuller had dressed exotically. He explained, "I interpret this repeated story of sumptuousness of dress, that this appearance, like her reported beauty, was simply an effect of a general impression of magnificence made by her genius, and mistakenly attributed to some external elegance; for I have been told by her most intimate friend [Caroline Sturgis, according to Capper], who knew every particular of her conduct at that time, that there was nothing of special expense or splendor in her toilette" (*Memoirs* 1:337). Here Emerson reverses the equation of dress=woman=intellect; but as in algebra, the commutative principle holds. His logic is binary: Either Fuller must be beautiful and well dressed or a magnificent genius. She cannot be both, because a beautiful woman would be, by extension, sexually desirable and married, thus not forced to earn her living. Nor would a beautiful woman want to run the risk of repelling potential suitors by challenging their intelligence. An intellectual woman, on the other hand, could not be beautiful, for presumably she would not wish to take time from studies to maintain surface appearances or to pursue sumptuary display. Thus Emerson opts for intelligence and relegates beauty to the status of mere illusion.

The intersection of dress, gender, and intellect finds its way into the work of twentieth-century scholars as well. For Mason Wade, as it had for Martineau, dress suggests the invisible economic underpinnings of Fuller's Conversations. Although he calls the Conversations "nothing less than a feminist manifesto" (70), he evaluates their meaning to contemporary scholars in these words: "Today . . . the Conversations . . . seem more than a little silly and ridiculous, a *homespun* imitation of the salon without its social charms and amenities. The very notion of paying for the right to share in conversation seems absurd" (77–78; emphasis added). The metaphor of homespun picks up the notion of counterfeit that dominated nineteenth-century debates about attire. Here the logic is that conversation itself is a kind of intellectual "drag," at best a counterfeit of the continental salon, and, because sham, not a marketable commodity. The reverse notion—that Fuller might have offered the Conversations as an economic venture masked as a social gathering—seems unthinkable. Apparently for Wade, Emerson might earn money presenting lyceum lectures, or Channing support himself by professing rhetoric at Harvard, but Fuller should have used her oratorical skills only as social currency.

Only one study of Fuller has sought to deal with her dress and appearance as manipulable signifiers rather than essential feminine attributes. Julie Ellison insists that "to restore the significance of performance—of gesture, costume, and voice—is crucial for an appreciation of Fuller's reimagining of the romantic" (219). Following Ellison, Fuller's dress might be read as costume for a multilayered performance. On the simplest level, her appearance underscored the topics and enhanced the occasions of her conversations. The conversation on Beauty, for example, was held at Christmas. To a woman trained by Eliza Farrar, both subject and season would warrant extra care and elegance in dress. More complexly, Fuller conceived of the Conversations in sartorial terms (as befits a woman who had read Carlyle's *Sartor Resartus*), announcing to Sophia Ripley that she wished to avoid "the cant of coterei [sic] criticism" and "that sort of vanity in them which wears the garb of modesty" (*Letters* 2:87). Thus her "elegant" dress may be read as pride in femininity, an assertion that a woman need not deny her gender by affecting either a falsely modest retirement (the plain attire and self effacement of the sort Hale affected) or an androgynous exterior in order to perform intellectually.

Indeed, Fuller's dress may be read as a performance in costume that to the conversationalists produced the effect of "watching a woman demonstrate the representation of a woman's body" (Doane 181). This kind of parodic and self-aware performance Mary Ann Doane terms *double mimesis*: "a divergence between voice and body in the representation of the woman. Her voice is mocking, distanced, while her body assumes the poses of idealized romance. . . . The image is false, and the woman's voice directs our reading of it. For her own purposes, the woman mimes the gestures and language of the romance" (182). The Conversations might be read in a parallel fashion, especially in light of the fact that they were an economic venture costumed as a salon. They represented Fuller's effort to support her family at a time in her life when she had hoped to be in Europe, when she was seen as increasingly desexualized and unmarriageable by her male counterparts, and when Emerson had already decided that she was not beautiful. Thus, a Conversation on dancing seems especially to exemplify the ironic double mimesis Doane describes, during which Fuller's body and dress declare the sumptuous contentment Martineau decried, while her ironic voice-over declares: "I love, I live, I am beautiful!—I put on my festal dress to do honor to my happiness" (*Memoirs* 1:336).

Fuller's and Hale's mimes of the dress codes signifying womanly elegance and matronly retirement suggest that Fern's play with cross-dressing may be read as a mime, as well—a public act interpreted by her columns as a material demonstration of the political, economic, and social issues related to dress. News of Fern's public but as-yet unpublicized excursion to the weighing-machine was spread by gossip initiated by "some neighbor" who "recognized" the Partons and "mentioned the circumstance to others" (Warren, *Fanny Fern* 184). Fern seized the initiative, telling her own version of the story to *Ledger* readers on page four of the 10 and 17 July 1858 editions. In print, the playful aspects of costume are subsumed to more serious issues associated with dress, for Fern points out that if fashion is a matter of feminine choice, that choice is limited by law. In a series of three columns on the dress issue she builds a cumulative argument; within each column, as well, she moves from less to more serious issues. In her first column Fern establishes that dress is not merely an issue of vanity but that it has serious consequences for women's bodies. She introduces the first column by noting the arrest of Emma Wilson "for wearing man's apparel," a figural juxtaposition of Wilson's mobility when dressed in trousers with the containment enacted on her by law. Such mobility, she argues, would not be dangerous; it would only contribute to women's improved health: "Now if any male or female Miss Nancy who reads this feels shocked, let 'em! Any woman who likes, may stay at home during a three weeks' rain, till her skin looks like parchment, and her eyes like those of a dead fish, or she may go out and get a consumption dragging round wet petticoats; I won't" (*Ledger* 10 July 1858). Fern's challenge to "any male or female Miss Nancy" insists that gender ambiguity, as well as health and physical comfort, are at the heart of this column. Dressed in "Mr. Fern's" attire and with her hair tucked up, she "looked into the glass, where I beheld the very fac-simile of a certain musical gentleman, whose photograph hangs this minute in Brady's entry" (*Ledger* 10 July 1858). At issue here is not whether women may wear trousers in bad weather but how far into men's territory women may intrude: in borrowing her husband's clothing, is she borrowing his masculine privileges as well? Calling him "Mr. Fern" is ambiguous, but suggestive—it may signal either Fanny Fern's proper wifely gesture of having taken her husband's name, or Sarah Parton's improper reversal of power by naming

Fern's husband after her textual alter ego. The "musical gentleman" whom
the short-haired Fern resembles is likely her brother, Richard Storrs Willis,
a composer, musician, music teacher, and editor of the *New York Musical
World and Times,* with whom she enjoyed a more cordial relationship than
with Nathaniel Parker Willis. Having slandered one brother by lampooning
his foppishness in *Ruth Hall* and imitating his career as a successful writer,
is she now usurping the very bodily form of the other brother? Or is her
act of counterfeit only a parallel to Brady's photographic facsimile? That is,
has she only written signs of masculine identity on her body as Brady has
written those signs on a photographic plate?

Fern returned to the issue in her next week's column, also entitled "A
Law More Nice Than Just." This column has an explanatory and reassuring
agenda, as if to remind readers that such cross-dressing does not "unsex" a
woman. Fern first implies that she has become reconciled to her feminine
attire, since cross-dressing deprives her of the advantages of both sexes.
Because she is not a skilled imitator of bodily gesture (the man at the scale
had to lift her leg for her), she is subject to "indecent" physical incursions.
But dressed as a man, she cannot object. In fact, she can claim none of the
"delicious little politenesses" extended to women by gentlemen. Nor can
she can indulge her "unstifleable feminine desire for adornment" because
she cannot appropriate its masculine equivalents: she must tie up her hair,
but she cannot wear a mustache. Yet, she claims, masculine masquerade
has its privileges, including the right "to pick up contraband bits of science
in Medical Museums, forbidden to crinoline, and hold conversation with
intelligent men, who supposing you to be a man, consequently talk sense
to you" (*Ledger* 17 July 1858). This column, immediately following her
first public acknowledgment of cross-dressing, reassures readers that dress
is indeed separable from bodily identity and demonstrates that when the
difference between dress and body is not honored, women suffer. It marks,
as well, the substantial intellectual privileges reserved to men even in an era
of increased women's literacy.

Fern dropped the topic of cross-dressing for a year, only to return to it
with renewed vehemence. Now she emphasized the connection between
legal strictures that prescribed gendered attire (propriety) and issues of
economics (property). As in the first column, she notes the arrest of another
woman for dressing as a man. This Englishwoman, who, after dressing and
working as a seaman for ten years, had been apprehended when "her sex was
by some means suspected." "It then appeared that she was a married woman;

and had undergone these incredible hardships to support a husband, who by a misfortune was forever disabled from doing it himself." In detailing the resulting scandal, Fern emphasizes that this woman, who had conducted herself "with perfect propriety" during the episode, was made to swear by a magistrate that she would "never [dress] so again" and was nearly mobbed by outraged observers. She asks, "had this woman supported herself, or her husband, or both, in her own proper attire, tinselled with the wages of shame, would the same discriminating law, through its magistrates, have considered it their business to interfere?" The magistrate and the law thus discount the sum total of manners, conduct, situation, and intent, and make the simplest equation of attire with person. Fern then recounts another related anecdote. A merchant of her acquaintance "dismissed all his men-clerks and substituted women." After a period of trial, he agreed that their performance was equal to the men's, and on certain points better, since they were less pugnacious, less likely to drink, and more pleasant to the customers. "After making this admission, he added, with a chuckle of satisfaction, *'and then, I get them for one-third less wages!'* " (*Ledger* 8 Oct. 1859).

This final column summarizes the meaning of the three, which is as much about wearing women's dress as it is about dressing as a man. To affect feminine dress has serious consequences: womanly attire limits physical mobility, contributes to ill health, and bars its wearers from intellectual challenge. Worse, it forces some of its wearers to exploit dress—their "own proper attire"—as a signifier of illicit sexual desire in order to make a living wage. The cross-dressed working woman, Fern demonstrates, is no more improperly attired than is the prostitute, "tinselled" in a gaudy feminine dress bought with her illicit earnings. Ultimately, Fern suggests, wearing "crinoline" is an economic privilege affordable only by women who can afford not to work or to work for substandard wages.

The examples of Hale, Fuller, and Fern thus demonstrate the variety of ways interpretation derives from a foundational equation of women with dress. The equation seems simple enough: a widow who dresses modestly writes conciliatory columns. A woman who dresses extravagantly or fashionably is frivolous and likewise incapable of being taken seriously; if she is, nevertheless, brilliant, her mind has illusorily illuminated her body. A woman who dresses as a man is an impostor, a sexual outlaw, and a threat to masculine economic systems. More complex readings, however, demonstrate that these women exploited and surpassed that simple equivalence. Costumed as a widow, Hale argued that dress could unite

American women who were differentiated by space, language, and economic privilege. Costumed as a beauty, Fuller mimed beauty. Costumed as a man, Fern demonstrated how legislated dress constricted women's physical mobility, ruined their health, and lessened their economic status.

Catharine Beecher held similar understandings, but the trajectory of her concern with dress had perhaps the most disturbing potential consequences. Like Fuller she understood fine dress to be mimicry. Like Fern, she sought to demonstrate its material consequences. Like Hale, she saw dress as an issue of national identity. But Beecher's agendas demonstrate the danger of such nationalistic fervor. Her alignment of fashion and national identity was much less egalitarian than Hale's. She held fashion magazines (presumably including *Godey's*, which was edited by her friend Sarah Hale) responsible for circulating and promoting fashions that Beecher blamed for the declining health of American women. Unlike Hale, she did not praise fashion's potential for linking city and country. She minced no words about the effects of nationally circulated grammars of fashion: "Into our rural towns, even, these pernicious customs of dress have been carried by mantua-makers from the city, and still more by the miserable fashion-plates in our literature, that set forth the distortions of deformity and disease as models of taste and fashion" (*Health* 107). This dictum presents the counterargument to Hale's asserting that fashion transcended geography, uniting country with city. Beecher's accusations carry a class coding; she blames working seamstresses for corrupting innocent country tastes.

Beecher wished women to unite not because they all recognized fine fashion but because they recognized the implications of dressing unwisely for their health. Because she was not employed by a magazine or newspaper whose profit depended on promulgating fashion, she was able to pursue a vigorous and outspoken campaign of dress reform. This is not to argue that Hale ignored dress reform; in the sections of *Godey's* she controlled, she advocated good posture, exercise, and abandonment of corsets and crinolines. Nor is it to paint Beecher's concerns as altruistic. Rather, they were part of her own economic agenda, which depended on selling books. Selling books, in turn, depended on readers' endorsing her tripartite equation of health, education, and nationalism, of healthy practices taught in schools by New England women who had been displaced from domestic occupations by foreign infiltrators. Thus patriotic women would at once reform their dress, contribute to education, and crush the foreign menace, for Beecher's campaign of dress reform invoked patriotic duty at the point of eugenics.

She explained in detail that fashionable dress could be linked to the "disease and deformity" of mother and offspring alike. Beecher decried crinolines, hoops, and wide skirts that required a compensatory "whalebone pressure" of corsets for balance, telling readers that these designs deformed "the most delicate and important organs of life." She concluded, "And the most terrible feature in this monstrous course is, that the evil thus achieved by a mother is often transmitted to her deformed offspring" (*Health* 88–89).

Beecher's objections exceed a concern for the health of American women, however, and remind us that a classless commonwealth of American fashion exists only because certain boundaries differentiate its citizens from others. If the "mothers and daughters of the nation" insist on wearing the latest fashions, which inhibit their reproductive organs and eventually might produce deformed offspring, a crisis looms. Those who do not have the money for whalebone corsets (that is, immigrant women and servant girls) will produce more and healthier children. In a democratic society, a simple numeric majority thus seems inevitable, a majority in which unentitled others may simply overwhelm the offspring of fashionable American citizens. This point Beecher argues forcefully in *American Woman's Home,* taking as her example the exodus of young New England women from kitchens to factories: "The foreigners who supplant them in kitchen labor are almost the only strong and healthy women to rear large families. . . . Thus it is that the controlling political majority of New-England is passing from the educated to the children of ignorant foreigners" (467). (In fact, the *American Woman's Home* argument does not mention fashion, but centers on unhealthy factory conditions. The line of logic, from class privilege through health, to political defeat is, however, constant in Beecher's writings and characterizes her arguments on both fashion and factory conditions.) Beecher's arguments, although disturbingly xenophobic, thus relocate the issues of dress from a somewhat abstract debate about intellect, or beauty, or costume, to an embodied, materioeconomic question of political majority. A concern with fashion is more than coincident with the move of foreigners into "kitchen labor." Both are the result of larger economic upheavals: industrialization, improved transportation, the rise of consumer capitalism, and the consequent debate about where women fit into such a landscape. Thus issues of economics and politics are inseparably linked to interpretations of the costumed womanly body.

The surface of that costumed body, however, like personal names and nominative identifiers, belies feminine essentialism. Ironically, whether women cross-dressed, dressed modestly, "tinselled" their attire "with the wages of shame," removed their corsets, or attended assiduously to fashion, they were liable to be read as vainly obsessed with their appearance. The best way out of this double bind seems clearly indicated by Hale and Fuller, who indulged in a kind of double-cross-dressing, parodying the already established signifying codes of True Womanhood. As code-literate "authors," possessed of the economic and subjective entitlement to comment publicly, in print and in performance, these women demonstrate the impossibility of a definitive interpretation of their "public images."

Chapter Five

THE DOMESTIC
MANNERS OF
AMERICAN LADIES

In 1841, as Catharine Beecher was completing her *Treatise on Domestic Economy*, her cousin Elizabeth Foote wrote from Ohio: "Catharine Beecher is with us but is expecting every day to go to Chilecothe—She is writing a book upon house keeping and domestic matters generally—if it were not for these maiden ladies instructing the married ones how to keep house and take care of children I dont know what would become of us" (28/29 Jan.; Foote Collection, Stowe-Day). In this letter Foote notes a central paradox that characterizes all four of these writers. Beecher was an unmarried, childless, and virtually homeless forty-one-year old woman writing a book on domestic practice. Foote's ironic separation of "maiden ladies" from "married ones" based on experiential authority suggests a beginning distinction that, if followed, demonstrates how the *Treatise*— as well as other similar conduct books—rests on unarticulated ideas about gender, class, location, and nationalism.

Foote assumes that heterosexual marriage produces important differences among ladies, and that her domestic experience as a married woman is significantly different from that of her cousin, whose domestic expertise was only as an older sister, aunt, and perpetual houseguest. These assumptions, in turn, depend on deeper markers of class identity. Married women, unlike their single counterparts who often worked to support themselves, derived their economic support from their husbands; their exemption from labor was a component of their own and their husbands' elevated class status. "Maiden ladies," like Catharine Beecher, although they might enjoy a certain respect for their dutiful acts of schoolkeeping and writing, were, nevertheless, objects of pity because they labored. Beecher's *Treatise* engaged these presumptions, pointing out that a married woman's class status depended precariously on her husband's health and financial stability. Should a man die or lose his fortune, his dependents might be forced to support themselves. Although advantages of literacy and race would qualify a fortunate woman to find respectable work as a writer or a teacher rather than as a seamstress, a governess, a domestic, a mill worker, or a prostitute, entering the labor market would nevertheless diminish her class status.

The address of the Beecher and Foote families in Ohio in 1841 also suggests the importance of location in determining the coding of social class. Ohio, part of the then-western frontier, was an area of great social ferment and racial/ethnic diversity; many of its residents had left the East in an attempt to better their economic status. This fluid situation, in turn, structured the details of the *Treatise's* marketing and of its ideological framing. Sold to female seminaries and common schools in the East and distributed throughout the western settlements by a network of teachers Beecher had trained, the book announced that its aim was to professionalize domestic practice on the frontier. Over the next thirty-five years it circulated nationwide. That the book was read by several generations of women nationwide suggests that the domestic practice it encoded as foundational to an American identity in 1841 continued to be viable as the nation expanded westward.

Nor was Beecher's *Treatise on Domestic Economy* the only such domestic handbook written during this period. After 1830 advanced technologies of print circulation, immigration and cultural diversity, urbanization, and proliferating consumer commodities called forth hundreds of similar texts that promised to guide women to social security. These books focus on deferential behavior (etiquette), practice (directions, recipes, and procedures), and custom (cultural uses and traditions). They spawned companion volumes that included almanacs, textbooks, handbooks of health, physiology and calisthenics, advice to servants, and recipe books.

The publication of Beecher's *Treatise* and Sara Josepha Hale's *Manners: or, Happy Homes and Good Society All the Year Round* (1867) frames a period of social differentiation fueled by internal U.S. expansion. Defining the conduct of a woman whose identity is uniquely American, these books establish that the duty of such a woman was to produce American citizens, either through the embodied labor of natural reproduction or the mind-labor of cultural reproduction. In support of this agenda, these books claim a class status for this woman independent of the men with whom she may be affiliated and relocate her class relative to mannerly behaviors that can be taught and learned. Their gendered version of class is also distinctly nationalistic, and articulated in contrast to other racial and ethnic groups then present in the United States. In fine, these books invent an American woman who transcends the circumstances of her birth, location, economic circumstance, or marital status. This woman is not everywoman, but a literate, middle-class, white, Anglo-Saxon, Protestant, and economically self-sufficient woman.

Both Beecher and Hale frame their books with an explicit articulation of their American context. They first differentiate the United States from Europe by how class functions in each society. Hale states that American domesticity stems from but is different than British tradition. Claiming that "the two Anglo-Saxon Peoples were intrusted with the holy duty of keeping pure the home of woman and the altar of God" (5), she vaunts their elevated respect for the home, wherein "are united the "characteristics and virtues of the Princely and the Popular . . . [,] the MANNERS that form the most perfect standard for social life and home happiness" (6). Hale equates and thus limits the status of "Americans" to those whose background derives from Anglo-Saxon heritage. Her book aims to preserve the best of the British class system (its manners) while celebrating the popular democracy of American practice. Beecher, as well, establishes her arguments about manners and class by differentiating European practice from American. She entitles the initial chapters of the early editions of *Treatise on Domestic Economy* "The Peculiar Responsibilities of American Women" and "Difficulties Peculiar to American Women." Here she considers the situations that might result in a diminution of class for women. Whereas in Europe's aristocracies, "all ranks and classes are fixed in a given position, and each person is educated for a particular sphere and style of living," in America, class status is not constant. "Persons in poverty, are rising to opulence, and persons of wealth, are sinking to poverty." Beecher noted particularly the geographic mobility that characterized antebellum America and further confused any system of class. "The sons of the wealthy are leaving the rich mansions of their fathers, to dwell in the log cabins of the forest, where very soon they bear away the daughters of ease and refinement, to share the privations of a new settlement. Meantime, . . . there is a mingling of all grades of wealth, intellect, and education. There are no distinct classes, as in aristocratic lands, . . . but all are thrown into promiscuous masses" (39, 40).[1] Although class and geographic mobility are foundational to democracy, Beecher worries that they produce a dangerous economic and political instability. Women in particular seem to have little agency under economic fluctuations that may ultimately expose them to social instability for which they have not been prepared and which they do not deserve.

One such situation is removal to the frontier. The *Treatise* is written to forestall the possibility that by such a dislocation a woman's class status would diminish. Having lived for several years in what was then the frontier West, Beecher argued that a change in location did not necessarily imply a lessening of status: "Few persons realize how many refined and lovely women are scattered over the broad prairies and deep forests of the West; and none, but the Father above, appreciates the extent of those sacrifices and sufferings, . . . amid those vast solitudes. If the American women of the East merit the palm, for their skill and success as accomplished housekeepers, still more is due to the heroines of the West, who, with such unyielding fortitude and cheerful endurance, attempt similar duties, amid so many disadvantages and deprivations" (47). Despite its self-serving and patronizing tone, this passage implies several important circumstances that determine social class: concentrated population, within which peers validate social standing; skill in managing a complex domestic establishment, again recognized by peers; and material possessions, which, if absent, constitute deprivation. All of these variables depend on a father's or husband's economic success. Part of the logic for the *Treatise,* then, is to establish that if a woman is forced to move to the West, if she must inhabit a log cabin in the howling wilderness, if she cannot own the material signifiers of class, she can nevertheless maintain her status from her practice of the household economies articulated in the *Treatise.*

Removal to the West is only one of the vagaries of station that may be visited upon a woman as a result of her masculine affiliations. Although Beecher admits that "such trials" as emigration may not befall "all American women," she also asserts that it is impossible to anticipate whom they will touch. She warns, "The reverses of fortune, and the chances of matrimony, expose every woman in the Nation to such liabilities, for which she needs to be prepared" (48). Although in this context, the referent for "trials" is the social dislocation of moving to the frontier, the mention of "liabilities" follows Beecher's introduction of other situations that may deprive a woman of economic support: having married unwisely, having married a man whose fortune fails, or having failed to marry at all, a woman may be forced to work. Unfortunately, most of the occupations for which a woman might be prepared entail a lowering of social class. Beecher acknowledges the class codes associated with labor, claiming that "young ladies" often "imagine that it is vulgar and ungenteel to know how to work." But she does not consider this to be an American attitude. Rather, it is "one of the relics of an aristocratic state of society, which is fast passing away" (67).

Knowing how to work, however, is not the only source of vulgarity, since an occupational hierarchy also carries codings of gentility. In other documents written at approximately the same date, Beecher clearly articulates this "principle of *caste*" as an issue that "bears heavily on our sex." To demonstrate the effects of such an invisible hierarchy, she challenges "any woman" of elevated class to "imagine that her son, or brother, is about to marry a young lady, whose character and education are every way lovely and unexceptionable, but who, it appears, is a *seamstress,* or a *nurse,* or a *domestic,* and how few are there, who will not be conscious of the . . . principle of *caste.* But suppose the young lady to be one, who has been earning her livelihood by writing poetry and love stories, or who has lived all her days in utter idleness, and how suddenly the feelings are changed!" ("Evils" 6). This passage strikingly illustrates Beecher's always present, but often hidden, attempt to separate writing women from other laborers. Here, although her tone is scornful toward dilettante women writers, she nevertheless divides their class status from women who ply sweated trades, placing writers in a conceptual category that also contains women who do no labor. More centrally, Beecher asks the reader to supply the unarticulated circumstances that would have made such a well-educated and respectable young lady liable for her own economic support, circumstances such as the failed or lessened economic status of a father, brother, or husband. Moreover, Beecher's way of framing this hypothetical case implies that "any woman" might be subject to the same circumstances.

Thus the *Treatise* separates the domestic and social codes by which an American lady might be identified from the economic uncertainties that determined her social and physical location. The argument of this book and of others like it is that a woman's social class is most reliably measured not by her masculine affiliates but by the qualities she herself displays. To be a lady, she need not be married. If forced to labor for her own support, a woman may continue to claim the status of a lady. Moreover, she may do so regardless of where she lives. This is not to say that Beecher and Hale argued for a perfectly democratic state wherein all claims to social class would be equally endorsed. Rather, they propose to replace one system of status with another: in place of basing social rank on wealth and its material signifiers, they locate it in character traits most appropriate to a democracy. Not surprisingly, these are qualities already possessed by entitled "ladies." Nevertheless, because they are able to be articulated, they can be taught to and learned by those who may experience an elevation in class as well.

For Beecher, the criteria that would found such a social hierarchy include an equal right to happiness; but this right must not be anarchically claimed. Rather, in a democracy, a rule of thumb prevails: "superiors in age, station, or office, have precedence of subordinates; age and feebleness, of youth and strength; and the feebler sex, of more vigorous man" (*Treatise* 140-41). The constituent principles of this "democratic rule" fall into three general categories—voluntary deference, noblesse oblige, and racial privilege—that also suggest the general structure and content of the conduct books that articulate the character of the new American woman. These principles, by which a class status deriving from character may be measured, are, in Beecher's and Hale's understanding, based in Christian principle. First, the strong voluntarily defer to the weak, the young to the elder, men to women. Second, to ensure that each individual is valued equally, those who are endowed with financial and/or cultural capital share liberally with others, practicing a kind of noblesse oblige. In their turn, those who have less capital agree not to resort to brute force to destroy the wealth of others. Third, voluntary deference is balanced by voluntary respect accorded to those who are evidently superior in "station or office." The meaning of these terms is vague, but strongly implies political, social, and racial privilege.

In books such as Beecher's *Treatise* and Hale's *Manners,* prescriptions of proper etiquette ensure that voluntary deference will obtain in a democracy. Both women assume that the etiquette of social relations is first and best learned in family situations, where those who are superior in physical strength, health, age, or political privilege learn to coexist with those who are weaker. Beecher's abstract of her chapter "On Domestic Manners" outlines the logic of voluntary deference: "Rules of Precedence to be enforced in the Family. Manners and Tones towards Superiors to be regulated in the Family. Treatment of grown Brothers and Sisters by Young Children. Acknowledgment of Favors by Children to be required. . . . Caution as to Allowances to be made for those deficient in Good-manners. Comparison of English and American Manners, by De Tocqueville. America may hope to excel all Nations in Refinement, Taste, and Good-breeding; and why. Effects of Wealth and Equalisation of Labor" (15–16). This brief outline demonstrates how, within the scope of a chapter twelve pages in length,

Beecher moves from the personal and local to the national. Hale's similar chapter is entitled "Domestic Etiquette and Duties." Here she enjoins husbands "Never [to] forget that the happiness of another is committed to your charge, and strive to render your home happy by kindness and attention to your wife, and by carefully watching over your words and actions" (320). She counsels wives to "deserve the beautiful commendation of Solomon . . . 'The heart of her husband doth safely trust in her: she will do him good, and not evil, all the days of her life' " (319). Thus, both writers envision a hierarchical heterosexual family situation in which mutual and voluntary deference prevails. Superiors respect those who are in their care; inferiors recognize and defer to the self-evident authority of their husbands, parents, and elders.

Such books also spell out practices of noblesse oblige whose purpose it is to ensure that such voluntary deference will be recognized. By rewarding deference with charity, these books imply, the circumstantial effects of an era of economic instability may be lessened; women may be protected from its worst effects; and class warfare, always a present possibility to Beecher, may be avoided. The *Treatise* contains chapters that articulate the requirements of "Giving in Charity," and prescribe how "superiors" are to care for domestics, infants, young children, the sick, and, in its 1869 edition, the elderly. Both the *Treatise* and *Manners* demonstrate that a component of noblesse oblige and a sure indicator of class is a respect for material goods, whether or not one owns them. Thus they detail practices whereby that respect can be demonstrated. If a woman is not rich, she may nevertheless display her few possessions tastefully, since her class status depends on a demonstrable mastery of household and domestic arts. According to *Manners*, "even a very simple home, filled with the evidences of taste and refinement, pleases and gratifies at once" since it "proves a love which has sought outward expression in bringing brightness and cheerfulness to the dear ones within" (81). Thus practice reinforces and demonstrates the principles of deference. Similarly, if a woman must accept domestic employment she will know how to care for another's possessions, having read the *Treatise*'s detailed instructions for domestic practice in chapters such as "On the Care of Parlors" or "On Starching, Ironing, and Cleansing." Or she may consult *Mrs. Hale's Receipts for the Million*, whose thousand-plus numbered entries provided a quickly accessible solution for every household eventuality. Thus a common repertoire of practice—based in the valuing of consumer goods and the knowledge of how to manage and care for feather beds, mahogany furniture, kitchen crockery, flower and vegetable gardens, and domestic pets—will characterize ladies, regardless of their economic status.[2]

A third category of American sociopolitical privilege undergirds voluntary deference (etiquette) and noblesse oblige (practice). In Beecher's and Hale's books it finds its articulation in chapters that consider "manners" as customs whose practice (or elimination or modification) constitute a uniquely American identity. In such chapters the meaning of American usage—from food to celebration—is clearly laid out, often in contrast to the curious customs of foreign lands, usually included as negative examples to establish that immigrants from these locations must not expect to rise to social prominence in America. In Hale's vision, a hierarchy of nations descends from those in which most citizens are literate and Protestant, and in which women occupy an elevated status (marked by chivalric respect; public, if limited, political participation; the right to education; and the ability to influence men's political behaviors). Hale's chapter "Heathen Homes" demonstrates these hierarchies. Its purpose is to establish by negative definition the blessings of what Beecher might call American "station and office." It is not insignificant that Hale has chosen Asian examples at a time when discussions of "The Chinese Problem" was beginning to fill East Coast newspapers. She takes "the state in which the Chinese women are kept" as evidence of the "debasement" of the "whole nation" of China, articulating in a chapter entitled "Heathen Homes" the practices of Chinese, "Hindoos," Burmese, Japanese, Tartars, and "all the swarming millions of Africa, and the inhabitants of the islands" to prove that in the "heathen world, . . . just in proportion as woman is lowered, just in the same proportion must man ever sink. The world shows no solitary instance of the highest form of national greatness, socially, politically, and morally, where woman's influence is ignored or systematically destroyed" (212). Hale here precisely reverses the tradition of linking a woman's class status to a man's. She argues implicitly that they must be separate. She argues explicitly that immigrants from lands where women are devalued must give up such habits and practices, as well, adopting in their place values Hale aligns with heterosexual American norms. These, she notes, derive from Germanic "tribes," who had, "according to Tacitus, kept the Eden idea of marriage and the sanctity of home-life, as Christians now understand God's law, while all other Gentile peoples had become corrupt and licentious. And from the customs and manners of these Germans . . . 'the original institution of chivalry has often been traced,' says Sir Walter Scott. So surely does the purity of the home-circle and the honor paid to woman elevate the minds and exalt the characters of men" (261). Hale invokes Anglo-Saxon and Teutonic norms to reinforce common cultural understandings that American identity was beneficially derived from "Anglo-Saxon" races. As well, Hale links Germanic uses with Protestant beliefs, thus effectively excluding Irish immigrants from any claim in Anglo-Saxonism.

These books do not apologize for a new social hierarchy of manners, since its context is self-evidently American, and democracy needs no explanation or apology. Rather, they justify the resultant social hierarchy by the guarantee that since these privileges are no longer linked to blood entitlement, they can be acquired by anyone. This context of social flux articulated by Hale and Beecher as a frame for their writings balances the threat of economic disaster with the possibility of social elevation. If a woman of lower caste can increase her status through a fortunately contracted marriage or through her own diligence, the conduct books assure her that if she has read them, she will know how to behave in a manner appropriate to her new economic status. Hale, for example, differentiates American from continental servitude (scanting, of course, racial slavery), since in the United States it is only a temporary expedient, a "present resource to obtain a living and a little cash, so that they may begin business or house-keeping for themselves. American *help,* therefore, should be very particular in their good behavior, and be careful to do by their employers as they will want help to do by them, when their turn to keep domestics shall arrive" (*Good* 123). Hale's injunction demonstrates how Protestant principles undergird the new hierarchy of manners. A theology of works promises that hard work be rewarded; the Golden Rule ensures that deferential behavior will prevail when social positions are reversed. The practice of noblesse oblige ensures that those who are elevated will likewise be generous and respectful of possessions. And an ideology of American exceptionalism implicitly argues that domestic servitude in America is not a negative condition but a way that immigrants can begin to ascend in class respectability.

To illustrate her point, Hale recounts the example of Julia, an ignorant Irish maid. For five years a kindly mistress has devoted herself to Julia's education. Julia, in turn, has "proved herself not only capable of learning to work, but willing and most devoted in the service of her mistress, whom she regarded with a reverence little short of what a Catholic feels for his patron saint." Hale's footnotes, tracing the details of Julia's life after her period of domestic service illustrate compactly the intersection of geographic location and upward mobility: According to Hale, Julia "only left her mistress to be married" (*Mrs. Hale's* 486); and she "is settled at the West, her husband a respectable mechanic, and she a good wife" (*Good* 136). Such promises, of course, make an elevation of class status an individual responsibility. Furthermore, it is quite likely that such elevation was rare. Julia and her husband, for example, could probably ill afford a "Christian house" similar to those Catharine Beecher shows in chapter two of *American Woman's Home*. Costing $1,600, the home may be shared by "two small families" if straitened economic circumstances so demand (41).[3] Nor does Hale note that Julia apparently employs no domestics of her own "at the West." Rather, the promise of class elevation and the apparent generosity with which the terms of its attainment were offered served to quell class dissent, while tales such as Julia's seemed to demonstrate that if one has not succeeded, it is only because one has not worked hard enough.

Certainly it could be argued that the terms of class status were explicitly and democratically available. The addressed audience for many of these conduct books was the pupils of the common school and the female seminary. The *Treatise,* part of the Massachusetts School Library, was "extensively introduced as a text-book into public schools and higher female seminaries. . . . Its sequel, *The Domestic Receipt-Book,* circulated . . . in every State of the Union" (Beecher and Stowe 15). Common schools presented notions of domestic economy, cleanliness, orderly behavior, as well as American patriotism and ideologically coded maxims to be memorized and practiced by new immigrant children. In the young ladies' seminary, such information would reach several constituencies: daughters whose mothers had not trained them in the fine points of domestic management; young women who, due to death, economic crisis, or geographic mobility were dislocated from the feminine elders who would have taught these skills; and the daughters of newly rich and upstart "genteel" social climbers of the sort Fanny Fern deprecated. Illiterate but willing students who could not attend school could also acquire the necessary manners at the hand of benevolent women employers who would educate them for a better station. If they could not purchase a conduct book, they could nevertheless have access to one in a library, or as a gift from social betters who were fulfilling their class obligation of noblesse oblige. Beecher, for example, addressed the foreword of her *Letters to Persons Who Are Engaged in Domestic Service* to "My Countrywomen," charging "all benevolent and Christian ladies" to "secure the reading of this book to at least one of those for whom it is written" (6).

These books of domestic management were disseminated to single and married women alike, through the curricula of schools in the Northeast, through the pages of mass circulation periodicals such as *Godey's,* and through informal networks of teacher-missionaries as well. Ostensibly used as school texts, they became instruments of enculturation, as well. Beecher's *True Remedy for the Wrongs of Woman* appends a chapter of testimonials from teachers who had been sent to the West by her American Woman's Educational Association (AWEA). Assuming the tone of enlightened missionaries bringing civilization to the cabins of the roaring wilderness, these testimonials frequently invoke the name of Beecher's *Treatise* as a primary component of the civilizing process. One such missionary-teacher writes: " 'I have read your 'Domestic Economy' through to the family, one chapter a day. They like it, and have adopted some of your suggestions in regard both to *order* and to *health*" (166).

Yet the promise that these books held out for social elevation and validation is deferred and contingent. For immigrant women, especially, the surest guarantee of social validation is neither hard work, nor economic success, nor mastery of the etiquette, practices, and customs of American women, but giving birth to American citizens. The full benefits of citizenship and social status are reserved for native-born Americans, the children of mannerly and hard-working immigrants. This is the moral Hale addresses to Irish housemaids such as Julia. Presuming that they have been so fortunate as to have worked for "benevolent and sensible ladies" who teach them to work, to sew, to read, and to write, Hale pontificates: "If you have had such a kind mistress, my poor girl, for the honor of old Ireland be grateful and faithful to your benefactress; and show yourself worthy to be the mother of American citizens; for to such good fortune your children, should you marry, will be entitled" (*Good* 127). The promise of citizenship is not held out to the woman herself, suggesting that most of the promises of upward class mobility were infinitely deferrable and dependent on voluntary deference. That deferral was guaranteed by the proliferation of editions of conduct books and their allied handbooks, a practice that suggests that the codes by which ladies might be identified could be and were continually reinvented.

Although such written recipes for class status made acceptable social behaviors teachable, learnable, and deferrable, their production did benefit literate, white, upper-middle-class women by promising them a stable class identity independent of men, and by assigning to them meaningful labor

as (re)producers of culture.⁴ Although this separation may be interpreted as
dangerous and demeaning, since it alienates women from "the corporeality
of [their] work" (G. Brown 80), it may also be argued that Beecher relocates
a woman's class status to a matter of surface performance and asks that
the body's location not be the determinant of its classed identity. Beecher's
argument does not disconnect women from their bodies since it assigns
them the task of (re)producing citizens, either through birth (body-labor)
or education (mind-labor). Indeed, chapters and entire books written by
Beecher present basic housework (although not sweated labor), physiology,
and calisthenics as essential to a mother's physical ability to bear healthy
children. Both mothering and teaching are direct effects of, and not separate
from, the womanly body. Both married and single women are charged, for
example, with the labor of maintaining their own and their family's health.
To this end they should have a "general knowledge" of the "construction of
the body, and the laws of health" (*Treatise* 69), as well as of "the subject of
exercise" (*Treatise* 129). In *Letters to the People on Health and Happiness,* a
book that supplements the *Treatise*'s initial attention to health, Beecher links
women to their corporeality in explicit detail, arguing the importance of
exercise, comfortable clothing, and fresh air. She recalls her own childhood
as ideal in this regard: "As to clothing, one loose garment next the skin [sic],
a warm flannel petticoat in winter, with a woolen frock, shoes and stockings,
were all that was worn in the house . . . No drawers around their limbs, in
those days, interrupted the constant air-bath which every little girl received
for her whole person" (113).

Letters to the People on Health and Happiness puts the care of bodies in
explicitly nationalist terms, as well: "If the American people were a strong,
hardy, unexcitable race like the German laborers that come among us, such
rules for the selection of diet would be of less importance" (96). Beecher had
charged American women with maintaining health through dress reform
as an important step in producing large numbers of healthy American
citizens so that the Anglo-Saxon political majority of the West might be
maintained. In support of this agenda, she argued that if "ladies" were to
produce large families whose "female members" would share "the labors of
the cook, the nurse, the laundress, and the seamstress," the need for foreign
domestic laborers would disappear. Moreover, the laborers would benefit
from a balanced regimen in which neither physical nor mental labor would
predominate, and "every muscle in the body would receive exercise." By
contrast, according to Beecher, under the present arrangement of household

tasks, "One portion of the women have all the exercise of the *nerves of motion,* and another have all the *brain-work,* while they thus grow up deficient and deformed. . . . And so American women every year become more and more nervous, sickly, and miserable, while they are bringing into existence a feeble, delicate, or deformed offspring" (*Treatise* 110–11).

Beecher does not advocate large families only as a means to political majority or as an efficient way of maintaining a household, however. Mere biological reproduction can be and is done by women of the lowest classes. Ladies must reproduce not only children but their own class entitlement. *Miss Beecher's Domestic Receipt Book,* a companion volume to the *Treatise,* promises that children brought up by careful mothers "will imitate your feelings, tastes, habits, and opinions, and . . . will transmit what they receive from you to their children, to pass again to the next generation, and then to the next, until *a whole nation* will have received its character and destiny from your hands! No imperial queen ever stood in a more sublime and responsible position" (279–80). This passage summarizes Beecher's entire philosophy of domestic reproduction: American women, unlike their European counterparts, do not partake of a heritable class ("No imperial queen"). Rather, they (and their children) acquire their social qualities and national identity through learning and overt instruction in behaviors that are uniquely American. Entitlement of blood is transmuted into entitlement of good birth, the result of learnable practices of health, exercise, and diet.

Hale, too, charged American mothers with the production of citizens, overtly using the language of statecraft in a holiday column entitled "The Glorious Fourth; or, the Home-life of the Nation." Her extended metaphor links motherhood with nationalism, arguing that the "nation" is also a "community composed of united households. . . . Every household is a little republic in itself. The husband and wife are the heads. . . . The children take their proper parts in the little community, according to their ages and characters, from the wee citizen of three years old, whose whole duty is to be as obedient and happy as possible, to the sprightly and busy maiden or youth of eighteen or twenty, who is an influential member of the household cabinet. And how truly do all together constitute a genuine 'commonwealth!' " (*Manners* 163–64). Father and mother together head this enterprise, for in Hale's own hierarchy of nationhood, women find a place in such deliberations only in civilized republics. The household becomes a site of political production wherein even "wee citizens" learn the etiquette, practice, and customs that entitle them to an enduring social heritage as Americans.

The responsibilities of mothers to produce citizens do not end with their own children, however. In the codes that structure all these manuals of domestic economy, servants are classed with, or slightly below, children as objects of an entitled woman's practical obligations. Hundreds of column inches in newspapers and entire sections of advice books are devoted to the troubles and responsibilities of mistresses who employ domestics, in turn unfailingly limned as ignorant, illiterate, and untrained. Beecher advises employers "to attach domestics to the family, by feelings of gratitude and affection," and to teach their servants to "make and take proper care of their clothes [and guard] their health." Employers are given the specific responsibility for their servants' literacy, even should that mean they must furnish them with books (including, presumably, *The Treatise* or *Letters to Persons who are Engaged in Domestic Service*). "In short," Beecher concludes, employers should be willing "to supply the place of parents" (*Treatise* 206–7). "Attaching" servants to the family thus includes them in an arena where the etiquette of voluntary deference holds sway. Servants' presence as family adjuncts positions them as objects of charitable practice. Thinking of them as family members also excuses any guilt an employer might feel about keeping servants, under the logic that they can be taught etiquette, practice, and customs that may allow them to rise in class at some unspecified future point. Hale's version of these responsibilities articulates the benefits employers might expect in return for such enlightened practices. Since educating domestics makes those "who would, if ignorant, become a burthen and a nuisance," into "useful, and often respectable members of society," Hale declares that "to educate a good domestic is one of the surest proofs that a lady is a good housekeeper" (*Good* 136). Like Beecher's her logic links noblesse oblige, patriotic duty, and the possibility of social elevation for the underclass to the guarantee of social class for entitled women.

If it be the responsibility of the married American woman to produce citizens, what of the "maiden ladies" and widows who have written these texts? They, too, may make American citizens, not as mothers, but as authors of the books of domestic advice that will inscribe upon the bodies of American children and upon unruly and disorderly servant bodies habits of etiquette, obligation, and custom. For writers, Beecher claims the special right to produce not bodies but representations of bodies. Representing women's bodies, as she does in *Letters . . . on Health, Physiology and Calisthenics*, and *Miss Beecher's Housekeeper and Healthkeeper,* unites bodily and mental labor in the task of social reproduction. These books incorporate illustrations of internal organs, musculature, and skeletal frames, as well as of calisthenic exercises. Such images accompany a composite textual representation of the state of women's bodies based on extensive sampling from her "widely-diffused circle of relatives, [and] with very many of my former pupils who had become wives and mothers. . . . I obtained statistics from about two hundred different places in almost all the Free States" (*Health* 121–22). Based on this information, which she reprints in tabular and anecdotal form, Beecher represents the general condition of health in "American women" through a taxonomy whose specimens descend from a "perfectly healthy" woman; to the "well" woman who becomes ill as a result of exposure or "great fatigue"; to the "delicate" woman of "frail constitution," "ill health," and susceptibility to "fatigue, or exposure, or excitement" (*Health* 123).

Through her ability, indeed duty, to represent American women, the unmarried lady author of school texts, like the unmarried schoolteacher, can specify the customs and behaviors that will be identifiable as American. Hale's *The Countries of Europe and the Manners and Customs of Its Various Nations* instructed children in the relative merits of geographic location and citizenship. A collection of verses whose ostensible purpose is to make geography palatable to little minds, this book constructs a taxonomy of acceptable ancestry. Thus Anglo-Saxon nations appear in the best possible terms, only slightly inferior to America, while other nations serve primarily as negative examples. Hale's interest in measuring a country's enlightened treatment of women is the apparent basis for a poem entitled "Turkey," which asserts that

> . . . for all the world I've seen,
> I would not be a Turkish girl,
> Nor a little Turkish queen;
>
> For 'mid the moss and daisies,
> I never then should play,
> But be shut, a weary prisoner,
> In dark houses all the day.
> . . . .
> But I do not like the turbaned Turk,
> For his brow is dark and fell:
> So to glittering crescent on the dome,
> And to long-robed Turk, farewell. (18, 21)

Hale's use of the first person invites her child readers to renounce the benighted social practices of Turkey (associated figurally with practices of slavery through words such as *prisoner, dark,* and *turban*) in favor of more enlightened democratic uses. Such representation slights, of course, the fact that any number of American women—women of lower classes, domestics, and housewives alike—were effectively prisoners in their own American homes.

Books such as these, then, were a part of the process of constituting American identity.[5] The domestic economies and conduct books offer, even entice, "foreign" readers to adopt new American praxes. They prescribe the customs, rituals, and observances that make Americans, including the celebration of its round of holidays—patriotic observances that inscribe, palimpsest-fashion, the calendar of patriotic devotion over the holy-day round of Catholic calendars. In Hale's words, "there are, in the texture of American life, certain threads, that, like telegraphic wires, reach across all obstacles, and awaken the sympathies of the world. These sympathies are drawn to us in our American holidays, that thus become exponents of the heart of humanity" (*Manners* 6). Hale's use of the figure of the telegraph is apt and shows the role of holiday celebrations to be yet another cultural practice that, like common possessions and common reading materials, contributes to a pervasive sense of national identity.

In fact, Hale organizes the entire book of *Manners* around a secular calendar, dividing it into seven sections of seven entries each, devoting the three remaining entries to "our three American holidays": "The Glorious Fourth," "Washington's Birthday," and "Our National Thanksgiving Day." Of Thanksgiving, a holiday celebrated (owing to Hale's promotion of it to several U.S. presidents) by all Americans, Hale writes that its "plentiful din-ner," its presidentially mandated common day of celebration, its "song[s], stor[ies], and sermon[s]," will "strengthen the bond of union that binds us brothers and sisters in that true sympathy of American patriotism which makes the Atlantic and Pacific Oceans mingle in our mind as waters that wash the shores of kindred homes, and mark from east to west the boundaries of our dominion" (331, 338). Hale's image of mingled waters suggests that the aim of such conduct books was to effect an undifferentiated American whole and allows for no regional or ethnic variants of the celebration. As the details of an "American" Thanksgiving suggest, these books take on the articulation of even the smallest details of citizenly identity, engrafting onto foreign bodies the tastes and appetites that identify Americans. Additionally, her articulation of the holiday's celebrants and their location within the "boundaries of our dominion" mark *Manners'* location at the beginning of a new period of conduct books that moved American praxis beyond continental boundaries in the service of U.S. imperialism. According to Hale, Thanksgiving is celebrated not only at home but also "in European cities, and wherever our countrymen could meet together,—on board our fleets in the Mediterranean, African, and Brazilian stations; by our missionaries in India, China, Africa; and, in 1860, it was observed by our countrymen in Japan, and also in Constantinople, Berlin, Paris, and other places" (335).

Perhaps the best demonstration of the process of replacing foreign with domestic taste can be found in recipes included in the sections of conduct books that prescribe practice and in the "Receipt Books" that often were published following or in tandem with manuals of domestic advice. Prefacing *Miss Beecher's Domestic Receipt Book,* Beecher claims that her work avoids promoting foods that are "so rich as to be both expensive and unhealthful," defects that have characterized other similar books "issued in this country, or sent from England" (ii). Hale's logic is similar, as her adaptation of one of those British texts indicates. Acknowledging that "the art of COOKERY in the United States is behind the age," Hale promises both to update Eliza Acton's *Modern Cookery* and to add instructions for the "preparation of those articles which may be regarded as more strictly American: such as Indian Corn, Terrapins, and some others" (xvii). Hale addresses her own *New Cook Book* to a multicultural population, and includes "the best receipts from the Domestic Economy of the different nations of the Old World. Emigrants from each country will . . . find the method of preparing their favorite dishes." Her apparently generous impulse here is undermined by syntax. The purpose of this book is not so much to make the recipes of "different nations" available to "our Republic" but to rationalize the preparation of those recipes, assimilating them to American tastes and practice. Hale then emphasizes that "the prominent features" of her book are "American," the result of the favors of "ladies, famed for their excellent housekeeping," who have donated "large collections of original receipts, which these ladies have tested in their own families" (xx). Despite the nod to other cuisines, then, the book's most characteristic features are the result of Hale's location at the center of a network of certified housekeepers, whose "original" (read Anglo-Saxon, not ethnic) and "tested" recipes are authorized by real "ladies."

The effect of such a concentrated attention to issues of class, geographic mobility, gender, and marital status is that these conduct books sought to revise one of identity's most basic components: that of social class. Freeing its determinants from economic fluctuation, they sought to revise work's relation to class, disengaging it from the tasks performed and linking it instead to a citizenly identity determined not by a woman's political rights but by her manners and her dedication to social reproduction. Therefore, it might be argued that these books present a paradoxical version of class. They certainly do not erase it, but argue for its dissociation from economics and its replacement inside a grid of womanly identity based in deference, charity, and commonality.

In this noneconomic version of class, women's mobility is acknowledged. Upwardly mobile women are promised a (deferred) class position as American citizen-mothers. The most immediate and tangible benefits of revised components of class, however, are reserved for already-entitled white women. Given that economic instability might reduce the amount of money she and her husband had access to, given the fact that she might not marry, that she might be widowed, given the increasing possibility of her geographic mobility, these books seek to secure a gendered identity that would transcend all these mutable factors. That identity will be the same whether women are married and reproduce children, married with no children, or single and working: as cultural laborers these entitled and mannerly women will produce the reproducing and reproducible American citizen.

Chapter Six

DOMESTICATED
ELOQUENCE

In her *Godey's* editorial of February 1836, Sarah Josepha Hale observed that
formalized systems of penmanship had blurred the surface differences of a
handwritten text so that "females of the same class in life, now write, as
they dress, nearly alike." Still, she continues, "the destruction of individual
character, by the adoption of the general type or form in manuscript, is really
but a trifling loss" when compared with the gain in readability. Although
handwriting may threaten to level individual differences, a written text
will still attest to the entitlement of its absent writer, for "the language is
a much better criterion of the writer's mental and moral qualities, than
the characters in which it is clothed" (12:57–58). Hale's observations here
encompass issues of upward mobility, social counterfeit, and the difficulty
of reading "character" in an age of increasing literacy. She metaphorically
equates orthography with dress, insisting, by extension, that although each
may be an unreliable indicator of character, a lady's true "mental and moral
qualities" may be measured in her language. Although Hale is vague here
about what she means by language, in other texts she equates it with style,
precise diction, and, of course, standard and grammatical English.

Although this editorial considered only one outcome of increasingly
available education, it anticipated the combined effects of industrialization,
state-mandated and state-supported education, and mass-circulation print,
as well, all of which combined to make literacy a less-than-precise indicator
of class entitlement. By 1850 in the increasingly homogeneous and industrial
northeastern United States, outward signifiers of social class—whether
material goods, manners, taste, or literate behaviors—were increasingly
available to anyone with cash, regardless of the entitlements of birth or

traditional class values. Newly-rich and sometimes foreign-born merchants and tradesmen could and did purchase clothing and household goods that equaled or exceeded those of their social betters. Their children attended public school or one of the increasing number of private academies. There they perfected their dress, their behavior, and their penmanship. There, as well, they acquired the common store of intellectual referents and literate behaviors once thought to mark an elevated social position.

The "destruction of individual character" that Hale attributed to standardized penmanship was only intensified by mass-circulation print. Books by learned authors rubbed covers with those penned by anonymous or pseudonymous writers, some with dubious social credentials. The literature of moral uplift competed with penny-press novels that featured lower-class lifestyles and even reproduced the "vulgar" speech patterns of the unentitled and unlettered. Dozens of conduct books offered instruction in mannerly speech. Handbooks of letter writing contained precomposed forms for every imaginable social situation. Mass-circulation periodicals, *Godey's* among them, printed suggestions for reading that replicated school curricula, gave directions for journal keeping, offered hints to writers who aspired to publication, and proclaimed the rules of social conversation.

Despite increasingly available print sources, the general public retained an interest in oral performance, attending lyceums, chautauquas, stump speeches, and even lectures by women platform speakers. Likewise, people displayed a remarkable appetite for instruction in elocutionary activities, an interest that was answered by numerous self-help manuals that offered instruction in public speaking. The general interest in verbal skill was echoed in elite institutions, as well. Although college professors had begun to shift their emphasis from verbal to textual rhetoric (Reid), from drilling students in public oratory to instructing them in a variety of written forms, they still sought to inculcate in them a unique diction and a characteristic style of speaking. At Harvard, for example, from 1820 through the midcentury, John Quincy Adams labored to "eliminate 'rustic' idioms and pronunciation from the Harvard scene" (Story 112). His successors, including Edward T. Channing, Edward Everett, and Cornelius Felton, emphasized a distinctive and class-marked "New England diction" characterized by "measured, dignified speech, careful enunciation, precise choice of words, and well-modulated voice" (Story 113; Morison 216–17).

Whether that "dialect" characterized women or other men who had not been educated at Harvard is not clear. It is clear, however, that the pace, enunciation, and tone that signaled elite privilege were not reproducible in print. Nevertheless these qualities could be described and linked to character in that medium, and, in the process constitute what people took to be an infallible signifier of "the writer's mental and moral qualities." This interest in verbal performance establishes the close connection of spoken language to class identity. According to Raymond Williams, "Our important sense of belonging, to a family, to a group, to a people, [is] vitally interwoven with the making and hearing of certain sounds—the making and hearing being a very large part of our social sense" (*Long* 214). The mid-nineteenth-century obsession with spoken language—with elocution, diction, pronunciation, phraseology, and tone—provided a basis for a hierarchical differentiation that promised to offset the leveling effects of print. The spoken word seemed to guarantee bodily presence, the speaker's availability to social surveillance, and her or his class status. Yet, as the century progressed, it became apparent that even in public speaking, "ethos was giving way to *persona*, or, . . . that character was disappearing for role playing" (Cmiel 27; see also Clark and Halloran; and Fisher "Appearing").

Studies of this shift have not considered how women hastened the process. Cmiel, for example, asserts that "ladies were excluded from public speaking; they were not taught to be orators" (29) and that "the initial impetus for the craze of verbal criticism . . . was a move by refined gentlemen to reassert their cultural authority over popular editors and politicians. The critics just did not fear women" (136). While these statements are not false, they nevertheless render only a partial picture of the effects of such an important shift in the understanding of voice's ability to guarantee character. Women did, in fact, speak in public; they learned oratory in women's seminaries. Moreover, they joined in the public discussion of the meaning of verbal performances, speeding oratory's "decline" from *ethos* to *persona*. In fact, women benefited from this shift, since they were able to exploit the ambiguity of *personae* to their own financial and professional advantage.

Taken together, the books, columns, and letters written by Beecher, Hale, Fern, and Fuller present a coherent, although paradoxical, position about the issues of verbal correctness. On the one hand, they argued, as did their peers, that control over voice constituted an ultimate and reliable delineation of class difference. They held that prescribing appropriate and correct speech to social equals or inferiors was a class-appropriate exercise of public power and that honoring these prescriptions was a sign of deference from social inferiors. Most important, they informed their readers that correct patterns of speech could not be mastered outside situations of social control and surveillance (such as public schools or literate families). For example, as *Godey's* literary editor, Hale encouraged the publication of numerous articles and series that offered extensive instruction in verbal behaviors appropriate to social elevation. Yet most of these essays also hinted darkly that counterfeit behaviors would immediately be detected.

On the other hand, through their own manipulations of speaking and writing, these women destabilized the connections of verbal and bodily selves. Hale and Beecher mimed womanly retirement, all the while making verbal and written pleas for public support of their projects. Fern overtly questioned the gendered codes that differentiated women public speakers from men. Fuller professionalized oral performance, promising her women students that joining her in formal intellectual conversation would make them better thinkers. Thus while these writers sought to make speech the guarantee of the speaker's sex, appearance, mental development, and social class, they also exploited and profited from the fact that such a connection was impossible to establish.

The *Godey's* articles that offer self-instruction in verbal literacy at mid-century follow a contradictory agenda. While holding out the promise that education might make class advancement possible, they also delimit a heuristic by which pretenders could be identified. As a major partic-ipant in the middle-class interest in spoken language, *Godey's* presented a sustained program of essays aimed at encouraging self-education. The magazine endorsed and promoted resources for self-study, now available to any literate person with money or access to a circulating library. Yet its essays were hedged with qualifiers intended to limit the social approbation that would accompany elevated speech to worthy—that is, native-born and genealogically entitled—Americans. Celebrating the publication of Webster's 1857 *American Dictionary of the English Language,* Hale points out that the book makes available the advantages of a classical education to "many people . . . who have either never been taught the dead languages, or who have acquired too superficial a tincture of them to be of any practical use." Yet such knowledge "will not, to be sure, give ideas where the power of thought is deficient or uncultivated" (54 [Mar. 1857]: 273). If one had learned etymology only by reading Webster's, for example, one would likely risk embarrassment during a conversation with one's social betters. Thus Hale also enjoined readers to "be what you say, and, within the rules of prudence, say what you are. . . . When we hear a person use a queer expression, or pronounce a name in reading differently from his neighbor, the habit always goes down, minus sign before: it stands on the side of deficit, not of credit" (70 [Jan. 1865]: 52). Social imposture, she warns, is always subject to exposure by incorrect speech habits that lie beyond the range of even the most detailed manual of self-help. This striking passage figuratively links bootstrap literacy to (bootstrap) economic advancement, as if Hale had intentionally chosen the metaphor most likely to address the motivating interest of the self-made entrepreneur. Yet she insists that, unlike economic fortune, social advance, accompanied or occasioned by autodidacticism, is not to be attained by mere force of will and hard work. A person's recognition of a lack of knowledge is admirable; a willingness to learn is commendable. But the motivation to self-education parallels the motivation for economic advancement, signals a troubling dissatisfaction with the status quo, and indicates a tendency to seek remedies outside of existing social institutions. To Hale's way of thinking, economic advancement might come as the result of wise or fortuitous investment in an impersonal market, but social position cannot be bought, speculated for, or attained by mere force of will and hard work. Coequal with the speaker's body, and refined in the crucible of a genteel home, the voice—its tone, diction, and grammar—seemed to offer a sure indication of the speaker's intent, identity, and entitlement.

Over some thirty years, individual essays and instructional series from the pens of *Godey's* editorial staff and from its contributing readers outlined the lexical qualities that would identify "genuine vulgarisms" and thus expose social pretense. Early on, Hale had replaced references to the *vulgar* tongue with the term "mother tongue," primarily as a way of claiming women's primary position in teaching language to their children. Such a shift in terminology also signaled her attempt to dissociate the vernacular (spoken by women, as opposed to Latin, the language of learning, which was largely limited to men) from the taint of debased class (see, for example, *Godey's* 84 [June 1872]: 572). In every case, the magazine emphasized the importance of refined speech and precise diction, always linking mastery of spoken language with facility in the finest points of social intercourse. The emphasis on correctness in language became so great that *Godey's* was forced occasionally to reassure "cautious writers who have avoided the use of ordinary forms [of diction] for fear of defacing their style with vulgarisms" (94 [Feb. 1877]: 186).

Vulgarity signified a "lack of elegance" accompanied by an inflated self-importance (Cmiel 133–34). Addressing this specific social infraction, the author of *Godey's* "Hints on Language" warns, "There is hardly any reproach which a writer or speaker dreads more than that of vulgarity." The writer reassures readers that incorrect speech does not signal debased class: "There are many colloquial expressions, used by the best writers and speakers, which do not accord with the strict laws of etymology or grammar, but which it would be highly unjust to term underbred." Among these technically inaccurate terms fall euphemisms, locutions that "usually surrounded biologically related phenomena with more circumspect associative meanings" (Cmiel 131)—for example, saying that a "mutual" [rather than a "common"] friend is in "delicate" health. "Hints on Language" informed readers that, carefully used, euphemisms did not indicate "either . . . ignorance or . . . vulgarity." Rather, such a verbal gesture "often proceeds from a sentiment which is of the very essence of good-breeding—the desire to spare the feelings of others." Then, as if fearful of having ceded too much ground, the column concludes, "There are, however, genuine vulgarisms, which have their origin in a disregard of the proper distinctions of language, and which cannot be too carefully avoided" (83 [Aug. 1871]: 181–82). This essay demonstrates how "mistakes" in speech take their meaning according to class. Mistakes made by unentitled pretenders are merely vulgar results of an ignorance of the "proper distinctions of language" (the choice of adjective here is no accident). "Mistakes" made by well-bred speakers, on the other hand, indicate their mastery of the laws of propriety, which transcend the mere laws of language. The difference lies in the voice's tone, a signal that the speaker has chosen intentionally to violate a law of language in the interest of good breeding.

Spoken language thus functions as the ultimate signifier of character in *Godey's* version of the social world. According to Hale, "There is a far deeper effect upon the moral character than many good people are aware from the habitual use of slang. Refinement of language falls first: but not less surely refinement of mind and thought, and of feeling falls also into the ruins caused by corrupt speech. . . . It is notorious that persons congregated together in vice and crime always use the slang modes of expression to each other" (73 [Sept. 1866]: 262). Hale does not indicate how she can be so sure of her facts, but that does not stop her from equating unrefined language, base character, and degraded class. This tripartite danger must be guarded against beginning in childhood. Hale herself demonstrated how a mother might monitor propriety in language by evaluating how books might contribute to their readers' language and character, especially were those readers children.

Reviewing several children's books whose writers had apparently tried to capture the tones of childhood speech through diction and orthography, Hale pronounced their language to be "very often low and vulgar. In the effort to make the boys and girls represented talk like children, the authors make them talk like street-sweepers. No child that is respectably educated uses the vulgar dialect put into the mouths of the Freddies and Lizzies of these fictions. . . . The literature of boot-blacks and newsboys should be kept away from imitative little ones." Unsecured by elevated tones, print representations of language imply either childishness or debased class. Hale warns her readers against buying these books, for if they are read in private, with no responsible social authority to separate vulgarity from innocent childish mistakes, the vulgarity—of speech and of behavior— may be imitated and repeated. Hale connects the debased language of these books with their dubious moral value, as well, warning that "the virtues inculcated, where the books are not directly religious, are what we may call those of tradesmen . . . little mention is made of the delicacy, magnanimity, generous fondness for friends, high-spirited endurance of evil that make up our notion of a perfect character" (79 [Dec. 1869]: 540). Mercantile ventures, apparently, are incompatible with sensibility, generosity, patience, and fine grammar.

Given the dangers of solitary reading and self-instruction, what is the ideal situation in which to acquire elevated language? For Hale, it is the affectionate domestic circle where a literate and devoted mother intimately supervises both vocal and social behavior. She enjoins mothers not to "tolerate" or "encourage" mispronunciations and grammatical errors in their children, else "others will think ill of them." She warns that any "slip of the tongue" may result in a person's being "set down as ignorant and ill educated—perhaps even be suspected of a rudeness and vulgarity in thought and feeling which they were far from being guilty of" (48 [May 1854]: 443). The error-free speech that would result from such maternal surveillance constituted, in Hale's opinion, a family inheritance. Unlike money and property, which often were deeded only to eldest sons, and which could be gained and lost through market speculation, linguistic mastery could ostensibly be equally and permanently available to all the children of a literate family; unlike material commodities, such cultural capital could not be counterfeited by newly rich pretenders.

Thus Hale claimed language education as mothers' special purview, assigning them the grand responsibility of teaching their children the interrelated virtues of good manners, taste, deference, and proper speech. Unlike the mere pretender, an entitled but impoverished son would thus be prepared for fortunate social advancement: "In our country, where the fusion of classes is . . . constantly carried on, where men rise from poverty and obscurity to the highest public positions, and finally where so much depends upon the faculty of speech, it is especially necessary that we should learn in the very cradle the grammar and the diction of our native English" (84 [June 1872]: 512). In its structure and logic this passage bears a striking similarity to *Godey's* observation that American women who had learned the grammar of fashion would be prepared even to be a president's wife. Here, Hale substitutes speech for fashion, but the dream of social elevation is similar. Here, as well, she establishes explicit and implicit boundaries to that dream: those to whom this promise extends have been taught from birth both linguistic and social propriety. They will always be distinguished from those whose origin is foreign and whose heritage is only poverty and obscurity.

Like Hale, Fanny Fern conflated the issues of literacy, speech, social mobility, and morality. She, too, charged mothers with overseeing the literary and moral nurture of their offspring. She particularly urged them not to abdicate that responsibility by sending their daughters to boarding school. There an impressionable girl might take for her "companion or bed-fellow" an "over-dressed, vain, vapid, brainless offshoot of upstart aristocracy." All the careful nurturing and training of the girl's home life could be destroyed by her association with the "child of [an] upstart rich mother," a child whose "priceless infancy and childhood have been spent with illiterate servants; . . . peeping into the doubtful books with which doubtful servants often beguile the tedious hours . . . lying awake in her little bed, hearing unguarded details of servants' amours, while her mother dances away the hours so pregnant with fate to that listening child. . . . It is *such* a companion that a true mother has to fear for her pure-minded, simple-hearted young daughter" (*Fresh* 69–70).

Illiterate servants and newly rich ("upstart") mistresses present a particular and intertwined social threat. One of the mistakes of the "upstart rich" is to hire illiterate and hence undisciplined servants. Barely literate themselves (and often self-taught, as well as self-elevated), these upstarts can only purchase the surface behaviors of elite entitlement (the servants, the parties, and the dancing). They have no idea of the obligation to train both children and servants that accompanies an elevated social position. The behaviors of the rich mistress are thus nearly indistinguishable from those of her servants. By contrast, the "true mother" speaks well, reads responsibly, educates her servants, and supervises her daughter "at a time when the physique of this future wife and mother requires a lynx-eyed watchfulness" (*Fresh* 68). This done, the need for boarding school disappears. Unsupported by the socially respectable, such institutions cannot thrive and will thus be prevented from aiding still more social pretenders in their upward progress.

In every instance, servants' illiteracy serves as a synecdoche for their failure to master a whole complex of cultural codes. Thus a servant's education is directly linked to her moral development, as Margaret Fuller makes clear. Her *Tribune* column entitled "The Irish Character" charges employers to oversee their servants' physical surroundings, moral development, and literacy training. According to Fuller, "good physical circumstances," are the first necessity, so that a servant may cultivate "different habits from those of the Irish hovel, or illicit still-house." In comfortable surroundings, "instruction . . . for the mind" may be undertaken. Employers must put "good books in their way, if able to read, and [provide] intelligent conversation when there is a chance. . . . Explain to them the relations of objects around them; teach them to compare the old with the new life. If you show a better way than theirs of doing work, teach them, too, *why* it is better. Thus will the mind be prepared by development for a moral reformation" (*Woman* 1855, 332). Fuller's developmental continuum progresses from physical comfort through literacy—both textual and verbal—to moral regeneration. Such development will correct shoddy household work, alcoholism, and even urban blight. Underlying the entire passage is the idea that illiteracy is central to other disabilities: the preference for "hovels," the reluctance to compare present with past circumstances, inefficient work habits, and immorality.

Here, as elsewhere, the agitation about literacy is linked to larger cultural fears of contamination—of cities, of kitchens and bedrooms, and of bodies. Beecher identifies the root issue: servants' incorrect speech must be eradicated so that it will not corrupt the speech of the children who are their charges. Directly addressing servants, she explains: "Parents, in the best society, wish to have their children trained so as to appear properly in the circles in which they move. For this end they strive to make them neat in dress and person, polite and respectful in manners, *particularly in the use of refined and grammatical language,* and careful to observe propriety in their behavior at table and in society" (*Letters to Persons* 87; emphasis added). Like Fern, she implies that parents' most careful training may be quickly undone by ungrammatical servants. She assigns the responsibility for making sure this does not happen to the servants themselves: "I hope therefore, that you will improve every opportunity you can gain to read and study, and I would advise you also to notice how well educated persons pronounce, and try to acquire a similar way of speaking" (*Letters to Persons* 152). Beecher's assumption that children imitate servants' speech rather than their parents' implies that servants are thus the child's primary associates, although she never attempts to remedy this situation. Rather, she concentrates on the inappropriate reversals of social deference and social genealogy such linguistic contamination might cause. Entitled children must not ape the language (and behaviors, since the two are irretrievably linked) of those who are their social inferiors. If they do, instead of reproducing their parents' speech, they propagate the infectious and vulgar language and morals of servants and tradesmen. Children, servants, autodidacts, and upstart mothers thus need to acquire their understandings of the fine points of verbal correctness—the manners, regulation of pronunciation, topics, pace, and tone—in social situations where regulation is provided by superiors in education, wealth, class, and where the need for appropriate deference is understood and honored.

These writers did not only attend to the speech of the socially unentitled, however. They also specified how fine speech could enrich society generally. An 1867 *Godey's* "Editor's Table" offers the best indication of how such skills were understood to benefit young ladies. In it, Hale quotes at length from a commencement address delivered to the Young Ladies' Seminary of Philadelphia. According to this speaker, a Professor Hard, "No instrument of man's devising can reach the heart, as does that most wonderful instrument, the human voice. It is God's special gift and endowment to his chosen creatures. . . . No music below the skies is equal to that of pure, silvery speech from the lips of a man or woman of high culture." Hard therefore advises the graduates to "cultivate assiduously the ability to read well . . . because it is so very elegant, charming, and ladylike an accomplishment. . . . The culture of the voice necessary for reading well, gives a delightful charm to the same voice in conversation" (74 [Feb. 1867]: 191–92). He then delineates the gender-linked norms by which young ladies could share this gift with those less fortunate than they. Hard allots to them the private skills of reading aloud and conversing artfully. (The public art of elocutionary display he reserves, by omission, for men.)

Hard begins by announcing that he recommends learning to read aloud "to all of your sex" because "it is the most effective of all commentaries upon the works of genius. It seems to bring dead authors to life again, and makes us sit down familiarly with the great and good of all ages. . . . In the hospital, in the chamber of the invalid, in the nursery, in the domestic and the social circle, among chosen friends and companions, how it enables you to minister to the amusement, the comfort, the pleasure of dear ones, as no other art or accomplishment can" (74 [Feb. 1867]: 191–92). By employing such words as *chamber, invalid, nursery, circle, chosen,* and *dear ones,* Hard limits women's vocal performance to circumscribed audiences. Within certain contained spaces, a woman may seek to entertain or to enhance social interchange, using her voice either to converse or to read aloud. If she chooses the latter, she reads words penned by others, using her voice to enhance the text. If a cultured voice is "the most effective of all commentaries upon the works of genius," it goes without saying such commentary extends only to sympathy of tone; it will never be the commentary of addendum and certainly not of disagreement.

Hard earnestly urged these norms upon a generation of seminary-educated women in an age when women like Margaret Fuller had begun to exercise their cultivated voices not only in parlors but upon lecture platforms as well. At first glance, Fuller does not seem to challenge the gendered assumptions Hard outlines. She wrote, for example, "Conversation is my natural element. I need to be called out, and never think alone . . . ; it is my habit, and bespeaks a second-rate mind" (*Memoirs* 1:107). She confined her conversation to personal encounters within her private circle of friends, never taking the platform. Yet not one of her contemporaries would have equated Fuller's conversation with the parlor chat that Hard promotes. James Freeman Clarke asserted that "all her friends will unite in the testimony that . . . they have never seen one who, like her, by the conversation of an hour or two, could not merely entertain and inform, but make an epoch in one's life" (*Memoirs* 1:107).

Nor could Fuller's verbal habits of abundant quotation and allusion in her speech and writing be termed an enhancement of others' genius that brought dead authors to life again. True, she may have revivified dead words, but in Fuller's mouth these words rekindled debates, recombined issues, and from the raw material of past genius, yielded new philosophical insights. As Julie Ellison explains, the "heterogeneity of Fuller's verbal performance refers not to a random mixture of styles, but to a structured

movement among certain discourses and the cultural positions associated
with them. . . . The *effect* of quotation or allusion . . . makes [Fuller's] most
ordinary utterance into a literary event" (283). That is, Fuller exploited
the cultural preference for speech, *ethos,* and presence by frequently using
quotation; her own use of others' words was to recombine them into a
new and coherent discourse, effecting their transmutation into a kind of
"literature." Such a practice also ensured that she would not be censured
for exceeding womanly commentary because her words were self-evidently
not her own; she "merely" quoted others.

Hale, Beecher, and Fern, too, simultaneously honored and parodied
the gendered prescriptions for women's use of public speech. They adapted
their own speech to accord with the rhetorical and situational demands in
which they found themselves, frequently in ways that were immensely more
complex than adhering to Hale's injunction to "be what you say." Rather,
they honored the qualifier Hale appended: "*within the rules of prudence* say
what you are." The rules of prudence, in their cases, seemed to dictate that
what they said accord with their public images; those personae, however,
were open to a number of interpretations.

Unlike Beecher, Fern, and Fuller, Sarah Hale had not been raised in
a family whose language had been filtered and refined by contact with
Harvardian elocution. Nor did she enjoy the social advantages of associ-
ating in the "highest circles" until comparatively late in her life when she
moved to Boston. Even there, because she worked for a living, she invited
social censure. Her interest in autodidacticism and social pretense signals
her dis-ease about her own social position as she became an increasingly
public figure. An immensely ambitious woman, she nevertheless apparently
avoided situations involving face-to-face encounters, preferring to conduct
her business behind the silent and ambiguous facades of letter writing or
print journalism.[1] Early in her career, for example, she wrote to a friend,
David Henshaw, to thank him for permitting her to use an illustration
in the *Ladies' Magazine* and entreating him to contact several men who
had promised to contribute written material. She explains, "it would be
a favor as I should thereby be spared the necessity of addressing them.
And I have a dread almost approaching to terror at the idea of addressing a
stranger, or in any way drawing on myself public notice. . . . I am sometimes
obliged to intrude on the notice of strangers; but I never do it without fear,
and without feeling how much deeper is the favor of meeting with respect
paid to the woman and the mother rather than the author" (18 Oct. 1827;

Ms. Ch. B.3.47, Boston Public Library). At issue in this passage is not the truth or falsity of the "terror" Hale claims to feel at public encounter, but the multiple advantages she claimed by reporting the feeling. Separated from hearers by Henshaw's ventriloquism, she demonstrated the demure retirement she proclaimed as ideal for women and enacted the respect for social norms she required of other autodidacts. At the same time, her wishes could be verbalized in a masculine voice; a man's bodily presence guaranteed cultural permission. Because she did not utter them publicly, her words would be evaluated separately from her personal life. The question of her public employment was thus subsumed under larger impersonal (but still ideologically inflected) categories such as motherhood and authorship. Professing a wish to be respected as a mother rather than as an author, Hale effected the claim that domesticity was her most important occupational identity.

Beecher used tactics similar to Hale's ventriloquism, especially in her ambitious projects on behalf of women's education. She enlisted her male relatives to write letters on her behalf and to solicit social and financial support whenever she judged that a masculine voice would further her aims. On her speaking tours to the East, she was accompanied by her younger half-brother Thomas and brother-in-law Calvin Stowe. According to Lyman Beecher Stowe's memoir, Thomas read her addresses as she sat in womanly and demure silence on the platform (*Saints* 127). In this report, Beecher's demeanor endorses both the words issuing from Thomas's mouth and larger, unarticulated cultural prescriptions about women's limited participation in public life. Yet such a recollection again has more force as trope than as truth. Such stories are told about the public women who were Beecher's contemporaries, as well. Emma Willard, for instance, is said to have sat upon the platform as a man read her speeches for her (A.F. Scott). Moreover, Kathryn Kish Sklar, Beecher's most careful biographer, offers a different version of the fund-raising campaigns: "Accompanied by Calvin Stowe or . . . Thomas Beecher, she visited almost every major city in the East, delivering a standard speech and organizing local groups of church women to collect and forward funds and proselytize her views" (170).

To the conservative public press, the lecturess was an anomaly, neither woman nor man. The standard journalistic response to a woman who spoke forcefully or controversially in public was to charge that she had "un-sexed" herself. It took the outspoken Fanny Fern to expose the hypocrisy of such a public condemnation: "The great bugbear cry of 'unsex-ing' is getting to be

monotonous" she declared (*Ledger* 12 Mar. 1864). She systematically exposed
the assumptions entailed in this label, chief of which is the idea that people
must (and do) talk differently because they are differently sexed. To Fern,
public speaking seems no more a masculine verbal behavior than gossip
is feminine. Thus she counters charges that women unsex themselves by
lecturing by showing that men engage in gossip with no parallel diminution
of their masculinity. In a column entitled "Tit for Tat-ing," for example,
she notes that the president has had to secure the telegraph wires in order
to control editorial gossip about Civil War strategies: "Our good President,
in order to keep the *national* secrets, is obliged to take possession of the
telegraph wires, and keep them from the editors, who, like a parcel of old
women, keep hinting about what they *could* tell, in such a transparent
way, that their promise *not to tell* is a dead letter" (*Ledger* 29 Mar. 1862).
Here Fern offers a parody of those reviewers who charged women lecturers
with unsexing themselves. By implication, men's conversational equivalent
to gossip is a kind of verbal one upmanship, wherein hinting that they
know more than they might tell about national defense policy counts as
superior masculinity. To Fern, however, they resemble nothing so much as
a sewing circle.

Fern's second mode of attacking the charge that a woman speaking in
public had unsexed herself was to demonstrate that "custom sanctions every
day a thousand things much more amenable than female lecturing to this
objection, about which no such hue or cry is raised" (*Ledger* 12 Mar. 1864).
She exposes the hypocrisy of "gentlemen who patronizingly and pityingly
allow every woman to speak in public, 'if she wishes to do so,' by no means
include on the list any female relative of *their own*. 'What! *my* wife! *my*
sister! *my* niece, to stand up to be stared at and commented upon by Tom,
Dick and Harry!—Never!' And yet these fastidious gentlemen make no
objection to taking 'my wife, my sister or my niece' to some public ball,
where their charms are displayed to the best advantage to be there stared at
and commented upon by anybody who can purchase a ball ticket" (*Ledger* 12
Mar. 1864). In this remarkable paragraph Fern exposes the logic of possession
that dictated the relation of men and women. The objection of "fastidious
gentlemen" to women's public activities is shown to stem from the fear that
their possessions would thereby be devalued, an interpretation supported
by Fern's relentless use of the adjective *my*. "Every woman" thus becomes, in
practice, every woman except *my* woman. She then argues that the bodily
presence of women on the platform was no different than their attendance

at social functions. Whether on the platform or in the ballroom, women in public are seen as objects, their bodies transmuted into texts available "to be commented upon" when displayed in public. One difference obtains, however. Women at a ball may not speak on their own behalf. On the platform, by contrast, they may be speaking subjects.

"Fastidious gentlemen" are only one segment of the public who undermine women's right to speak in public. Reporters who write about "Women on the Platform" (the title Fern chose for this essay) present a different challenge. Neither group, however, is able to see women as anything but objects. Fern asks, rhetorically, "Can anybody tell me why reporters, in making mention of lady speakers, always consider it to be necessary to report, fully and *firstly,* the dresses worn by them?" (*Ginger-Snaps* 114). Reporters' inability to grant women their own subjectivity means that they can never concede that women could be skillful public speakers. When women resist objectification by mounting the platform, when they undertake to speak, rather than be spoken about, their acts are judged in terms of the commonplaces Hard had articulated. Reviewers of a woman's public address expected to hear a woman's voice ornament preexistent texts: " 'What can *she* have to tell us that we did not know before?' I heard some one say, as we took our seats in the Lecture-room to hear a Female Lecturess" (*Folly* 210). Fern reminds readers through her redundant and capitalized diction that women in public may exceed the conventional. She insists, as well, that women may speak—and think—differently: "And is it not worth while, sometimes, to look at a subject from an intelligent *woman's* stand-point?" (*Folly* 210). To conventional understandings, a woman's platform monologue violated her obligation to facilitate social interaction. Apparently rejecting the give and take, the social monitoring implied in conversation, a lecturess bore no interruption, again behaving in a fashion deemed more appropriate to men than to women. This objection, too, Fern counters: "We deny that a woman who can reason or argue, and who prefers to do her own thinking, cannot love, and warmly too" (*Ledger* 12 Mar. 1864).

As in all issues revolving around voice, objections to women on the platform centered in issue of economics. "Women on the Platform" begins with this brief journalistic interchange between an unnamed source and the *New York Tribune.* The source had noted that "MISS MARIANNA THOMPSON, now a student at the Theological school, received, during her summer vacation two invitations to settle with good societies, each of which offered her twelve hundred dollars per year. Pretty good for a school-girl, I think."

To this anecdote the *Tribune* replied "Yes, that is very good; and we trust Miss Thompson will accept one of these (or a better) and do great good to her hearers. And, should some excellent young man ask her to 'settle' with him as wife, *at no salary at all,* we advise her to heed that 'call' as well." Fern then joins the conversation: "Well, now, Mr. *Tribune,* I don't." Rather than allow the *Tribune's* comment to stand as a representation of commonsense heterosexual norms, Fern retorts, "I differ from you entirely. I advise no woman to refuse twelve hundred independent dollars a year for good, honest labor, to become such a serf as this" (*Ginger-Snaps* 111–12). While the *Tribune* endeavors to demonstrate the cause and effect logic of public lecturing, financial independence, and the threat of women's refusal of their bodily destiny, Fern disrupts this logic. She reminds readers that the profession of wife, which bears "no salary at all" is a medieval notion, entirely unsuited to life in a capitalist society. Women like Miss Thompson, who are strong enough and intelligent enough to command a handsome salary, are much safer to remain single. As a successful public figure, herself a mother and three times married—twice to men who defaulted on her financial support—Fern gives the lie to such sanctimonious pronouncements.

For all their advocacy of women's right to speak in public, Beecher, Hale, Fern, and Fuller customarily avoided the podium, preferring to style themselves not as lecturers but as conversationalists. Fern rarely engaged even in print debates like the one she entered into with the *Tribune.* Rather, she took quotations from other books and newspapers as conversational openers, anticipating responses, answering imaginary questions, and posing other questions in return. Her breezy prose style suggested informal chat caught in print. *Harpers,* for example, noted—with some ambiguity and in terms recalling oral performance—that her writing style showed "that the day for stilted rhetoric, scholastic refinements, and big dictionary words, the parade and pomp, and the pageantry of literature, is declining" (qtd. in Warren, "Introduction" x). Beecher and Hale affected the conversational style, as well. Beecher wrote several of her books as fictional conversations with her sister Harriet, thus claiming to address a circumscribed and private audience of women, while simultaneously capitalizing on Harriet's enhanced reputation. Similarly, Hale naturalized her threatening act of publishing a magazine addressed exclusively to women and claimed a ladylike social role as hostess by calling her editorials "*Conversaziones*" (14 [Jan. 1837]: 2).

Fuller, however, offers the best demonstration of how a skill thought to be a natural endowment of refined women—particularly of the wives, daughters, and sisters of Boston intelligentsia schooled in both formal elocution and elegant pronunciation—was in fact an artifice. In the process of making womanly conversation a profession, she effectively separated the fact of her own economic dependence and (potentially) reduced class from her skill in talking. In other words, her conversations sealed the separation of her *saying* from her *being*.

A primary component of subsequent generations' understanding of Fuller was what Rufus Griswold termed her "incorrigible faith in high talk" (qtd. in Cross 23). The very fact that Fuller could conceive of supporting herself by selling what so far had seemed merely to be a social accomplishment depended on the culture's taste for elocution. Ralph Waldo Emerson's success on the lyceum circuit demonstrated the willingness of the new rich and upwardly mobile middle classes to pay for verbal entertainment and instruction. Fuller successfully offered two conversational series annually for four years to more than two hundred women, an accomplishment that demonstrated both her own local reputation and the willingness of people of "high" culture[2] to pay for such instruction.

In the Conversations, verbal and economic exchange became conflated. Fuller's students, a chosen few, who had attended "superior nonevangelical private girls' schools in or around Boston" (Capper, "Reformer" 511), paid $20 per series for the Conversations at a time when an average Lyceum season membership cost $1.50; they often brought gifts to Fuller as well (Ellison 242). In return they received a confirmation of their upper-class identity and their (potential) intellectual abilities. Fuller described the women she wished to include in her group as "thinking women in a city which, with great pretensions to mental refinement, boasts at present nothing of the kind" (*Letters* 2:86). It is likely Fuller's charge of "pretensions" here refers to the Transcendental Club, whose meetings Fuller had attended with Elizabeth Hoar, Sarah Alden, Sophia Ripley, and Lidian Emerson. None of these intelligent women felt as challenged or as rewarded by those associations as they did in the Conversations, perhaps because their identities in the Conversations did not derive from their male relatives. Fuller saw her women students as individuals. In planning the Conversations, she had conceived her "office" to be "to turn back the current when digressing into personalities or commonplaces so that—what is invaluable in the experience of each might be brought to bear upon all" (*Letters* 2:86–87). In other words, in exchange for the salary Fuller received, which enhanced her economic status, Fuller offered a similar transvaluation, sifting each student's unique and "invaluable . . . experience" from the dross, allowing each to be not a wife, a sister, or a daughter, but simply a brilliant discussant. In turn, her recognition of their "invaluable" qualities marked her as a woman of superior taste and discrimination.

Within the context of the Conversations, Fuller transformed the office of teacher, as well, from that of a drudge or assistant to something more exalted. Fuller chose topics, set times, assigned her social peers to roles as students, gave them permission to speak, and challenged their assumptions. She performed her mental mastery for them in terms a contemporary theorist of education, Pierre Bourdieu, links to the way a teacher "exalt[s] the quality of [her] office and the culture [s]he communicates by the quality of [her] personal manner of communicating it." According to Bourdieu, the most important component of a teacher's "symbolic attributes" is "the *livery* of the Word" displayed in "the most typically charismatic feats, such as verbal acrobatics, hermetic allusion, disconcerting references or peremptory obscurity, as well as the technical tricks which serve as their support or substitute, such as the concealment of sources, the insertion of studied jokes or the avoidance of compromising formulations" (125; emphasis added). Fuller had as her audience women who had lived with this behavior all their lives and knew enough to be awed by it, especially when they saw it enacted on and by a body gendered feminine, literally garbed in elegant clothing, and metaphorically affecting the "livery" of her exalted speech. The effect of the Conversations, then, was to create a space in which women could display their entitlement to each other and in which a differential calculus of entitlement based on oral acuity prevailed. Heading this hierarchy, despite the undeniable fact that she worked for hire, was Margaret Fuller.

Ultimately, Fuller demonstrates that the very practices of literacy and pedagogy depend on differentiation. Fuller's project of bringing literate and wealthy Boston matrons into a situation where learning oral mastery would be accomplished in company with the performance of complicated rituals of social deference is strikingly parallel in its terminologies, its procedures, and its effects to those carried forth by Hale in *Godey's,* by Beecher in her advice to responsible mistresses who employ servants, and by Fern in her scorn of upstart mothers who send their daughters to boarding school. In her Conversations Fuller effectively claimed that orality—the ability to think on one's feet and to talk faster and better and with more obscurity and refinement than one's audience—was still a more convincing indicator of entitlement than physical appearance, money, or social position.

Although the practice of these writers seems to indicate that they endorsed the culture's assumption that voice could indicate character and that women could not and should not speak in public, it must be remembered that they did not refuse to participate in public, nor did they deny other women the right to do so. They chose to exploit verbal ambiguity to their own considerable advantage. When it served their purposes to retire from public view and conduct their business via ventriloquized texts, all four of these women did so. When it served their purposes to challenge the public presumptions that women could not and should not speak publicly, they did so. And when it would profit them to teach other women to speak publicly, they did so. As women who worked for a living but who continued to claim that such public labor did not diminish their status as ladies, they thus hastened the general trend in public speaking to see elocution as a performance that might or might not guarantee the *ethos* of its source.

Chapter Seven

THE DIFFERENCE
BETWEEN AUTHORS
AND SERVANTS

The nonfictional texts penned by Beecher, Hale, Fern, and Fuller constructed a composite portrait that claimed to describe "the" American woman.[1] That representation, however, obscured differences of occupation, age, marital status, race, social class, and geographic location among its referents. The illusion of a singular version of American womanhood recedes under an interrogation of its place in a triad of reciprocal and hierarchical dependency among the professional woman writer, within whose prescriptive texts the domestic woman gained her political and social specificity, and the invisible servant woman, whose labor maintained them both.

As several studies have established, in the tidy, well-organized, and self-contained bourgeois household the invisible labor of servants maintained the domestic woman as a home-centered counterpart to her manager/businessman husband. However, the connection of the intertwined figures of mistress and maid to the writing woman who invented them remains unremarked. As their own contemporaries noted, the writing woman bore little similarity to the domestic woman she inscribed. Paradoxically, she had more in common with the servant woman she inscribes as peripheral to the ideal domestic configuration. Thus the domestic woman is the textual creation of the professional writer, a figure whose inscription at the center of domestic handbooks performs a crucial rhetorical function, a necessary middle term that separates servant from writer—a distinction that is otherwise by no means self-evident.

Unlike unmarried women before them, Beecher, Hale, and Fern followed a comparatively new path. Rather than live with married relatives and trade her household labor for financial support, each invented a career for herself as a writer. This change anticipated and characterized a similar phenomenon among bourgeois single women in the Northeast generally, a move away from family-centered units of economic production into re-munerative employment in expanding capitalist arenas, including factories, schools, and publishing. As a result of this shift, paid domestic servants supplanted and eventually almost completely replaced unmarried female relatives as household adjuncts. At the period during which the initial wave of household handbooks were published, the transition between the two forms of domestic adjuncts was not yet complete, nor were the ideological formations that differentiated unpaid unmarried relatives from waged do-mestic servants completely articulated. Writing by Beecher, Hale, and Fern helped to encode those differences.

Suspending for a moment the very real and highly important differences that separated authors from immigrant servant women—differences of social class, affiliation, ethnicity, and educational advantage—it is possible to argue that these groups shared a striking number of characteristics, especially in contrast to married bourgeois women. Both authors and servants, if unmarried, were legally responsible for their own property, while a wife's political and property rights devolved through her husband.[2] Both were ex-cessive to the nuclear family constellation: Unlike racial slaves or indentured servants, domestic servants' relation to the families they lived with was not secured by legal fiat. Similarly, unmarried relatives' relation to the family was based only on ties of affection or obligation, but not mandated by law, as was the relation of wife and husband. The domestic woman occupied the stable center of her home; these other women were mobile: as unmarried relatives, they were guests in a series of host families; as servants, they were seen as itinerant laborers. By virtue of their work at the center of the household, as well as because they were presumed invisible, servants were party to the family's most intimate workings. Similarly, guests like Beecher could insin-uate themselves into the confidence of their hostesses, making their "secret domestic histories" (*Health,* 121) the raw material for their prescriptive writ-ings on domesticity. Writers who were less widely traveled established the same kinds of womanly identification with their readers, and thus were party to numerous unsolicited feminine confidences.[3] Both servants and authors used their knowledge of a variety of domestic practice—and of domestic secrets—as capital, stock in trade to better their positions as wage earners. It is the similarities—in relation to mobility and capital in property and information—that handbooks of domestic practice seek to occlude, thus

inscribing stability, silence, and fiscal irresponsibility on servants and encoding a relation of social hierarchy among authors, mistresses, and servants.

In the process of regularizing American domestic practice based on information they had gathered from their hosts and correspondents, Beecher,
Hale, and Fern invented a domestic woman who inhabited and maintained
the homes wherein these practices centered. As a composite creation, this
domestic paragon claims representative validity because her qualities are
based on the individual practices of "real" women. But since no one woman
embodied all these qualities, her fictionality was acknowledged by these authors at the same time they were promoting her. To call their representations
fictional is not to deny their force, however. Assembled as composites they
claim a transcendent and normative "truth" against which deviation may
be measured.

Hale's *Sketches of American Character,* an early collection of essays
purporting to document the "types" that constituted a national identity,
amply demonstrates these claims. Introducing a sketch of "the Village
Schoolmistress" (its generic title signaling that this is a composite, not
"realistic" portrait), Hale proclaims,

> the peculiar characteristics of females, being less distinctly marked,
> are much more difficult to be delineated than those of the other
> sex. There are various pursuits by which men may hope to obtain
> happiness and distinction—for women there is but one path—her
> success in life depends entirely on her domestic establishment. . . .
> In every station the object of female ambition is to marry well. This
> similarity of purpose produces a similarity of thought, feeling, action,
> and consequently *character,* which no uniformity of training could
> otherwise bestow. And then, the business of married women, though
> varying in *ceremonials,* according to the circumstances or rank of the
> respective husbands, is essentially alike. (102)

The grammatical tension evident here in Hale's vacillation between the
plural *women* and the immediately following singular—"*her* success"—
signals the distortion that results from her attempt to subsume a plurality of
women into the composite singular. The fiction of compositeness, however,
undermines Hale's overall aim of delineating *varieties* of national character,
since it leaves her with little to write about individual women. Thus
Sketches of American Character contains no definitive portrait of "the"
married woman; instead Hale "sketches" a number of young single women,
whose lives she follows only until marriage, when their separate identities
apparently merge into the domestic ideal.

In contrast to Hale's rather abstract delineations, Catharine Beecher's descriptions are drawn from close observation of hundreds of "domestic establishments." As does Hale, Beecher frames her discussion of married women's identities with a brief meditation about the different "intellectual capacity" of men and women, with the aim of establishing "the relative importance and difficulty of the duties a woman is called to perform" (*Treatise* 155). The enumeration of these duties gives specificity to married women's character, which, since it is a composite fiction, emerges primarily by negative definition, "according to the circumstances" (to use Hale's phrase) of husbands and other domestic intimates. Beecher presents the following outline of the domestic duties of "a well-educated and pious woman":

> She has a husband, to whose peculiar tastes and habits she must accommodate herself; she has children, whose health she must guard, whose physical constitutions she must study and develope [sic], whose temper and habits she must regulate, whose principles she must form, whose pursuits she must direct. She has constantly changing domestics, with all varieties of temper and habits, whom she must govern, instruct, and direct; she is required to regulate the finances of the domestic state, and constantly to adapt expenditures to the means and to the relative claims of each department. . . . She has the claims of society to meet, calls to receive and return, and the duties of hospitality to sustain. She has the poor to relieve; benevolent societies to aid; the schools of her children to inquire and decide about; the care of the sick; the nursing of infancy; and the endless miscellany of odd items, constantly recurring in a large family. (*Treatise* 156–57)

The rhetoric of this meticulously detailed yet abstract list is precisely calculated to emphasize the married woman's lack of agency in the face of nearly overwhelming obligation. This litany of responsibilities is recited not in active verbs—she guards, studies, regulates, governs—but in a curiously passive possessive imperative. Amid the swirl, mutability, and chaos of the home and its larger society, "she," the domestic woman, is a unified and singular (if characterless) constant. She must accommodate herself to a husband whose actions are not predictable; to children who grow, learn, and depart from her home; to temperamental domestics who come and go; and to fluctuating social responsibilities. Even property has more agency than she; she does not own property but must adapt its management to "claims" made by each "department" of her household. It should be emphasized that Beecher acknowledges the impossibility of any woman's actually attaining this ideal. Rather, this description of a married woman rhetorically founds her project of redefining a position outside domesticity for *unmarried* women. Rather than give the single woman identity as a domestic adjunct who echoes her married sister's household functions, Beecher will reverse the process, establishing that the married woman can escape her lack of subjectivity and the confusion of her domestic situation only by imitating her single writing counterpart.

Thus she acknowledges the effects of her encyclopedic gathering of representative praxis from all the "best" households nationwide. For example, "Words of Comfort for a Discouraged Housekeeper," a chapter included in the 1846 addendum to the *Treatise*, admits that "It is probable that many of those who may read over the methods of thrift and economy adopted by some of the best housekeepers in our land, and detailed in this work, will with a sigh exclaim, that it is *impossible* for them even to attempt any such plans" (*Domestic* 276). Such statements have occasioned several important studies linking Beecher's domestic texts to the larger national issues of slavery and suffrage. Positing that these works affected her sister Harriet's writing, they compare Stowe's presumed hysteria (which they interpret as the effect of her helplessness in the face of proliferating details of domestic management) to the loss of "integrity of the self" implied in racial slavery and in the conditions of patriarchal marriage. Lora Romero, for example, argues that "Beecher understood hysteria to result from absorption in details" and offered "systematization [as] the domestic skill that allowed women to displace the patriarch from the home, [conjoined] faculties dissevered by patriarchal government and in so doing [repaired] the self-division that, for Beecher, defines hysteria" (718). Yet Beecher did not use the term hysteria to describe the psychic effects of domestic disorder. Nor is it clear that Stowe's crisis of illness in the 1840s was an hysteric episode.[4] Rather than pursue an argument about women's health, however, I wish here to emphasize two points in relation to their authorship, attending not to Stowe's biography nor to the argument of *Uncle Tom's Cabin,* but to the full extent of Catharine Beecher's quite different project of inscribing a hierarchy of American— meaning white northeastern—women.

In the first place, although domestic disorder undoubtedly existed in individual households prior to its inscription in handboooks of domestic management, the books themselves proliferate and multiply the details that threaten to overwhelm the "discouraged housekeeper." Their encyclopedic quality is the direct result of their author's ability to gather a representative sample of *all* ideal domestic praxis in the "best households of the nation." Thus Beecher acknowledges that a lack of organization may produce a pathology peculiar to domesticity: "It is impossible, for a conscientious woman to secure [a] peaceful mind, and cheerful enjoyment of life . . . who is constantly finding her duties jarring with each other. . . . In consequence . . . there will be a secret uneasiness, which will throw a shade over the whole current of life, . . . till she so efficiently defines and regulates her duties, that she can fulfil them all" (*Treatise* 167). The pathology of housework, it is clear, Beecher attributes to the lack of agency inherent in current understandings of domesticity. Because "woman's pursuits" are of a "peculiarly desultory nature" (*Treatise* 157), "most women are . . . driven along, by the daily occurrences of life, so that, instead of being the intelligent regulators of their own time, they are the mere sport of circumstances. There is nothing, which so distinctly marks the difference between weak and strong minds, as the fact, whether they control circumstances, or circumstances control them" (*Treatise* 160). Noting that a "weak mind" may keep a woman at the mercy of circumstances surrounding her, Beecher's books categorize those duties and provide steps for their accomplishment, offering the managerial housewife a way to control and regulate their performance. Hence, although the books create the situation of domestic disorder and allude to its resulting pathology, they also offer the domestic woman a position outside the disorder, a place of agency and control that echoes in small the superordinate view of the well-traveled author. Beecher cautions that this position cannot be attained easily or immediately, and that any attempt to do so will result in "bafflement" and "discouragement" and produce a "relapse" into "former desultory ways" (*Treatise* 165). A definitive movement into systems of habit and order entails a rationalized and orderly redefinition of the housekeeper's subjectivity. No longer can she be entirely at the mercy of such passive and negatively defined lists as the one Beecher outlines at the beginning of her chapter. Rather "let her select that hour of the day, in which she will be least liable to interruption. . . . At this time, let her take a pen, and make a list of all the things which she considers as duties. Then, let a calculation be made, whether there be time enough, in the day or the week, for all these duties. If there be not, let the least important be stricken from the list, as not being duties, and which must be omitted" (*Treatise* 166). Here Beecher begins to allow a switch in agency in an attempt to move domestic women from being at the mercy of circumstances to being in control of them. Through writing a woman may control circumstances and redefine, even resist passivity, negation, and desultoriness. She determines when best to plan; then (as the syntax implies), under the direction of an outside theorist, whose act of authorship she imitates, a list is made, and a relative determination of priorities reached.

In offering the domestic woman this control over her circumstances, Beecher simultaneously justifies the single woman's move out of her position of household ancillary. Echoing the Word of creation with her scriptural diction ("let her choose," "let a calculation be made"), Beecher establishes the woman author as omniscient, if not omnipotent. She has surveyed the practices of the nation's best housekeepers, judged them, systematized their praxis and, in the handbooks, passed the information on to other, less mobile women. To them will be allowed the choice of appropriate method of organization (in this case, whether according to task, to category of obligation, to time of day, or to day of week—all options outlined in this chapter). Thus these books extend to domestic women a chance to echo— and, by extension, to endorse—the act of authoring, maintaining their control of their own circumscribed domains while justifying the departure of those women once thought most qualified by blood, (lack of) marital status, and custom to assist her.

Of course, not all the "duties" entailed in running a middle-class family would be performed by the woman whose written plans had designated them as important. Undergirding Beecher's rationalized household was a network of servant labor. These servants, unlike their southern counterparts, were not, either in bodily appearance or legal status, self-evidently "inferior" to their employers. In fact, the relation of servants and mistresses to the master's property were equally distant: neither legally owned the home, land, or household accoutrements that sustained them, although both were supposed to have an interest in maintaining them. Furthermore, servants' legal rights exceeded those of their mistresses. As single women they were legally responsible for their own property. They also retained the right to separate themselves from the household when necessity—or will—dictated. Hence, much of the writing that delineated servant-mistress relationships was compensatory, seeking to establish mistresses' status as superior to servants'.

Accordingly, writers of domestic texts advised a division of household labor, assigning most physical labors—propagating plants, cultivating fruits, caring for domestic animals, carrying water, washing, ironing, mending, baking pies and bread, deodorizing earth-closets, tending fireplaces, cooking meals, and preserving food, with their attendant dirt, sweat, and toil—to servants, while they reserved administrative functions—supervising servants and managing the household, and orchestrating sumptuary display—for mistresses. The effect of this division was to establish "white" married women who had surrendered their property rights and their (potential) mobility at marriage as naturally superior to wage-earning ethnic immigrant women whose physical and social mobility was legendary.

This differentiation of privilege is grounded in the contrast between a mistress's literacy, which she was to use in administering the household, and the literal-mindedness of her servants, a quality that derived from their unfamiliarity with the domestic codes governing ownership of consumer goods, but which was held to signify their general incompetence. The gap between literacy and literal-mindedness produced innumerable jokes and anecdotes such as those promulgated by Hale in a *Godey's* editorial entitled "Help." She begins the essay with a definition of "help" from *Webster's*: "That which gives assistance; he or that which contributes to advance a purpose; a hired man or woman." By invoking the dictionary to establish as correct the dominant cultural understanding that help are "hired" to "assist" or "advance a purpose," Hale appeals to the literacy of readers whom she figured, as did Beecher, as "well-educated and pious" women (*Treatise* 156). This passage also elides the issue of race. As Hedrick points out, "the operative distinction between 'help' and 'servant' was race: help was white, servants were black" (118). To the dictionary definition Hale counterposes a series of anecdotes, including the following: "A friend of mine once told her cook to grate a lemon, and she did 'clean through,' rind and pith. Another, who had ordered eggs boiled soft for breakfast, was greeted, after having waited with exemplary patience, with 'It's no use your ringing for them eggs agin; I have had them down an hour, and they won't bile soft!'" (32 [June 1846]: 288). In such anecdotes as these, the ungrammatical and literal-minded "help" emerge as hopelessly ignorant and childishly literal. Both lemons and eggs are wasted as a result of servants' inability to master figurative language and domestic custom.

Based on the proliferation of such accounts of servant incompetence, Beecher concluded, "The old New-England motto, *Get your work done up in the forenoon,* applied to an amount of work which would keep a common Irish servant toiling from daylight to sunset" (*New* 311). The implication is clear: literate New England housekeepers, possessed of supervisory abilities, are rightfully given the responsibility of overseeing the work of those who cannot regulate their own activities. Because new immigrant servants had not mastered codes of domestic practice held to signify literate competence, and because literacy was so closely aligned with good character, it was held to be a mistress's moral obligation to educate her servants. The practical benefits were several: if mistresses could leave written instructions for servants, the connection of writing to household organization was complete. The practice held the additional benefit of documenting servant (ir)responsibility.

In prescriptive domestic writings that articulated the relative duties of mistress and maid, Beecher, Hale, and Fern—all of whom had seen or directly experienced the results of married women's limited rights in property, and who had written specifically to the issue in other print venues—were curiously indirect. Their paradoxical reluctance to engage such a discussion in domestic handbooks presumably is related to genre, journalism being considered more appropriate to political discussion, while handbooks were deemed to represent socially established practice. Thus, rather than argue relative property rights, the domestic handbooks separate mistress from maid by elevating her managerial functions while figuring servants as spendthrift and larcenous. Such a figuration is contrary to the documentable fact that "domestics were the largest single occupational group among the depositors in antebellum savings banks" (Dudden 222).

Nevertheless, to a mistress fell the primary responsibility of regulating the consumption of household resources—particularly of clothing and food. The energy and specificity of the advice written to a managerial mistress concerning these matters suggests that the differences between family and "help" were not self-evident. Whereas in an earlier period, *family* had signified "those sharing a roof and a table," by midcentury the usage had contracted to designate only those sharing "blood ties and emotional bonds" (Dudden 251, n. 39). Quantities of prescriptive ink marked the borders separating private family from help, mistresses from maids, and entitled managers from spendthrift servants. Promiscuous interminglings of outsiders with family were prohibited, for example, at the washtub, as Fanny Fern points out in this anecdote: "When Mrs. Jabez, the washerwoman, comes in of a Monday to help do the washing, where's the harm, I'd like to know, in her bringing her own husband's soiled things, and her children's too, and doing them, convenient like, all together, where soap and starch and coal are plenty? Besides, in that way, she gets wages for *two* days' work instead of one, and sure no 'real lady' would make a fuss about that, or be poking her nose into the wash-tub, to see what was there" (*Ledger* 17 June 1871). As this passage suggests, promiscuity and property are intermingled concerns. Not only does the clothing of "outsiders" mix with the family's, not only does Mrs. Jabez use resources belonging to the privately enclosed family, but she also receives money for doing private work (her own family's laundry) for which she should not be reimbursed.

Even more worrisome than whether the laundress was kiting soap was the issue of where and what servants might eat. As with the laundry, these deliberations, presented as part of a mistress's managerial duties, simultaneously produced social distinction. Beecher explains in her *American Woman's Home* that "for a generation or two there was, indeed, a sort of interchange of family strength,—sons and daughters engaging in the service of neighboring families . . . always on conditions of strict equality. The assistant was to share the table, the family sitting-room, and every honor and attention that might be claimed by son or daughter. When families increased in refinement and education so as to make these conditions of close intimacy with more uncultured neighbors disagreeable, they had to choose between such intimacies and the performance of their own domestic toil" (319). Beecher's miniature history of the change from live-in "help" to domestic servitude delineates two moments: a prelapsarian interchange among egalitarian communal families and a later moment when literacy (the result of education and the guarantor of refinement) separated privately enclosed and entitled "families" from their "uncultured neighbors."

Assigning servants to dine at separate tables and at separate times had both practical and symbolic functions. According to Hale: "The taste and management of the mistress are always displayed in the general conduct of the table; for, though that department of the household be not always under her direction, it is always under her eye" (*New* 210). At table the proper management of domestic resources is demonstrated in choice and display of tableware, healthily planned meals, and prompt delivery of appetizing dishes, all items for which the a good mistress could take credit without having had to sweat over their preparation. By assigning servants to dine separately, a mistress might also supervise their diet, ensuring that they eat food appropriate to their status, while justifying such a practice as devolving from her moral obligation to oversee their health and to apportion household resources. Here, then, a mistress' obligations of management and display intermingle, for by enforcing culinary economies on the servants, she might be able to offer her guests a more elegant and sumptuous meal above stairs.

Yet separate dining produced as many problems as it solved, since if a mistress did not "direct" the kitchen, its resources often escaped her "eye." Domestic writers raised a universal outcry against servants who dispensed food and especially liquor from the kitchen to relatives and friends not employed by the family. To servants, this practice may have represented a continuation of "traditions of relatively free-handed charity or mutual assistance among the poor. A well-to-do Irish farmer's servant might distribute food daily to dozens of paupers who came to the farmhouse door, but an old-country style of generosity could get an Irish domestic into trouble in the United States" (Dudden 178). To these writers, however, such largesse suggested that servants were making judgment calls about disposing of excess resources, in the process intruding on a mistress's managerial obligation; and infringing into the family's rights in sumptuary display. While charity given from the hand of the mistress signified her munificence and her husband's financial ability, charity dispensed out the back door of the home by a servant suggested only a want of proper supervision.

In any case, the energy devoted to regulating servants suggests how important—and how difficult—it was to distinguish "uncultured" domestics from their employers. Because those engaged as domestic servants did not signify their so-called "degraded" status through evident codes such as skin color or bodily configuration, authors of domestic tracts gave a great deal of attention to other outward displays of status. While they condemned the use of livery in the name of democratic equality, these writers nevertheless enjoined servants to dress appropriately and sympathized with mistresses when they did not. Unlike a well-dressed wife, an elegantly attired servant signified not her master's wealth but rather an unseemly permeability of borders. A servant's finery, it was understood, was unlikely to be her own; she had more likely "borrowed" it from her mistress's closet than purchased it by saving her wages. If this was the case, it suggested troubling gaps in boundaries of discipline—around the family's possessions, as well as around the places "disguised" servants might circulate. Fern, for example, notes that "occasionally, your spangled opera-fan spends an evening out, where you yourself never had the felicity of an introduction" (*Ledger* 20 Feb. 1864). At issue here is not that a well-dressed servant might "pass" at the opera but that the servant will carry the fan to degraded places where its rightful owner would never presume to expose herself and where she might be mistaken for her mistress, whose status as a "real lady" implied that she did not circulate unaccompanied and unintroduced. If, by contrast, the finery did belong to the servant, it implied not thrift but a breach of decorum arising from a lack of respect for class boundaries. The money of servants, it was universally held, should be spent on *service*able attire. If a servant could afford such fine dress, it placed a back-pressure on her master to array his wife and daughters even more elegantly. Or, most problematically, it suggested that a woman being paid to do private household work could afford to dress more sumptuously than women whose economic status derived through men.

In an effort to establish the mistress's superiority to her servants, domestic writers consistently characterized servants as spendthrift or criminal. As she did with the issue of laundry soap, Fern terms the use of family resources by servants for their own good "Domestic Thieving": "According to Betty's code, it is not 'stealing,' constantly to use your thread, needles, spools, silk, tape, thimble and scissors, unlimitedly, to make or mend her own clothes. Is it not just so much saved from her pocket, toward the purchase of a brass breast-pin, or a flashy dress-bonnet?" (*Ledger* 20 Feb. 1864). In reading such condemnations of "thievery," it becomes clear that in many, if not most cases, the act results from the fact that "Betty's" relation to domestic property is the same as her mistress's. By law, the thread and scissors, like laundry soap, belonged no more directly to the mistress than to the maid. Hence, when an employee used them to enhance her own possessions, the resulting display did not redound to the husband's economic credit; instead, it indirectly enhanced the employee's own net worth, and by extension counted as larceny.

Other instances of domestic thievery delineated in this same column emphasize that if a servant had legal property rights, her mistress, who did not, must have compensatory rights of disciplinary supervision. According to Fern, "Chambermaids and nurses too often consider that everything that drops upon the carpet is their *personal property,* from a common pin to a pair of diamond ear-rings. '*I found it on the floor,*' is considered by them sufficient excuse when detected in any felonious appropriation" (first emphasis added). Since a servant could thus appropriate a mistress's goods by petty theft, Fern proposes a compensatory strategy: "Once in a while, to be sure, you may be fortunate enough by making a sudden and successful foray among her goods and chattels, to seize [a] lost treasure." Paradoxically, such an act performed by one whose domestic duties charge her with managing family property does not count as "felonious appropriation." An unannounced raid on "goods and chattels"—personal property legally owned by a servant—is simply good domestic management.

Of course, the most worrisome thing that might happen is that the felonious appropriator would leave the household before such a raid could be effected, for it was commonly held that servants lacked loyalty to their employers. This tendency toward mobility, although nominally endorsed as democratic opportunity, marks a second inequality between supervisors and serving women. Earlier, the legal status of servants was as legally fixed as was the relation of married couples: wives assumed their husbands' name, protection, and financial obligations; the terms and responsibilities of bound and indentured servants (like slaves) were fixed by contract or deed of sale.[5] By midcentury, however, servants had become paid employees without legal or emotional obligation to a family's economic fortunes. Nevertheless, these mercurial "strangers" still lived with the family, shared their domestic space, ate their food, and were involved in all its most intimate functions. It was therefore hoped that servants also had the family's best interests at heart and would demonstrate an appropriate filial loyalty. Yet the tone of writings about domestic management suggests that mistresses and the authors who advised them suspected this was not the case.

In response to the issue of servant mobility (and mistresses' containment), writers adopted a twin strategy: to mistresses, whose economic fate depended on their husbands', they assigned household production; to servants, who could and did leave when economic or personal problems arose, they addressed encomia on loyalty and injunctions of silence. Thus, some sweated labor, logically the province of servants (or so it would seem to the contemporary reader), was given instead to women bound by blood and law to the nuclear family. For example, Hale declares that "there are some sorts of domestic work, that of dairy work is one, which no hired help would be competent to discharge. This must be done by a wife or daughter, who feels a deep personal interest in the prosperity of her husband or father" (*Mrs. Hale's New* 483). Dairy work, by midcentury, was one of the last vestiges of home production. The logic here is that such labors must literally derive from the body of a family member, not a paid surrogate, to "count" as domestic (not manufactory) production. Moreover, as this passage suggests, a wife's direct "interest" in her husband's economic well-being exceeds that of a servant, who cannot be depended upon to work in support of another family's economic betterment. Finally, this passage suggests the connection of economic independence to mobility: if a male householder did not succeed economically, that household's servants could (and did) move to other employment. According to Dudden, servants comprised "an especially high percentage of new depositors" in New York savings banks "between 1837 and 1844, reflecting the relative steadiness of service work in hard times" (324 n. 162). Wives' fortunes, by contrast, were almost inexorably tied to their husbands'; their labor, therefore, is more self-interested.

The issue of servant mobility is most frequently framed in terms of how much work it is for the mistress to find and train their replacements. Fern, for example, concludes "Domestic Thieving" with this observation: "To make the moon-struck *master* . . . comprehend that his wife cannot at once upon the entrance of a bran new Betty dismiss dull care, would take more breath than most mothers of young and rising families are able to spare" (*Ledger* 20 Feb. 1864). In an effort to restrict the ebb and flow of servant populations, Beecher suggests that their duties are the result of divine injunction, beginning a chapter entitled "Friendly Counsels for Domestics" with the proclamation that "the duties committed to you by God . . . are indeed most solemn and important" (*Miss* 280). As Beecher's direct address to servants makes clear, the trouble of training hew help is only part of the issue. In counseling servants to remain faithful, for example, she inadvertently exposes the counterdiscourse to the common understandings of servants' disloyalty: "It is a bad thing for you, as well as for your employers, to keep roving about from one place to another. Stay where you are, and try to make those things that trouble you more tolerable, by enduring them with patience" (*Miss* 281). Beecher's recognition that servant life may not always be "tolerable" is echoed by most domestic writers. But in each case, its rhetorical function is to mark a minor concession in the interest of gaining a larger argumentative point and is followed by the direct—or implied— threat that things might not improve in another situation.

The most worrisome issue about servant mobility emerges in Beecher's following counsels. Not only are servants not to "form a habit of roaming about to see company," they are "never [to] tell tales out of the family, nor tell to . . . employers the bad things [they] have seen, or heard in other families, for this is mean and ungenerous" (*Miss* 282). Beecher seems especially able to mark the danger of servant circulation because it so closely approximates her own practices. Literate or not, both servants and single authors/houseguests like Beecher had access to "secret domestic histories" that they could use as capital. As family intimates with no legal obligations to the family, both authors and servants could exchange their knowledge for personal enhancement—servants to negotiate for a better position, or as simple blackmail, and authors as the basis for domestic handbooks that catalogued the practices of the "best American families."

The similarities between authors and serving women are not immediately evident in a cursory survey of nineteenth-century domesticity, especially if textual constructs of marital status, literate privilege, and ethnic superiority are taken as impermeable signifiers of difference among women. Yet servants were as necessary to the professional woman writer as to her domestic sisters. Not only did the labor of servants give these women time and sufficient intellectual distance from domesticity to rationalize its practice, but "the servant problem" also provided them with an infinity of topics: they defined servant duties, usually by detailing and lampooning their supposed imbecilities; addressed (and inscribed) servant subjectivities; and in the process differentiated them from others whom they threatened to resemble—from other waged and impressed labor; from wives' unremunerated domestic labor, and, most important, from themselves as authors.

Seldom do writers refer directly to their own servants, although biographical sources establish—usually parenthetically—that each grew up in a family that employed "help"; that each attended schools that employed servants and that, as school administrators, each perpetuated the practice; that as adults they were served by the domestic help in the families with whom they lodged; and that, as married women, they employed seamstresses, cooks, laundresses, chambermaids, and nannies. When these writers do directly acknowledge that their work is derived in any way from servants' labor, it is often by way of complaint. Fanny Fern's "A Voice from Bedlam" is typical: "Is my article for the *Ledger* ready? No sir, . . . it is NOT! Have I not been beset, since I left my bed this morning, with cook, chambermaid and sempstress? . . . the settling of the thousand and one little matters which take up, and *must take up,* the precious morning hours, which, alas! show for nothing, and yet which no housekeeper may dodge" (*Ledger* 26 Oct. 1861). In this column, Fern poses her multiple domestic helpers as obstacles to her literary production. The irony, of course, is that her article for the *Ledger,* is indeed, finished; the very situation that Fern bemoans provides the material for her trademark humor. In addition the anecdote establishes her as an author who, unlike her servants, can settle minor domestic matters efficiently, and, in addition, can transcend these trivial but overwhelming details to spin the straw of domestic drudgery into literary gold. Such writing encodes her as an understanding and compassionate domestic woman, one who is very much like her readers, and who (only incidentally) makes a handsome salary as a writer.

In addition to making more time available for literary pursuits, servants also stood as the objects of these writers' attentions. The fine points of managing servants occasioned at least a chapter in every housekeeping manual. Beecher discovered, as well, that money might be made by writing directly to servants themselves. Undaunted by the fact that she generally posited them as illiterate in order to establish the mistress's superior domestic entitlement, she wrote a conduct book entitled *Letters to Persons Who Are Engaged in Domestic Service*, possibly the first and certainly one of only a few manuals addressed directly to this group. She publicized the book by cross-referencing it in editions of her *Treatise* and by marketing it not to servants directly but to women most likely to have the means to purchase it. In its preface, addressed to "My Countrywomen," Beecher writes: "The persons for whom I write, have few opportunities to know what issues from the press, and seldom buy books. . . . I would therefore appeal to all benevolent and Christian ladies, [to] . . . secure the reading of this book to at least *one* of those for whom it is written. If housekeepers will supply those they hire, if travellers and visitors will use this, to present as a token of good will to those who serve them, where they temporarily sojourn, if . . . this may be remembered as a suitable present to those who do so much to aid on festive occasions, then if this book is fit for the end designed, there will be many who will be joined, in the best of all fellowship, with their friend and countrywoman, THE AUTHOR" (6). *Letters to Persons Who are Engaged in Domestic Service* was published in a period when conduct books flooded the popular press. The authority of such books derived from their author's perceived status as exemplar of the subjectivity the book sought to document. Thus while ostensibly addressing the needs of a population who seldom were the subject of such manuals, Beecher also necessarily differentiated herself from them, establishing herself as one of the "benevolent and Christian ladies" who is entitled by her expert superordinate knowledge, not by her experience as a domestic worker, to write such manuals.

Letters, unlike *Treatise on Domestic Economy*, is not a handbook of household practice. Rather it spells out the details of acceptable servant conduct, in the process differentiating actions performed by single, mobile servant women from similar behaviors associated with single, mobile, "benevolent and Christian ladies." Although in other books addressed to employers Beecher had argued that servitude was a respectable occupation that could be used as a foundation to upward mobility, in this direct address to them, she enjoined them to stability. For example, in *New Housekeeper's Manual*, advising readers against affecting to dress their servants in livery, she argued that service was an occupation, not an obligation, declaring that a servant "must be a fellow-citizen, with an established position of his own, free to make contracts, free to come and go, and having in his sphere titles to consideration and respect just as definite as those of any trade or profession whatever" (333). (The generic pronoun here may mark a gendered distinction in Beecher's mind. Or the content of this pronouncement may be determined by the audience of "housekeepers" Beecher is addressing.) Beecher advises a woman servant to choose her employment carefully, making every effort to "seek a place where she will be willing to stay *for life*, if she does not get a home of her own" (169). Once employed, she should exercise utmost circumspection in her conversation, never revealing family secrets. "Do this, and every body will respect you for your sense of propriety, and feel reproved if they have tempted you, by questions, to so ungenerous and wrong a course" (170).

As a conduct book, *Letters to Persons Who Are Engaged in Domestic Service* establishes a uniquely American definition of service that is different both from indenture and from slavery. The first step in this differentiation is to establish a nomenclature appropriate to the national ethic. Thus Beecher instructs her readers:

> We find that it is common to call persons who have wealth and education, "*ladies*," and persons who have no education, and labour for a support, "*women*." And if a person who considered herself among the first, should hear a person say, "there is a *woman* in the parlour," instead of saying, "there is a *lady* in the parlour," she would in some cases feel offended. What is the reason of this? She *is* a woman, why is she not pleased to be called so? Why simply because persons whom she regards as below herself are so called. Now this is exactly the case with you. You do not like to be called by the same name as is given to slaves in this land, and to the degraded servants of other countries. . . . But you must not allow yourselves to be offended because people do not always know your feelings on this point, or do not always remember to regard your wishes. (164–65)

This passage establishes a hierarchy of service by acknowledging that servants should not be confused with slaves or with "degraded"—that is, bound—servants. And thus, Beecher proposes a new designation, "domestic," a word derived, she explains, from *domus*, and "[signifying] one employed in doing the work at home, and therefore it has a very pleasant idea connected with it" (166). Not incidentally, the passage constructs a parallel argument in favor of servants' observing an exactness in language that would demonstrate their respect for their social betters. Servants must not confuse "ladies" with "women," nor should they aspire to the status of *woman*. To do so would be to think of housework as labor that yields a living rather than as a domestic, residential, and moral obligation, with its attendant implications of loyalty and stability.

Beecher was not the only author to devote her writing to stabilizing and classifying servitude. Among *Godey's* regular and numerous features— letters, advice, fiction, and opinion—regarding servants appears an item couched as a news bulletin and reporting a new classification of servant: the "lady-help." Designed to provide relief to mistresses who must keep unmannerly servants above stairs, this servant, more entitled to respect because of her elevated manners,

> has a bedroom to herself. She is not to scour floors, black-lead grates, clean pots and pans, or shoes. She will, however, kindle fires and remove ashes. Those who do not wish to employ two classes of servants, can employ char-women for the rougher work. . . .
>
> There are said to be great advantages in this system . . . greater refinement in the home, dishes more daintily cooked and served, the rooms kept neater, and the drawing-room more tastefully arranged. There are various other advantages which can be easily imagined, of sympathy and intelligence, in place of mere cupidity and ignorance. It is an interesting problem, and we shall watch carefully its development. (94 [June 1877]: 547)

This item is interesting precisely because it undoes what it pretends to endorse. On the excuse of increasing the refinement of the home by elevating the class of live-in help (and changing the nomenclature in the process) and consigning the sweated labor to day workers, Hale does not consider whence the lady-help originated. Who but gentlewomen fallen on hard times or unmarried female relatives might provide the dainty and tastefully refined services this lady-helper would render? Significantly, Hale stops short of endorsing this position, a sign, perhaps, that she recognized how difficult it would be to distinguish such women from those they assisted.

The project of differentiating categories of household service from slavery and marking the relative status of ladies, women, and domestics was complete only when the position of the woman author in this hierarchy was established. In Beecher's taxonomy, one category is missing, the very combination that best describes her—an educated woman who labors for her support. In *Letters,* lest her status remain ambiguous, she marks it in a less-than-subtle fashion by announcing, "Probably if I were in your place, I might not wish to be called *a servant,* just as many persons I associate with, choose to be called 'ladies' instead of 'women'" (165–66).

But Beecher's estimation of the superior social status of unmarried women authors is best demonstrated by an undated memoir she penned, ostensibly to demonstrate her sister Harriet's "combined exercise of . . . literary and domestic genius" (Stowe and Stowe 87). The anecdote, a perfect example of the "secret domestic histories" Beecher collected, makes clear, as well, that if Stowe is a genius-writer, she has succeeded only because of Beecher's even more superior ability to organize both domestic proceedings and authorial output. As Beecher tells it, she observed the incident "during a visit to . . . [Mrs. Stowe]" (87). Almost immediately, however, it becomes clear that the "visit" is part of a larger agenda of brokerage: Catharine has come to collect a "piece for the *Souvenir* which I promised the editor I would get . . . and send him on next week" (87). The "piece" is incomplete, having been put aside in the face of Stowe's more immediate domestic pressures—teething babies, house-cleaning, a "great baking down in the kitchen," and, most grievously, "a green girl for help" (88). In response to Harriet's objections that writing "is really out of the question," Catharine pontificates, "I see no such thing. I do not know what genius is given for if it is not to help a woman out of a scrape. Come set your wits to work and let me have my way, and you shall have all the work done, and finish the story too" (88–89). Catharine proceeds to organize the chaos, direct Harriet, prompt her muse, distract the children, take dictation from Harriet, and superintend Mina, the "dark-skinned nymph waiting for orders" in the kitchen (89). The incident concludes as Harriet dictates the closing lines of her story:

> She continued to dictate,—
> "You must take them away. It may be—perhaps it must be—that I shall soon follow, but the breaking heart of a wife still pleads, 'a little longer, a little longer.'"
> "How much longer must the ginger-bread stay in?" asked Mina.
> "Five minutes," said Harriet.
> "'A little longer, a little longer,'" I repeated in a dolorous tone, and we burst out into a laugh.
> Thus we went on, cooking, writing, nursing, and laughing, till I finally accomplished my object. The piece was finished and copied, and the next day sent to the editor.
> No wonder Mrs. Stowe describes her writing as "rowing against wind and tide!" (93)

This memoir depends on a complex handling of narration that produces a double definition of genius. Catharine becomes the administrative heroine ("I accomplished *my* object," the completion of Harriet's writing), and Harriet becomes the literary and domestic genius, an able housekeeper (in contrast to her domestic help who are more a problem than an aid), who is also able to complete her writing of a "piece" that transmutes the mundane details of household trivialities into "Art." The contemporary framing of the incident—in a biography of Stowe compiled by her son and grandson—uses the memoir to establish Stowe as a literary genius. Separate from this context, it delimits a hierarchy that includes married and unmarried women who perform domestic duties for various material and immaterial rewards. The single mobile writing woman possessed of superordinate skills comprehends and exceeds her sisters lower on the scale. Next in the hierarchy stands the married woman who also writes, a living demonstration of the "combined exercise of literary and domestic genius." Her status, in turn, exceeds that of the married woman who effects the smooth management of her household by written agendas and the married woman who does not write at all and is thus at the mercy of household circumstance. Finally, making the entire hierarchy possible by her supposed illiteracy, incompetence, and instability is the servant woman. To recognize her foundational position in this hierarchy is to mark a complexity and interrelatedness among these women heretofore obscured by standard accounts of nineteenth-century literary and domestic practice. It suggests that studies of feminism's theoretical engagement with abolition need to be paralleled by a similar emphasis on conservative domesticity's entanglements with ethnic oppression. Finally, it illuminates the absolute dependence of our mythical accounts of gendered authorial genius on carefully assembled and invisible substrata of class-based literacy and gendered labor.

Chapter Eight

DOMESTICATING PEDAGOGY

In 1843, as Margaret Fuller returned from her trip to the western prairies and began to prepare the manuscript of *Summer on the Lakes,* the book that recounted her journey, she conducted much of the supporting research for her writing in the Harvard University Library. She was, according to biographer Thomas Wentworth Higginson, the first woman to be allowed that privilege. As he recalls, she sat "day after day, under the covert gaze of the undergraduates who had never before looked upon a woman reading within those sacred precincts" (194).

Some thirty years later, when Catharine Beecher was in her seventies, she decided to enroll in a course at Cornell University. As her biographer recounts, when she announced her decision to Andrew White, the university's president, he replied, "with some embarrassment,"

> "I regret to say, Miss Beecher, that as yet, we have no courses open to women."
>
> "Oh, that is quite all right, Doctor White, in fact I prefer to take it with men," she disarmingly replied.
>
> That question seeming to be settled, Doctor White inquired whether he could be of service in finding her a place to lodge in town?
>
> "No, thank you, Doctor White," she answered, "I shall room in . . ." one of the dormitories on the campus.
>
> "But, Miss Beecher," protested Doctor White, "that is a dormitory for young men, it has no accommodations for ladies!"
>
> "I have inspected the accommodations and find them entirely satisfactory," imperturbably replied Miss Beecher, "and as for those young men, who are of appropriate ages to be my grandsons, they will not trouble me in the least." She stayed, took the course, roomed in

> the dormitory and became one of the most popular inmates of the
> building. (L.B. Stowe 129–30)

The presence of these two women in the innermost sancta of elite educational institutions marks the approximate temporal boundaries of a
period during which educational arenas once understood to be exclusively
masculine became increasingly available to women students, teachers, administrators, and theorists. Fuller's and Beecher's acts were unique enough to
earn the notice—and even the grudging admiration—of their biographers;
but the negotiations and arguments that led to those accomplishments are
only hinted at by the bemused tone of their retrospective accounts.[1]

Two interrelated factors brought these women to the center of educational theory and practice. First, a process of educational and disciplinary
reform helped open the dormitories, curricula, libraries, and administration
of higher education to women. Briefly stated, this new "disciplinary intimacy" (Brodhead, "Sparing" 18) substituted loving motivation for corporal
punishment; it mandated that discipline, whose result was understood to
be a strong character, be carried out by personalized and affectionally moti-
vated authorities. Such reform allowed for the possibility of women—older,
maternal (but not married), and desexualized women—as its agents. Fuller's
work in Harvard's library, one of the earliest such instances, demonstrated
that the presence of certain women in such formerly monastic sites need not
result in sexual anarchy but might also result in the spread of civilized and
civilizing knowledge. Such incursions continued until, in 1870, Beecher
could insist on being allowed to study and live with the young men of
Cornell. Although she had never married and did not have grandsons, her
biographer figures her residence in the Cornell dormitories as an extension
of normal intergenerational family relationships, a domestication of a space
formerly marked as utterly masculine.

Not just any woman would have been welcome at Harvard or Cornell,
however. A second important factor in the process of educational reform
is that the women who were its first theorists and practitioners enjoyed
considerable public reputations as journalists and literary women. Both
Fuller and Beecher had been teachers; significantly, however, each had
deliberately and speedily separated herself from daily classroom labor to
take up more theoretical and literary pursuits. Fuller's work as editor of
the *Dial*, which had published the writing of many of Harvard's graduates,
made it unthinkable that Harvard's library would be barred to her. Likewise,
by 1870 Beecher had published dozens of essays on education in popular

journals, as well as several best-selling books of domestic and educational theory; Andrew White could not easily dismiss her request.

Fuller and Beecher, like their contemporaries, Sarah Josepha Hale and Fanny Fern, had used writing—and particularly the journalistic venues addressed to women—to publicize carefully crafted versions of their experience as mothers, daughters, and sisters, ultimately arguing that such domestic expertise qualified them to theorize and to effect educational reform, not only for common schools and women's seminaries but also for the most venerable and elite universities. As journalists, they instructed readers in the fine points of disciplinary intimacy, arguing that learning best thrives when school becomes coextensive with home and when educational administration is subject to the public scrutiny of literate men and women who hold positions of respect in the larger intellectual community.

The reforms associated with disciplinary intimacy and promoted through mass-circulation journalism addressed a class- and gender-coded educational practice. In the early nineteenth century, advanced schooling had been the business of a select few men, agents of and responsible to male administrators. Their Latin-based collegiate training included rote learning, agonistic debate, heightened competition, and violent physical discipline. They later perpetuated these methods as masters of common schools, preparatory schools, and early women's academies, as well as in men's colleges. By the third quarter of the century, many such schoolmasters had been replaced by women teachers who practiced a discipline that was private, personal, and emotional, rather than public, impersonal, and corporal. The work of these women was subject to public scrutiny, discussion and review, not only by a male school board but also by public institutions of mass-circulation journalism who had both invented the idea of a loving middle-class family and styled themselves the agents of that family's interests.

Because disciplinary intimacy depended on personalized and loving attention, it was fairly easy to include women as its agents in common schools, since women were presumably fitted by nature to nurture children. Women journalists took up this logic, promoting the heterosexual urban middle-class family as the model for a new pedagogy that substituted a desexualized woman teacher as mother and an ambisexual journalistic voice as paternal supervisor. For example, by the time Fanny Fern had established her reputation as a columnist for the *New York Ledger,* she no longer had young children; nor had she ever taught school. Yet in her *Ledger* columns, she wrote authoritatively about affectional child rearing and education.

In so doing, she claimed to represent the opinions of a broad audience of middle-class readers. As support for these new ideas, she invoked the patriarchal and institutional authority of Robert Bonner and of the *Ledger,* occasionally concluding her more radically outspoken columns with such ingenuous disclaimers as this: "I can only grasp warmly by the hand those women who have the nerve to witness the effect of their own words; while I watch mine at a safe distance on paper, with Mr. Bonner to back me in the NEW YORK LEDGER" (23 May 1863).

In dozens of *Ledger* columns, Fern argued that young children and adolescents required an educational experience adapted to their ages. She advocated modifications to physical environment, disciplinary strategies, pedagogical expectations, classroom procedure, and administrative supervision, all with the idea in mind that childhood was an identifiable stage in a developmental journey to maturity. Her reform-oriented columns presume that the pupils who suffered under the abuses of an outmoded pedagogy came from happy, intact, heterosexual, suburban families (quite unlike the family in which she had been raised) in which discipline was effected by a lovingly persuasive, even indulgent, mother from whom school had separated her reluctant child. The best schools, according to Fern, reproduced this family ideal. Kindergartens should have child-size furniture, participant-oriented art projects, "music, and other studies and amusements, varied, and of short duration, follow[ed] with intervals of rest" (*Ledger* 28 Nov. 1863). Teachers—"married mothers," not "old maids"—would be supervised by kindly paternal administrators, never "dried up old bachelors" (*Fern,* Second Series 259). Since Fern did not advocate that mothers of small children work, the "married mother" teacher she imagines here must be either a widow laboring for her own support, an older woman whose children are grown, or a young woman trained in a women's seminary where ideas of childhood development and affectional discipline were theorized. Fern uses the phrase less as a literal descriptor than as a device for defusing the sexual tension suggested by the association of men and women as professional educators.

In the details of educational reform linger the biases of the middle-class writers who promoted it. Even the reform of composition instruction was framed by middle-class assumptions. Fern, for instance, advocated a developmental approach to writing, recommending that teachers assign to children topics appropriate to their age and experience. She deplores requiring "little children" to write about "The Nature of Evil" or "Moral Science"—topics routinely assigned to young students two generations earlier, but that now seemed to presume a moral awareness characteristic of much older persons. Nor does she endorse assignments such as "hydrostatics" that characterize a more pragmatic trade-oriented general education. In an assertion paralleling Fuller's emphases on age-appropriate curriculum, Fern declares, "A child should never be allowed, much less *compelled* to write words without ideas" (*Fresh* 266, 267). Titles from *Fresh Leaves,* the collection containing this essay, illustrate topics Fern might have suggested as more conducive to enthusiastic writing: "Visitors and Visiting," "Our First Nurse," and "Summer Travel," activities and experiences most familiar to upper-middle-class children.

Not surprisingly, Fern herself was the best exemplar of the approaches to writing that she advocated. Many of her arguments with the traditional composition curriculum betray her occupational bias as a journalist who had gained a reputation for writing pithy, humorous sketches. She challenges standardization in favor of individual ability and inclination, insisting that "to return a child's composition to him with the remark, 'It is very good, but it is *too short*' " is "stupidity." "If he has said all he has to say, what more would you have? what more can you get but repetition? Tell him to *stop when he gets through if it is at the end of the first line*—a lesson which many an adult has yet to learn. . . . Always consider one line, intelligibly and concisely expressed, better than pages of wordy bombast" (*Fresh* 267).

Fern implies that such expectations are the product of teachers pursuing now-outdated classic norms—of amplitude, agon, imitation, and profusion—and of socially ambitious parents who want their children to acquire these class-marked aptitudes but who have little or no understanding of newer theories of childhood development. The effect is to caution parents to keep out of educational business while retraining them to expect a new kind of public writing—one that replaces tradition, conservatism, and complexity with immediacy, creativity, and simplicity.

In fact, Fern advocated a process of composition that she had learned at Hartford Female Seminary where Catharine Beecher had modified classical education's discipline and subject matter to meet what she understood to be the needs of young middle-class women. As part of this concept, Beecher employed a developmental approach to composition that gave students a foundation in vocabulary; required them to read widely in texts translated from Latin or originally written in English; assigned them exercises in textual, grammatical, and syntactical analysis; and allowed them to imitate structural and argumentative forms before asking them to write extended original compositions. Beecher's students wrote about topics both personal and abstract but always modified (as Fern would later advocate) in experience appropriate to their age, sex, and social class. For example, although a composition entitled "A Description of Hartford Female Seminary" echoes the mnemonic exercises of classical rhetoric, which links ideas to precise locations, it is also literally grounded in the student's present domestic surroundings. Another, despite its imposing title, "The Governing Principle of the Mind Affects the Associations," takes a personal approach, illustrating its contentions with the example of a "lady . . . whose *sole* desire is to be admired" (Mary Kingsbury Talcott, 1832; Memoranda Books, Stowe-Day).

The class biases that inform Fern's journalistic opinions about pedagogy and composition also determined the modifications she advocated for educational administration. She implicitly argued that reform based on developmental and domestic models would succeed only if ill-informed and lower class social climbers did not insist on using schooling as a means of class elevation. In a column entitled "Stand by the School Teachers," she points out that abusive and unreasonable pedagogies often persist because parents demand their continuance. Enjoining such parents to have reasonable expectations, Fern writes: "I can understand that . . . parents, feeling every day, in their own experience, the want of early education, which a sudden money elevation, perhaps, has made painfully apparent to them, may commit, and that not from want of love to their offspring, just this fatal mistake. . . . I say let parents be more *just* to teachers. Let parents give more honorable credence to the suggestions of those conscientious servants of the public, whom they tie hand and foot, to make bricks without straw" (*Ledger* 19 Jan. 1867). Simply put, Fern argues that newly rich adults who have grown up in an environment barren of intellectual capital should not expect the public schools to provide it. In calling for more authority to be ceded to teachers, Fern marks a moment of increasing professionalization that limits the right of private citizens to influence pedagogy and curriculum. That right belongs not to ignorant parents who may have ephemeral monetary entitlement but to trained teachers and administrators: those teachers are women like Fern and men of similar educational background who may be less inclined—indeed, less able—to offer and administer a classical curriculum. Their supervision belongs, in turn, to their peers—professional administrators, school boards composed of parents with enhanced community reputations, and to the organs of mass media who represented the interests of these educated constituencies.

Fanny Fern's journalism addressed educational reform in the classroom; Catharine Beecher's demonstrates how reform addressed educational administration. Although she first worked as a teacher, Beecher quickly realized that success lay in directing the activities of others. As she wrote her brother, Edward, "I am not going into *partnership* with any one—I shall be head & pay salaries & *I mean to make money by it*" (March 3 [1827]; Acquisitions, Stowe-Day). Yet Beecher built a career not as an administrator but as a writer and theorist. Her practical experience served as the pretext for the written theories she published in dozens of magazines, newspapers, pamphlets, and full-length treatises. For example, in her *Suggestions Respecting Improvements in Education* (1839), she recounted her pedagogical experiments less to demonstrate their developmental and educational benefits than to buttress her argument that such procedures demanded a division and hierarchy of labor. Written composition, for example, could best be taught by several trained specialists directed, supervised, and evaluated by a well-paid and securely employed administrator. While lesser talents could teach, she argued, "there must be one directing mind; one whose business it is to devise plans for others to execute, and to see that nothing is left unattempted. . . . None but a *principal* can take such a station in this institution" (*Suggestions* 67). Beecher, at the apex of the disciplinary hierarchy that her theory promoted, publicized her reform agenda through strategically placed publications. In return, she claimed public respectability for such personal and institutional efforts by referring to their public acceptance as evidenced by the breadth of readership, the status of her readers, and the institutional imprimatur of publishing houses such as McGuffey and the Harper Brothers.

Ultimately, these journalistic discussions of theory-based pedagogy fueled a growing public support for educational reform and placed an increasing number of women in the classroom and in administrative positions in women's academies and seminaries. So successful was the work of reformers like Fern and Beecher in arguing that elementary and women's education be ceded to women that by 1868, even the conservative Sarah Josepha Hale declared that "by common consent, in our country, the office of teacher of children is held to be peculiarly proper for woman. It is a noteworthy fact that the older a State becomes, and the more widely education is diffused in it, the more general is the employment of women as teachers. . . . It is easy to see that the time will come when this profession will be almost as entirely surrendered to them as some other professions are and must be appropriated to men" (*Godey's* 77 [Dec.]: 541). Invoking the democratic principle of "common consent" and statistics that "prove" the numerical majority of women in the profession, Hale confidently predicts an irresistible tide of changed opinion. The political context for this change parallels new developmental understandings of childhood: Hale suggests that such enlightened reforms are the inevitable result of increasing sophistication of the "older" states. Thus younger states and territories could also aspire to similarly enlightened policies as they mature.

Three years later Hale amplified this stance, claiming that educational administration was also ideally suited to women and using a domestic metaphor to buttress her argument. She advocated that women be included on separate school boards, "bearing much the same relation . . . that the wife bears to the husband in household affairs." This meant, presumably, that the men's board would see to the administrative and financial details, while women would supervise domestic issues such as facilities, discipline, and curriculum. Skirting issues related to the franchise, Hale suggests that women should be not elected but appointed to such boards by school trustees. "If several respectable matrons were required to visit frequently the buildings in which . . . children . . . were confined for five or six hours every day, we may be sure that they would not long allow the little creatures to inhale a poisonous atmosphere, or be oppressed with excessive tasks, or tortured with cruel punishments; nor yet would they permit them to be left in idleness and disorder" (*Godey's* 82 [Feb. 1871]: 189). This passage demonstrates the unevenness with which reform proceeded. It charges public schools to adopt domestic and sentimental ideals; it also maintains domesticity's hierarchies.

Hale's proposal is not entirely modeled on heterosexual domesticity, however, since she recommends that *respectable matrons* should supervise women's school boards. Gender is the crux of this issue. If the classroom plagued by poisoned air, excessive work, and cruel torture is under the supervision of a man, a woman administrator necessarily derives her authority to correct these abuses from the parallel board of male supervisors. If, on the other hand, the classroom is under the care of a woman with supposedly innate nurturant abilities, why had she not already eliminated the abuses Hale catalogues? The answer can only be that although feminized education opened both teaching and administration to women, it nevertheless promulgated hierarchies of professional expertise. Thus Hale's argument depends on a self-evident assumption about class that cedes to "respectable matrons" even more enlightened sensibilities than those possessed by mere classroom teachers.

Thus reform agendas associated with disciplinary intimacy allowed women to move into elementary teaching and public school administration. Because these reforms were modeled on the power dynamics of the heterosexual family, however, women's professional gains reinscribed and perpetuated that dynamic, reserving economic power and theoretical supervision to men, while making women responsible for carrying out such theories. The practices of disciplinary intimacy that brought women into elementary school teaching had different resonances when applied to the management and teaching of older children, however. Physical size, age, and developing sexuality mitigated against women's employing disciplinary intimacy in classes containing young men. Yet to think of men supervising women's schools either by physical force or by disciplinary affection implied an unhealthy and disturbingly sexual energy. The sexual dynamics of coeducation were early publicized by journalists interested in reforming higher education. They urged that the instruction and supervision of adolescent women be given over to women, since it presumably would be untainted by sexual desire. In the process, they exposed the interconnection of pedagogy with sexual desire and economic power.

Disciplinary intimacy hastened the proliferation of single-sex schools and moved women into positions that equaled men's, not only as teachers but also as administrators and theorists in women's institutions of higher education. In such single-sex institutions the "natural" hierarchies of sexual difference were replaced by moral and intellectual hierarchy. Single-sex education did not efface adolescent sexual energies, however. Rather, it strove to sublimate that energy into reform and revivalistic fervor. These modifications of hierarchy and desire, combined with the secure economic basis afforded professional women as teachers and administrators, allowed educated women to argue from experience that families and occupations might be restructured. Invoking their intellectual and professional expertise they suggested that men need not leave home for higher education, since they could receive equivalent training from their mothers. Moreover, economically successful and morally upright women reformers argued that family need not follow the traditional heterosexual model but that same-sex couples could claim the social, economic, and moral respectability of heterosexual partnerships.

Women's control of institutions of higher education devoted to women was made inevitable by journalistic intervention. Chief among the magazines interested in women's education were those edited by Sarah Josepha

Hale. A self-taught woman who had briefly taught young children before she married, Hale determined that part of her journalistic calling was to promote the interests of formal higher education for women to her middle- and upper-class readers. Thus in both the *Ladies' Magazine* and later in *Godey's Ladies' Book*, Hale inaugurated and maintained a regular department entitled "The Ladies' Mentor" whose purpose was to "give reports of the present state of female education in Europe and America; Sketches of the most celebrated Female Seminaries in the United States; and notices of such literary works as are particularly designed for women, and peculiarly calculated to advance the improvement of our sex, by enlightening public opinion respecting the importance of female influence" (*Godey's* 14 [Jan. 1837]: 45). By comparing America with Europe, Hale could argue for hastened reform in the United States; by publicizing women's educational institutions, she indebted their administrators to her and expanded her base of subscribers; by promoting appropriate and select "literary works," she could surround her own opinions with sympathetic journalistic and public opinion. Her magazines thus assumed the responsibility of publicly monitoring all aspects of women's education.

Journalists who argued that women should be teachers and administrators of higher education followed two logics, one from sexual tension and one from economic necessity. The exigencies of boarding and teaching young women brought to the fore the sexual dynamics of pedagogy that had been naturalized in the processes of educating boys. These sexual energies stemmed from the practice of removing boys from their homes during their higher education. Since not every town had a preparatory school or academy, such young men lived in dormitories affiliated with or sponsored by their schools. Boarding in a dormitory was not, however, merely a matter of geographical necessity; it was also predicated on the assumption inherited from five centuries of pedagogy that boys would most effectively learn their lessons away from the emasculating sympathies of women (Ong). At prep school, and later at college, they were subjected to rigorous physical and mental discipline that included beatings, physical and psychic humiliation, excessive competition, and little or no emotional sustenance. Such emotional deprivation and physical abuse necessarily fueled a certain amount of rebellion, usually acted out in the privacy of the dormitories, where students would let off steam in pranks, horseplay, and sexual experimentation.

Such schools could not easily be made coeducational. Once young women began to leave home in pursuit of higher education, the ceding of that training to women was inevitable. It was unthinkable that young women would be removed from their families and put under the continual supervision of men who would administer physical discipline as a means of inducing mental rigor. It was equally unthinkable that a "softer" approach, one that substituted emotional discipline for physical, could be administered by men. The double bind presented by early experiments in coeducation became the matter for columns and essays that exposed both the sexual and economic implications of such educational ventures. Fern's "On Male School Teachers" omits such words as "sexual energy," yet demonstrates that a dangerous amount of it drives any encounter between a male teacher and a "frolicsome girl. . . . who *feels* her power without yet being old enough to understand it, and with an instinctive coquetry gets on his blind side, turning all his fore-ordained frowns into ill-suppressed smiles."

As Fern suggestively points out, sexual energy both drives and undermines pedagogical discipline. It is socially inappropriate, and even dangerously sexual, for a male teacher to think of "taming" feminine misbehaviors by resorting to physical discipline: "How can he box those little round ears? How can he disfigure those soft, white palms?" He may turn to gentler modes of discipline, but with little success. Fern continues in a more openly suggestive mode: "How can he—sending all the other pupils home—trust himself, after school, alone with those bright eyes, to put them through a subduing tear process?" Alternating the suggestive with the conventional, Fern suggests that these sentiments are based in her own experience with a " 'Reverend' gentleman, who once kept me after school for a reprimand, and spent the precious moments rolling my curls over [his] fingers, while my she-comrade was bursting off her hooks and eyes as she peeped through the key-hole." Again, the passage is suggestive in its innocent details—of curls, fingers, reprimand, bursting out of clothing, and key-hole peeping. A pious and socially entitled older man is unable to administer discipline, overcome by the girlish beauty before him. Meanwhile, the scene is observed by a feminine voyeur who is scandalized and/or titillated by what she sees. Retreating from this suggestive tone, Fern digresses into a page-long listing of more general educational abuses—too much work, inadequate ventilation—but concludes by returning to her original example: "Meantime our male teacher stands there, with his hands in his pockets, waiting to see what is to be done with *him*. Well, his pockets are the best place for his hands when he is keeping a girls' school, and with this advice I leave him" (*Ledger* 27 Nov. 1858). Fern's concluding allusion to hands in pockets is doubly suggestive of masturbatory and of economic gratification. Such connections were noted not only by the sometimes risqué Fern but by more conservative women journalists as well, in their investigation and promotion of women's education.

The apparently conservative Sarah Josepha Hale, for example, anticipated Fern's column on sexual tension by some twenty years. In 1837, Hale declared flatly that schooling that removed women from the bosoms of their families belonged to women alone. Affecting a reticence to mention anything to do with sex, Hale nevertheless announced to her readers: "We shall steadfastly insist on this point, (and we intend to carry it) that no *man* shall be permitted to name himself alone as responsible for the *education of young ladies at a boarding school!* It is a contumely to the delicacy, moral sentiment and mental ability of our sex" (*Godey's* 14 [May 1837]: 228). Hale's uncharacteristic vigor and elevated rhetoric of emphasis mark the degree to which the intimate proximities of women's boarding schools required the presence of women—at least as house mothers or chaperones—from their inception. Yet Hale also points out that women's functions often exceeded maternal supervision. Her critique exceeds mere Victorian prudery and insists that readers and parents alike recognize the economic implications of allowing men to monopolize this new and increasingly lucrative enterprise:

> If the *father's* influence is of such paramount importance in the training of a daughter that she must, when sent from home, for the completion of her education, be placed ostensibly under the care of a man, (we say *ostensibly,* for no man presumes to assert that he is the sole teacher of young ladies under his care—he keeps female assistants—but then *he* gains the *praises* and the *profits*) surely we may claim that the *mother's moral influence* being so indispensably necessary in the formation of the character of her sons, *women* should be employed as teachers in the Colleges for our young men. . . . In our opinion, no *man* can fulfil the delicate and responsible duty of training the young female mind and heart so well as an affectionate, sensible, intelligent, accomplished and pious woman can do. (*Godey's* 14 [Apr. 1837]: 185)

Hale's comments make clear that the training of women presumed affection. In turn, this allowed her to invoke arguments of respectability ("no man presumes to assert") as a means of exposing the economic consequences of leaving women's education to men ("he gains the . . . profits"). (For the logical extension of her argument—that women could teach college men— see below.) Thus, to assume that disciplinary intimacy was a pedagogical practice appropriate to women implied, as well, that women's schools must be led by women whose theoretical expertise and economic remuneration approximated or equaled that of their male counterparts.

At Hartford Female Seminary, disciplinary intimacy had the public effect of fueling Catharine Beecher's economic independence and professional status. Its less public effects can be measured only at an historical remove. For example, at the school, practices of affectional discipline sublimated sexual energy into revivalistic fervor; it did not, however, mitigate horseplay of adolescents. Unlike the random and sometimes violent misbehavior of their male counterparts, Hartford Female Seminary students' pranks often had overtones of feminine assertiveness, resistance, and critique, qualities engendered and perfected by details of the system of discipline Beecher had developed. Disciplinary intimacy may have produced compliant subjects, but these subjects were also individual, self-confident, logical, resistant (re)interpreters of the seminary's rules and regulations.

In founding Hartford Female Seminary, Beecher did not waste energy arguing that women should teach and administer such enterprises. She simply assumed the right. Although the Seminary's catalogs list male trustees, the principals and teachers are almost exclusively women, a staffing arrangement that suggests that from the beginning Beecher had presumed that affectional discipline would prevail. The unique benefits of this system were summarized in an October 1823 address by Catharine Beecher to the seminary's first class. She lists the progress the students have made in the first six months of their studies, then turns her attention to the "entire harmony of feeling which has subsisted in the school the season past." Complimenting her students on their "politeness & attention to our requirements," she asserts that "what might have been a source of care & anxiety, has proved to us a labour of love, prompted not merely by a sense of duty, but by the affectionate interest we have felt for every individual committed to our care." She continues, "It has also been pleasant to observe that there has been nothing like rivalry or ill will among you, but always apparently a spirit of kindness & good will & the manners & conduct becoming young ladies; & often I have realized when surrounded by you all, 'how good & how pleasant it is to dwell together in love' " (18 Oct. 1823; "An Address Written for the Young Ladies of Miss Beecher's School," Beecher-Stowe Collection, Schlesinger).[2] The principles Beecher enumerates here—of individual attention, (apparent) absence of rivalry, and the sense of a community of women disciplined by love and dwelling together in affection—mark the regime of disciplinary intimacy at Hartford Female Seminary.

The seminary's growth determined the relative speed with which such reform proceeded. Until boarding facilities could be financed and built, students lived with local families, who were responsible for their supervision and who became de facto supporters of Beecher's reforms. As she multiplied the number of her associates and students and as she perfected her notion of the division of academic and supervisory labors, Beecher also replaced the corporal discipline that obtained in Hartford's brother institutions with an elaborate system of monitorial reporting and self-surveillance, giving students the primary responsibility for their personal and group discipline. Additionally, and as part of the same shift in emphasis, she abolished the practices of competition and emulation that characterized men's education in favor of an ethic of affection that sought to balance individual development with community responsibility. But in other ways, girls' schools persistently resembled boys'—as they naturally would in the artificial situation of bringing so many adolescents together in one place— including a more pointed and intentional pranksterism and a continuation of sexual experimentation, in this case fueled by practices of disciplinary intimacy and sanctioned by a rhetoric of religious fervor.

From the beginning, Catharine Beecher's version of disciplinary intimacy was modeled on the corporate family in which she had been raised. Like Lyman Beecher's loosely amalgamated household of father, mother, children, servants, boarding students, itinerant clergy, and visiting relatives, Hartford Female Seminary included administrators, teachers, students from across the nation, servants, and townspeople that Beecher assumed— indeed, encouraged—to consider as mutually bound by familial affection and obligation. However, Hartford Female Seminary was primarily a family of women wherein Catharine Beecher occupied the father's position as the school's master theorist and chief administrator. Because the seminary was a private and not state-sponsored school, she had little accountability to agencies external to the school. The male trustees to whom she reported were fathers of her students whose major responsibility was to provide funding but who had little say over the curriculum or the theoretical direction of the school.

Beecher's family model was related directly to the exigencies of boarding and teaching young women in a regime of affectional discipline. In the seminary's early years, its students lived with local families because no boarding facilities were available. Rather than cede authority to the families with whom students boarded, however, Beecher effected an institutional

supervision that extended the school's authority into the privacy of patriarchal families. According to Beecher, "the pupils [who came to Hartford]
from abroad, numbering 120 to 160, were distributed into such private
families as would co-operate in promoting a healthful moral influence, and,
in most cases, with a teacher in the same family. . . . Ladies of high position,
culture, and religious principle . . . were happy to aid in this good work by
receiving a teacher, and from four to ten scholars as boarders, and . . . proved
invaluable helpers in all efforts for the good of the school" (*Educational
Reminiscences* 46). Significantly, Beecher extends credit for the success of this
arrangement only to the "ladies of high position" who opened their homes
to teachers and students, suggesting that their gentleman counterparts had
no part in the "moral influence" exerted upon these young women.

Under this arrangement, the definitions of appropriately "moral"
behavior remained under control of the school, as represented by the
personalized—if delegated—authority of teachers who boarded with the
pupils. Community leaders became, in their turn, co-constructors of a
"healthful moral" environment for students and, by extension, implicitly
approved Beecher's entire educational enterprise. Such arrangements, according to Beecher, corrected the "defects" of "those large establishments in
our country called *boarding schools,*" wherein "a large number of youth, of
all ages, characters and habits" are collected together "in one promiscuous
family, associated in an unrestrained manner, at school, in the chamber, at
table, and in hours of amusement" (*Suggestions* 55). Thus Beecher's practice
of out-boarding professionalized the institutional structure of women's
education, the families with which students boarded, and the abstract
concept of family that Hartford Female Seminary pretended to approximate.
Students were brought under the control of a family regime by the logic of
divide-and-conquer under the constant supervision of patriarchal families
who resembled their own but who, at the same time, were accountable to
Hartford Female Seminary.

Even later, as the growth in the school's enrollment forced her to
consider making Hartford Female Seminary a boarding school, Beecher
sought to avoid the abuses of conventional room and board arrangements,
wherein "influence" might be passed in an unrestrained manner upon "pliant
childhood and youth," stipulating that no more than two pupils share a
room and that at all social interactions teachers be present. Thus Beecher
proposes both to maintain the configuration of "family" and the discipline
of affection and hierarchy encoded therein and to professionalize the family's

function of character formation: "Let us suppose an institution where the pupils are all members of the same family, and in this establishment one teacher of suitable qualifications devoted to the formation and regulation of the moral character and the social feelings. . . . Let her come to them with all the authority of a teacher, the affability of a companion, and the affection of a friend, and what might she not accomplish in correcting bad habits and forming good ones?" (*Suggestions* 46). This professionalized family is ultimately superior to the heterosexual families with whom students had formerly boarded because it combines the affection presumed natural to family interactions with detached professional supervision. This family is a precursor to an ideal that Beecher would attempt to achieve in various ways for the rest of her career—a community of women in a moral hierarchy, headed by trained, professional, single women. Beecher is straightforward about the disciplinary advantages such an arrangement has over traditional family-centered education: "And what peculiar advantages teachers enjoy, who, unbiased by the partialities of parental fondness, can observe their charge when thrown into collision with all the various characters that meet in the school-room and play-ground, where often are developed peculiarities of character and temper, that escape parental notice and care" ("Essay on the Education" 11).

Such a system was not monolithic, however. Within the close supervision assumed by teachers and administrators, students were significantly involved both in monitoring their own adherence to the rules of the school—by interpreting them, by presenting themselves in their own terms and in advancing their own interpretations of the rules—and even in critiquing the administration's own compliance with those rules. A comparison of the 1828 and the 1831 catalogs of the seminary demonstrates both the rigidity and the fluidity of such a system. In 1828, Beecher had assigned individual teachers to document student infractions in a "school journal," which they met twice weekly to collate. By 1831, the system had changed to a more private, but probably more effective, system of notes and self-reporting that centered around a daily assembly in which "the school journal is read aloud, in which is recorded an account of the behaviour and recitation of the several classes during the preceding day. The *cases* are stated of those who are faulty in each class, but the *names* are omitted." After this public reading, the assembled scholars were "requested to forward to the Governess, on slips of paper, an account of all the rules they have violated since the preceding morning, which are to be recorded by the Governess." Then, after all students had stood, those "who can recollect that they have violated no rule, are requested to sit. This gives an opportunity for the teachers and scholars to notice those who remain standing, and thus learn whether all have recollected the rules they have been observed by others to neglect" (12–13).

Such details demonstrate that Beecher's version of disciplinary intimacy "require[d] authority to put on a human face," a process that, according to Richard Brodhead, characterized a particularly American incarnation of discipline ("Sparing" 19). At Hartford Female Seminary, however, both agents and objects of discipline assumed an individual and feminine face. While such procedures as the oral confessional implied by the ritual of reading aloud from school journals may reinvoke the Foucauldian panopticon, they also afforded to women for whom self-effacement had been deemed essential a new opportunity for self-fashioning. Women who had perhaps never before represented themselves in writing now were asked to document their own behavior, recounting private and heretofore unnoticed details, particular combinations of weakness and strengths that, when narrated, produced the effect of moral development and a unique personality measured against criteria understood to comprise ideal womanly intellectual and behavioral ideals.

These disciplinary arrangements call forth the individual from the group. Beecher herself put it most effectively to the trustees of the seminary when she presented the details of this boarding arrangement with its close personal supervision to the trustees: "There are few, except those who have tried some experiment on the subject, who can realize how much can be done to *form a conscience* and to regulate the conduct by its dictates, even before religion regulates the soul" (*Suggestions* 47). Catharine Beecher, whose own Calvinist upbringing depended so much on the presumption of conscience, does not classify conscience as a "natural" part of individual personality, but asserts, rather, that it can be formed—manufactured— through the close supervision and affectionate monitoring of teachers who had the specific charge to measure their students' behavior at all times and under all circumstances.

While the disciplinary tone of Hartford Female Seminary was thus quite different from that of its masculine counterparts, its regime of disciplinary intimacy seems to have retained, duplicated, and/or intensified other behaviors that characterized boys' schools—pranksterism, same-sex affectional alliances, and hierarchical divisions and administration. Student reminiscences of Hartford Female Seminary, combined with the biography of its most famous alumna, Fanny Fern, suggests that even the constant supervision of disciplinary intimacy did not always produce compliant and self-disciplined subjects. Rather, it may have taught women to effect ambiguous behaviors—at once appeasing teachers and administrators with womanly regret at not having behaved appropriately, at the same time participating in typical adolescent rowdiness, and even mounting significant critiques of the institution that housed them. Sarah Willis's accounts of residence at Hartford Female Seminary, not surprisingly, emphasize nurture, both psychic and physical, in school contexts. Willis was the apparent perpetrator of a number of student pranks around stealing food as a way of protesting the principal's rather draconian economies and experiments with Graham diets (E. Parton, "Fanny Fern"). Ethel Parton recounts an episode in which Willis supposedly ended the housekeeper's practice of giving students food of a lesser quality by exchanging the students' butter plate with Beecher's. When Beecher complained that the butter was "not the same as usual; there was something the matter with it," Fern immediately exchanged the dishes, explaining "it is just as usual, only there has been a mistake; we have your dish, and you have ours" (96). Since Willis could not possibly have been accused of inciting rebellion, nor of being openly confrontational, this episode effectively demonstrates that even under the constant supervision of disciplinary intimacy, its subjects have power to use its devices to further their own ends. Disciplinary mutuality and supervision were open to discussion and critique by students who became skilled in imitating and deploying its forms of morality.

Beecher's plans balanced the individualism produced by these systems of self-reporting and monitoring with a compensatory strategy whereby communal feelings would be built, but that was consistent with her philosophy of affectional discipline and moral development. When the seminary began, Beecher used a version of the system of emulation and competition employed in traditional boys' schools. The 1828 catalogue, for example, announces that "at the close of the term, those who in the estimation of the Teachers, are *in all respects* the best scholars, will receive the *First Honour* of the Seminary [and] Those who are *improved* the most, will receive the *Second Honour,* and other prizes may be given according to the discretion of the teachers" (13). By 1831, on the other hand, the catalog announced that although the closing examinations of the school are still open to "parents and friends of the teachers and pupils," the practice of a public "*Exhibition*" had been "dispensed with," as had "the principles of competition and emulation." It then elaborated on the differences this change in policy has engendered. "No prizes are given; no reward is offered for any degree of *comparative* merit; no emulation has existed in any department of the school; and yet it never was so orderly, so regular, so faithful in the discharge of every duty. The Principal can testify, that it is much easier to govern a school of one hundred and fifty without emulation and competition, than it ever was, by their aid, to control one of twenty or thirty" (20).

The pedagogical change here is analogous to that effected in the school's boarding arrangements—no longer is disciplinary power demonstrated through public display; discipline has become internalized. No longer could one be sure that the "best" students of the seminary were those who were reading publicly or those who received certificates. Rather, success came to consist in producing private behaviors that met the approval of the supervisors. The principles that Beecher listed as having replaced the disciplinary function once occupied by emulation and competition were the "*personal influence of the teachers*," the "co-operation and assistance of the *pupils* who are most matured" in aiding the teachers; "*constant faithfulness* in observing every dereliction from duty," and the "*correct tone of moral sentiment*" that "[pervaded] the whole school" (20–22). While it may be easy enough to imagine abolishing emulation and competition in coed schools, it is more difficult to imagine how principles of personal influence, constant observation, and moral tone could have existed in women's schools headed and taught by men. Furthermore, it is virtually certain that such constant and intimate supervision produced the occasion for heightened same-sex affectional episodes. In a situation apart from family, and fueled by the heightened passions associated with revivalism (a project that Beecher inaugurated beginning in 1826 as yet another way of proving herself the ecclesiastical equal of her brothers and father), it is likely that Hartford Female Seminary students engaged in what has been termed "smashes" with each other and in crushes on older teachers.

These homosocial affections flourished in the feminine families in which Hartford Female Seminary students lived; they were furthered by the emotional intensity of Beecher's revivals. Sheaves of affectionate and monitorial notes, passed among students, teachers, and even the principal hint at the aroused state of the young ladies. Sarah Terry, a Hartford student in the late 1820s, received dozens of notes from friends, student-teachers (including Harriet Beecher), and from Catharine Beecher herself, pleading, exhorting, even demanding that she measure her progress toward salvation and report that progress in writing to each concerned and loving friend. Finally, Sarah capitulated, writing "I am placed in a *very* responsible position—for the children all look to me. I . . . *resolve* to read a portion of Gods [sic] word every day & to take the portion I read for meditation thro [sic] the day" (Day Collection, Stowe-Day). The terms of her response demonstrate the very combination of individual sensibility and community responsibility that Beecher sought to foster.

Terry's cousin Ann replied to this declaration in a note that measures the intensity of emotion this sort of monitoring might produce and sustain:

> Dearest Sarah—My feelings when you told me of the change which you hoped you had experienced, are indescribable [sic]—I have lately felt as though I could not smile or appear with usual cheerfulness, my anxiety for you has been so very great—I think I have *wrestled* for you at the throne of grace, and I can assert that I am not the *only one* who has thus felt for you—My dear S—I know your feelings by *experience*— Yes—I know your *hopes* and I know your *fears*—Do confide *all* to me—and be assured that in me you have a friend who can *rejoice* with you in your *joys* and *weep* with you in your *sorrows*—I have passed through it all—and if we are in truth Christians I feel as if we had been converted in a very similar manner—If, my beloved friend, you have *in truth* been enabled to give yourself to *God,* you have *reason* to *rejoice*— . . . Again I ask you to confide *every* feeling in me—Yours with *increased* affection Ann. (Day Collection, Stowe-Day)

In the nineteenth century, such emotional intensity would surely have been unthinkable in a coeducational residential and educational situation, although it was deemed appropriate in a women's seminary in the throes of religious revival that was aided by disciplinary procedures that presumed intimate interpersonal supervision.

It is possible that Beecher herself was not aware of the erotic overtones of such intense relations, for she recalls in a later book, written more than twenty years after she left Hartford Female Seminary, that even as the headmistress of a boarding school she had not realized the potential for sexual experimentation such situations presented. According to her recollections, "In the early part of my experience as the principal of a large boarding-school, I had an English work put into my hands containing warnings in regard to certain dangerous practices, especially at boarding-schools, which are indicated in Mrs. Gleason's article. The whole thing was perfectly unintelligible, and when I went to several of my matron friends for information, I could not find any one that had ever heard of such a thing" (*Health* 158). In the present day, by contrast, according to Beecher, "such ignorance as this can . . . rarely be found. . . . On the contrary, the children at this day, to a wide extent, know far more than the parents ever learned in a former generation through their whole lives" (159). In case, however, that parents still have not apprehended her intent, she reproduces in the Notes the "Communication from Mrs. Dr. R. B. Gleason" "of the Elmira Water Cure, . . . a regularly educated physician, [who] has practiced, in connection with her husband, for ten years, confining her attention chiefly to patients of her own sex" (*Health* Note I, 1*). Here Mrs. Gleason gives several paragraphs of attention to "Peculiar Instruction needed by young Children" and gathered not from her own practice but from "my husband, from other physicians, from teachers, from medical writers, and from the reports of insane hospitals" (12*). According to Gleason, "a secret vice is becoming frequent among children of both sexes, that is taught by servants and communicated by children at school." This "vice," she names only as "any fingering of the parts." (12*–13*). She concludes this section with the example of "a little boy . . . of very delicate mind and susceptible temperament, [who] was sent to the country to a private boarding-school" who learned the vice from other students who had "threatened to kill him if he ever told any one." Gleason cautions, "Parents whose young sons are at boarding-schools *can not* be too much alarmed on this subject" (14*).

Gender plays a part in classifying which boarding-school behaviors count as "vice." Gleason assumes masturbation to be a vice common to boys' schools; Beecher extends her observations to remark that she had never been aware of such practices among her family of young women. Yet the passions and friendships that were formed in the context of this school/home led Hartford Female Seminary students to conclude that heterosexual marriage offered only a limited venue for erotic, emotional, and professional fulfillment for adult women. These conclusions could only have been reinforced by Beecher's increasingly well-articulated proposals for the reorganization of patriarchal institutions—family chief among them— in a broader, community sphere. Beecher's proposals for woman-centered families justified homosocial affiliations among women, whether in the guise of single-sex educational institutions modeled on Catholic nunneries ("Something") or in the increase in the number of women who did not marry and/or who may have taken female partners. The details of these effects form the subject matter of the concluding chapter, "Domesticity with a Difference."

As important, such dissociation of women from the imperatives of heterosocial marriage made possible their entry into a number of professional venues where they could claim effectiveness (if not salaries) equal to men's. Elizabeth Blackwell, for example, may have been spurred in her decision to enter medical school by her acquaintance with the Beecher sisters in Cincinnati. Beecher herself traces the success of the women she trained as teachers for the West. Such women frequently appropriated to themselves functions generally attributed to men, finding themselves "in the office of teacher and clergyman" (*Duty* 129). Trained in a school where these offices were combined with that of parent in the person of a single woman, and following that example, these frontier teachers apparently performed remarkable feats. Of one such teacher Beecher writes, "Her instructions in the day-school and in the Sunday-school, and her influence in the families, were unbounded, and almost transforming. *No minister, however well qualified, could have wrought such favourable changes in so short a time*" (*Duty* 129; emphasis added). Whether this be the literal truth, it is worth pointing out that although Beecher did not support suffrage as the means by which women might gain political/economic sufficiency, she nevertheless was centrally involved in proving their fitness to effect social change as well as men did.

The extent of the incursions made by educated women into traditionally patriarchal domains of education, family, and professions, is well illustrated by Fuller's presence in Harvard's library and by Beecher's study and residence at Cornell. Yet their acts were those of private individuals who, as single women, had begun to establish reputations as writers and educational reformers. Nor were they extensively publicized at the time they happened. Their acts did not immediately or significantly alter policies or curricula to accommodate women generally. It remains, therefore, to account for the broader effects of affectional discipline, professionalization of education, and the model of strong women mentors on women students and on the elite institutions of higher education. These included the well-documented reforms of the last half of the nineteenth century: coeducational admissions, a liberalized English-based curriculum, and an emphasis on practicality, including more homely topics for writing. Journalism sped these changes both by informing the broad population of the new trends and by advocating continued, speedy, and sometimes radical changes in men's institutions of higher learning. Not only did those processes result in institutional reform, but to a limited extent they also claimed for women who did enter heterosexual alliances a professional recognition and respect as educators of their children (sons and daughters alike) within the family circle.

Some twenty years after her initial pronouncement (which seems to have been advanced primarily for its rhetorical effect) that if men were an indispensable influence in women's colleges, women should be equally central to the administration and teaching efforts of men's schools, Sarah Hale followed through on the logic. The intervening years of steady progress and incursion of women into fields heretofore seen as men's, including teaching, educational administration, curricular reform, and even the most sacred functions of revivalism and ministry, all done under the guise of womanly and affectional discipline, had made her initial argument less ridiculous. Thus, after chronicling nearly a quarter-century of such changes, in 1853 Hale announced that it was time men ceased leaving home to go to college. Crowded college dormitories lacked a softening feminine influence, warns Hale, subjecting young men to " 'evil communications' which the influence of one depraved heart or character will spread through such a community. At a time, too, when the influence of example is most deep and lasting. . . . It is a mother's place to watch over the development of her son's temperament and the natural bent of his mind, as well as the heart. . . . Gentlemen, and even elegant scholars can be found who boast no *alma mater* save the affectionate care and judicious training of the home circle in their boyhood, and every year blots out the old prejudice for that genteel necessity, 'a college education' " (47 [Dec.]: 567).

Hale's account summarizes the logical outcomes of affectional disciplinary arrangements. Her first line of attack is to emphasize the dangerous sexual tension that arises in the absence of "female influence." Whether the "evil communications" Hale alludes to are simply Beecher's "fingering of parts" or more blatant homoerotic experimentation, Hale is sure that a mother's "influence" will curb such behaviors. More significantly, Hale implicitly argues that if a young man is kept in women's company, whether of a mother or other young women of his age, his heterosexual orientation will be assured.

Hale's second line of defense is to argue that the Latin-based classical education of the early century has been outdated and does not prepare a young man to enter any number of new professions—as a businessman, for example, or an engineer, agriculturalist, or journalist. This kind of advanced training, she argued, a young man could acquire while remaining at home with his mother. If Hale's proposal were taken to heart, a significant realignment of class would result: the privileges of elite education would be tamed, since even well educated but not economically entitled women could now teach their sons at home; this expanded and homogenized upper class would thus be even more distinguishable from lower classes who could not provide these signifiers to their children.

What Hale does not point out but what is inevitably and safely implied is that such modified educational arrangements would also eliminate the persistently antiwoman bias encoded in single-sex masculine education, bringing sons back under the sphere of their mothers' influence, expanding the bond that would unite father and sons who had enjoyed the same prep school experience to include the mother and perhaps sisters trained under the affectional discipline of women's colleges. Thus the designation *alma mater* would ultimately belong to the literal mother.

By 1874, Hale had overtly proclaimed the demise of traditional university education. Significantly, that end was effected by women. In 1866 she had noted the opening of the Syndicate of Cambridge University examination to young British women. Eight years later she noted American plans to adopt the Cambridge system. Not unexpectedly, she claimed that American women would perform as creditably as their British counterparts in the examinations, pointed to the advantage afforded women who could combine home study with public university certification, and even predicted that women who earned the Cambridge certification would be better able to find good employment. She commiserated with young men that they could not enjoy the same advantages: "It is doubted by many whether the present collegiate system is one which should be encouraged either for young men or young women. . . . a system of education which withdraws young people from home at the most impressionable age and confines them for three or four years chiefly in the companionship of persons of their own age, is contrary to the social laws designed by nature for their benefit, and cannot be conducive to their moral improvement or future well-doing. Our colleges . . . are modelled upon the monastic institutions of the middle ages—are, like them, temporary in their nature—and are likely to be swept away, like them, by the advance of society" (88 [Apr.]: 378). Of course, men did not cease going to college. But the advances made by women in the educational professions and the increasingly common structures of familial and affectionate discipline made such a proposal feasible enough for Hale to propound it as a reasonable alternative.

Thus by adapting and modifying the hierarchies of traditional patriarchal family structure to the institutional goals of women's education, Beecher and others who educated young women both ensured the success of these institutions and laid a foundation for later and more radical redefinitions of patriarchal family structure and for women's incursions into more traditionally masculine bastions of elite culture. This inevitability of women teachers and administrators was proclaimed from the very beginnings of women's education in surprisingly direct terms both by those who were carefully conservative and by those who were more fearlessly forward. Because these arguments were promulgated under the metaphor of family nurturance, it effected not only a revision of education of men and women but also new models for family relationships.

Chapter Nine

DOMESTICITY WITH
A DIFFERENCE

The most important implications of the domesticity prescribed by Beecher, Hale, Fuller and Fern are contained in their texts that critique the economic and legal inequities of traditional heterosexual marriage and family organization. Their revisions of heterosexual domesticity addressed the concerns of women in an era marked by high death rates and volatile economic circumstances, when a white, middle-class woman's conformity to the patterns of normative domesticity might be interrupted at any time by widowhood and/or economic disaster. As hedges against these possibilities, each of these writers explored domestic and affectional configurations that would accommodate women like themselves—upper-middle-class, self-sufficient, and excessive "women of genius" who did not marry, as well as those who were widowed or divorced. The alternate domestic arrangements they proposed echoed dominant patterns of domesticity, while offering the women who entered them respectability equal to that of their middle-class sisters and the emotional sustenance that was ideal but often in fact missing from heterosexual marriage. At the same time these arrangements would protect a single woman's rights of self-determination and financial independence.

These writers learned early that intellectual feminine subjectivity might be nurtured outside patriarchal families by women who were neither married nor "natural" mothers. And as adults who reached their majority in an era marked by utopian experiments with family structures, they made significant personal experiments with alternate affectional and family structures, either choosing emotional relationships with other women, or significantly modifying traditional expectations of marriage. These affiliations were not, however, merely the result of private circumstance; rather, they were theoretically based actions that became the basis for written public critiques[1] that were read, noted, commented upon, and critiqued by their contemporaries. But subsequent scholarly paradigms and practices have occluded these important and sometimes radical acts: a paradigm of "separate spheres," for example, had no room for revisions of heterosexual households; studies that have noted their alternative affectional arrangements have not understood those acts to have been a systematic political challenge; and studies of organized reformist efforts have overlooked the cumulative effect of writings by individual women unaffiliated with such groups.

Whether Beecher or Fuller—or any of these writers—were lesbian in the physical, contemporary, sexual sense of the term[2] is less important to the argument of this chapter than the way the writers themselves understood their same-sex affectional relationships and how they used these relationships as the basis for social critique. To date, these passionate attachments have been read as examples of sororal bonding or as a prelude to "normal" heterosexual unions. It is crucial, however, not to naturalize these alliances under a developmental hypothesis, presuming that heterosexuality is the normal goal of affectional and erotic development. Nor should they be read as the inevitable result of a society divided into "separate spheres." To read them as a phenomenon of a women's world does not adequately describe the political valence these relationships had in the lives of these women and many others like them. Neither explanation considers the very important understandings that heterosexual "development" is imbricated in an economic system of unequal political and economic power and that a questioning of normative binary heterosexuality, either transient or permanent, should be considered a political as well as a personal resistance.

Both Catherine Beecher and Margaret Fuller, women whose later lives followed divergent paths, recall similar childhood experiences in which older women who were not members of the immediate family led them to understand that a woman might combine the intellectual acuity commonly attributed to men with the emotional understanding they desired from their mothers. As adolescents they continued to form emotionally intense relations with other women, interpreting these relations as the equal of any they might form with men. For example, during her engagement to Alexander Fisher, Catharine Beecher wrote her friend Louisa Wait regarding a third, mutual friend, also about to be engaged, "I believe if there is any such thing as one womans [sic] *falling in love* with another that I was *in love* with Matilda—She is a sweet dear girl & will ever seem *dear* to

me as a sister." Later in the same letter Beecher enjoins Wait to "write
me particularly about Loring & Matilda-I believe they are made for each
other & will come together at last" (25 Mar. 1822, Beecher-Stowe Collection,
Schlesinger). This letter apparently supports a developmental thesis, since at
this point, despite their close attachment, Beecher seemed destined to marry
Alexander Fisher and Lucretia Matilda Moore to marry Loring Hubbell.[3]
Yet after Fisher's death, and for the rest of her life, Beecher consistently chose
to form affectional ties with women. Her choices do not suggest that those
relationships were a compensation for failure to marry; rather they seemed
to be experiments in forming same-sex alliances that were equivalent to
heterosexual marriage.

The friendship between Catharine Beecher and Matilda Moore was
enabled and nurtured by their association with Miss Sarah Pierce's Litchfield
Female Academy. Moore boarded with the Beecher family while attending
the academy in 1819 and 1820. The intensity of their friendship is typical of
the alliances that women formed in such schools and suggests that parental
attempts to correct deficiencies in socialization by sending their daughters to
female academies for "finishing" were in some cases undermined by those
same institutions. Boarding school did little to dampen the intellectual
ardor of its women students, nor did it mitigate their attraction to women
who embodied both intellect and affection. In fact, the very structures and
procedures of these schools reinforced the idea that the unique combination
of these qualities existed most comfortably outside heterosexual families.
Beecher wrote retrospectively that she had "had occasion to observe frequently . . . the power which a teacher, even of the same sex, may exert on
the affections and susceptibilities of pupils, so that in some cases they may
become morbid and excessive. There is a period when the young, especially if
highly gifted, find an outbursting of sensibilities that they have not learned to
control" (*Health* 160). Although this passage most clearly refers to Beecher's
Hartford Female Seminary, it is also likely that her early friendships, such as
the attachment to Matilda, gave this observation a more personal inflection.
Aware from her own early experiences of the extraordinary emotional energy
present in boarding school situations, Beecher had, in fact, designed the
disciplinary codes of Hartford Female Seminary to take advantage of the
lines of power as well as of affection between teachers and students and
among students.

The heightened sensibilities present in single-sex educational institutions were familiar to Margaret Fuller as well, who had been sent at age

fourteen to Miss Susan Prescott's Young Ladies' Seminary. Her parents hoped that this institution would correct what they saw as their daughter's inappropriate social forwardness and lack of interest in proper womanly pursuits, both the result of her intense childhood devotion to study. Fuller's short roman à clef "Mariana" is based on an emotional crisis that occurred while she attended the school. The narrator of this sketch tells of her attraction to the title character, an emotional relationship that has its roots in the intellectual/erotic pleasures of reading. The narrator attributes this attraction to her "sentimental" childhood when, because of "early ill health, [she] had been indulged in reading novels. . . . The heroine of one of these, 'The Bandit's Bride,' [she] immediately saw in Mariana." Like the Bandit's Bride, Mariana is "born to be 'misunderstood' by all but her lover." Nevertheless, the narrator determines that "until [Mariana's] lover appeared, [she her]self would be the wise and delicate being who could understand her" (*Summer on the Lakes* 88). The narrator tells of fetching Mariana's handkerchiefs, turning the pages of her piano music, sitting close to her, and offering her bouquets of wildflowers (88–89), ritual behaviors that scholars such as Vicinus have since established as formulaic elements of boarding-school "smashes." When these actions fail, the narrator takes more drastic action: "One day meeting her alone in the entry, I fell upon my knees, and kissing her hand, cried, 'O Mariana, do let me love you, and try to love me a little.' But my idol snatched away her hand, and laughing . . . ran into her room" (89). The boarding school section of this sketch concludes with Mariana's humiliation at the hands of her schoolmates for her indulgence in "calumny and falsehood" (89); her illness and restoration at the hands of an older teacher who "had never well understood her before, but had always looked on her with great tenderness" (91); and her reacceptance by classmates who "not only forgave her, but . . . vied with one another in offices of humble love to the humbled one" (92).

This tale is an excellent demonstration of the intense affections such single-sex living arrangements engendered. As did Beecher's Hartford Female Seminary, Miss Susan Prescott's school fostered emotional alliances among students and between students and teachers. The teacher figure in this sketch is generally thought to be Susan Prescott herself, of whom Fuller wrote "Miss Prescott has honored me by allowing me to call myself her adopted daughter" (*Letters* 1:146). The intensity of this teacher-student alliance is best demonstrated, however, by the fact that some ten years later Fuller wrote Prescott, perhaps of an incident similar to that narrated in

"Mariana," "Your image shines as fair to my mind's eye as it did in 1825, when I left you with my heart overflowing with gratitude for your singular and judicious tenderness. Can I ever forget that to your treatment in that crisis of youth I owe the true life,—the love of Truth and Honor?" (*Letters* 1:160).

During her late teen years Fuller became the center of a large circle of friends in Cambridge. She attended parties and dances, engaged in flirtations, and fell in love with her cousin George Davis, a law student, and his close friend, James Freeman Clarke, both of whom appreciated her intellect but did not reciprocate her more romantic advances. Indeed, young men seemed confused by her intellectual intensity. They persisted in seeing her as a platonic friend but did not pursue sustained romantic alliances with her. At the same time she displayed such a talent for nurturing women's friendships that Emerson would later coyly write in the *Memoirs* that "it is certain that Margaret, though unattractive in person, . . . with her burly masculine existence, quite reduced [the 'girls' with whom she was friends] to satellites, yet inspired an enthusiastic attachment. I hear from one witness, as early as 1829, that 'all the girls raved about Margaret Fuller' " (1:280).

Even as she exchanged intellectual confidences with Clarke, Channing, and Davis, Fuller had initiated a relationship with Anna Barker, probably her most intimate woman friend. Of Barker, Fuller later wrote, "It is so true that a woman may be in love with a woman, and a man with a man. . . . It is regulated by the same laws as that of love between persons of different sexes, only it is purely intellectual and spiritual, unprofaned by any mixture of lower instincts, undisturbed by any need of consulting temporal interests" (Chevigny, rev. ed. 112–13). Although this passage seems to deny the physical basis for such friendship, in the second phrase Fuller directly asserts that emotional bonds between women may allow them to escape "temporal interests." In this case it seems clear that those "temporal interests" were courtship and marriage, for it was also at this time that Fuller first confronted the possibility that she might not find a man who could accept having such an intellectual paragon as a wife. For Fuller, as for Beecher, earlier womanly attachments offered a pattern for a life that would not follow the traditional patterns of marriage and childrearing.

Beecher and Fuller, Hale and Fern solved the twin problems of emotional and economic support by drawing on their earlier experiences as the models for new personal arrangements that apparently conformed to normal domestic expectations: marriage as a young woman to a man older and better educated and who was to be the sole means of economic support;

reproducing and raising the children produced by that union; living in a suburban nuclear family; and, in the case of a spouse's death, remarrying after a decent interval of mourning. Their solutions, however, may also be read as italicizations, or parodies,4 whose intensity or variation exposed the limits of what passed for normal domestic arrangements. They were not merely contingent, personal, and individual choices, but reasoned experiments that each woman wrote about publicly.

In 1822, Catharine Beecher had become engaged to marry Alexander Fisher, a Yale-educated scholar, after his return from a year of study in Europe. Her hopes were dashed, however, by his accidental drowning. Fisher's death precipitated a complex emotional crisis in Beecher, since her father chose this occasion to force her to profess Calvinist conversion. Aware that Fisher had died unregenerate, and pressured by her father to avoid a similar fate, Beecher discovered that theological rigor did nothing to assuage emotional pain. Further, she realized that if she did not marry she must either remain financially dependent on her father and siblings or provide her own sustenance. As she helped set Fisher's papers in order, she discovered that his education had far better prepared him to be self-supporting than had hers. The mourning, the moral questioning attendant on Fisher's death, and the realization of her inferior intellectual preparation made Beecher intensely aware of the inadequacies of patriarchal systems of theology, economics, and education. She devoted the rest of her life to finding remedies for these shortcomings that would allow women to work productively and live independently of men if they wished.

On a visit to Boston the year following Fisher's death, Beecher sought solace from a cousin, Julia Porter. This relationship was an early incident in what was to become a series of experiments in how couples or groups of women might claim the emotional and economic privileges of married life. In all these relations, Beecher took the position of the intellectually and physically superior partner, forming alliances with younger unmarried women, frequently of lower social status and/or suffering from physical disabilities, rationalizing the intensity of the mutual attraction as a form of feminine "duty," either of nurture, rehabilitation, or education. In 1823 Beecher nursed Porter through an extended illness, writing her brother Edward that she planned to linger in Boston until Porter recovered because "it seems my duty to be with her." Of this constant companion, Beecher wrote, "She is a very interesting girl . . . I don't know where I have ever come in contact with one more congenial in habits, tastes and feelings. . . .

The more I become acquainted with her, the more I esteem and love her"
(22 Oct. 1822; Beecher-Stowe Collection, Schlesinger). Beecher's friendship
with Porter, combined with the physical distance from her father, offered
her a refuge from Lyman's probing of her spiritual state.

After she recovered from her bereavement, however, Beecher did not
abandon her preference for friendships with women. Instead, she increasingly explored ways in which women might form alliances that would
offer them emotional and affectional support, respect for their intellectual
capacity, and economic stability—while securing their respectability outside
the institution of marriage.[5] Although the family metaphor that structured
Hartford Female Seminary may initially have been intended to secure its respectability as a boarding school, Beecher eventually italicized the metaphor,
replicating within this womanly community the hierarchies of intellect and
power that had prevailed in her own family and that characterized the leading
men's educational institutions. Here Beecher was able to experiment with
planning a community wherein feminine friendship would supplement the
mere rule of law but that aspired to claim the intellectual respectability
associated with "the division of labor and responsibility peculiar to our college system" (*Educational Reminiscences* 34). A regular curriculum, Beecher
hoped, would also ensure financial stability. As the theoretician of these
structures, Beecher thus assumed a position analogous to that of patriarchs
within nuclear families, to clergymen, and to college presidents.

In her personal life, as well, Beecher found a balance between apparent capitulation to womanly norms and groundbreaking freedoms for
single women. She pursued several emotional/intellectual relationships with
younger women, establishing them as her companions or secretaries. On
their surface these arrangements appeared to be quite conventional arrangements of apprenticeship, charity, mentorship, or womanly companionship
that characterized the normal behavior of unmarried women who had the
financial ability to live independently. However, they may also be read
as a series of intentional choices, in which physical mobility and public
activism emphasize the immobility and intellectual deference expected of
conventionally married women. In the mid-1840s, for example, Beecher
undertook a sustained relationship with Nancy Johnson, who served as
her private secretary and traveling companion. Johnson's correspondence
suggests the attitude the two shared during their travels in the Mississippi
River Valley. To her sisters, she wrote: "A trip taken in this way is worth
ten taken in the ordinary way of travelling & stopping at hotels among

strangers. We stop in some pleasant family and all other pleasant families call upon us & invite us to spend a day or dine at their houses. So we see all the richest & most intelligent people & learn all the best things as well as all the worst about the country & people." Apparently not all the intelligentsia of the West approved of the independence of these self-assured travelers, however, for later in the letter Johnson declares: "Some ladies seem to think that all the *honors* as well as all the *privileges* of life belong to those who *marry*. . . . If [a young lady] does not get *married* it is her *duty* to stay forever at home, to find *there* all her means of pleasure & improvement. But I have no religion or Philosophy that teaches me this doctrine" (Mar. 25, 1848; David Johnson Papers, Connecticut Historical Society). Johnson's words capture the attitude that propelled this couple through a series of journeys under travel conditions that can only be described as harrowing. She implies that the feminine disapproval of their behavior originated in formal systems of masculine thought—"religion and Philosophy"—that maintain that women are naturally suited for a circumscribed and placid life. Her letter echoes the substance of her conversations with Catherine Beecher and the defensive strategies they must have taken vis à vis those married "ladies" who disapproved of their peripatetic and independent life.

Seeking to combine the emotional comfort of these private relationships with the financial security of a profession, Beecher experimented with new institutional arrangements that might replicate for adult women the sororal and affectional relations that had characterized her regime at Hartford Female Seminary. These new communities she modeled after two unrelated institutions: the water cure and the Catholic convent. Initially introduced to the water cures as she sought relief from a series of ailments, Beecher continued to visit them after she recovered, finding in these resorts a model for a feminine community. To married women these spas promised an escape from the strictures of patriarchal marriage, while to single and married women alike they offered an outlet for physical and emotional energies. Both Joan Hedrick and Kathryn Kish Sklar have suggested that Harriet Beecher Stowe's frequent retreats to the water cures offered her an effective method of limiting the size of her increasing family (*Harriet Beecher Stowe* 185; *Catharine Beecher* 184; 215; 318, n. 8). If Harriet found relief from marital "duties," Catharine seems to have relished living in a community that encompassed so many of the reforms she herself had advocated—vigorous exercise in the fresh air, a graham diet, intellectual stimulus, and close feminine friendships. Visitors to these enclaves found, as well, an unusual absence of sexual prudery. According to Sklar, "Under the guise of restoring their health, women could indulge their otherwise forbidden desires for physical sensuality, and some descriptions of water-cure treatments seem to express covert sexual feelings. Nudity and exhilaration were, in any case, frequent experiences during a water-cure treatment" (*Catharine Beecher* 206–7). This combination of mental and physical stimulus so pleased Beecher that she visited thirteen different establishments during the 1840s, either traveling by herself or with a female companion.

The difficulty with water cures, however, was their expense, which limited their clientele to women of upper and upper middle classes. How single adult women might establish and financially maintain similar communities began to obsess Beecher. Her plan to establish normal schools in which to train teachers for the West was thus not only the result of her concern for education but also related to her hope to establish institutional locations where the administrators and teachers who prepared the western instructors might establish a permanent and financially stable community. To this end she actively cultivated the friendships of women who had money at their disposal, proposing to them that they fund a series of such schools.

Beecher saw the Catholic convents of Cincinnati as the ideal of such financially secure adult enclaves. Convents seemed to offer adult women a venue for intellectual pursuits and social reform free from both the economic and behavioral restrictions of marriage. The reasoning that Beecher used to request such funding is best illustrated by a letter she wrote to her recently widowed sister-in-law, Sarah. (Not coincidentally, Sarah Beecher had recently inherited money from her mother.) Catharine writes:

> I thought of the Catholic communities of nuns I have met even in Cincinnati—where women of rank & wealth & learning consecrate themselves, to the cause of education & come to this land as "lady abbesses"—& "lady patronesses"—with their . . . young lady associates to educate our people in a false & slavish faith—And I mused whether a time might come when *Protestant* communities would not take some measure to employ the piety, education & wealth among American females that now is all but wasted for want of some such resources as the Catholic church provides for women of talents enterprise & piety—In the Catholic church there is a notch for every one—the poor girl can find her post as a working nun or teacher—the rich & noble have places provided as heads of great establishments

where in fact they have a power & station & influence which even
ambition might seek. (20 Aug. 1843; Acquisitions, Stowe-Day)

It is clear that Beecher intends to convince Sarah—now a woman excluded
from patriarchal support and obligation—to engage her energies and money
in works of benevolence. In two manuscript pages devoted to this plea,
Beecher uses words such as *wealth, money,* and *resources* at least ten times.
The logic by which she intends to accomplish this transfer of wealth is
somewhat more subtle. Catharine begins the letter with a conviction held
in common by that generation of Beechers—that in the West the "great work
of national education" would be staged. Similarly, Beecher's suggestion that
the Catholic Church might model a structure for community and financial
support plays on family prejudices, as George Beecher, Sarah's clergyman
husband, had supported his father's campaign to rout the infidel Catholics
from Ohio. Most significantly, however, Beecher offers Sarah the possibility
of finding a position wherein a widow might be more than a social cipher.
Sarah Beecher's claim to such an identity, of course, would be eased by her
comfortable financial position.

Although Beecher contacted a large number of potential supporters,
the chain of schools she had envisioned for the West did not materialize.
Despite this failure, she remained committed to mitigating the contradictory
status of single women. After it became apparent in 1856 that she could
not transform the domestic department of Milwaukee Female College
into a retirement home for herself, she invented yet another solution
to this dilemma, the details of which she included in the 1869 revision
of her best-selling *Treatise.* Drawing both on her own reputation as an
educator and domestic theorist and her sister Harriet's increased notoriety
as a best-selling author, Beecher reissued the *Treatise* as *The American
Woman's Home.* Updated to account for technological improvements in
household management, the book included, as well, a significant statement
regarding the status of unmarried women in relation to this domestic ideal.
In the *Treatise*'s two introductory chapters, Beecher had demonstrated
how de Tocqueville's American ideal was being enacted in the western
United States. In *Home* she replaces those chapters with two essays on
the Christian home and family. These chapters do not merely rehearse
Calvinist encomia about heterosexual domesticity, however. Early in the
first chapter Beecher asserts: "The blessed privileges of the family state are
not confined to those who rear children of their own. Any woman who can
earn a livelihood, as every woman should be trained to do, can take a properly

qualified female associate, and institute a family of her own, receiving to its heavenly influences the orphan, the sick, the homeless, and the sinful, and by motherly devotion train them to follow the self-denying example of Christ, in educating his earthly children for true happiness in this life and for his eternal home" (20). This statement encapsulates and summarizes positions she had been formulating over the past quarter century. At last, having proved to herself the feasibility of the concept, she advanced it as an unarguable proposition, a logical configuration of "The Christian Family."

The notion that "family" is a mutable concept that is not limited to "natural" reproduction stems from her youth, when the Beecher household included boarders and servants who were not related but who were treated as family members. The idea that women should be trained to earn a livelihood, which had characterized all of Beecher's educational efforts, here is linked not only with personal economic support in the case of death or financial emergency but also with the financial stability that ensures that a family can remain together. Beecher does not imply here that this womanly "family" is compensatory or to be considered only after other, more "normal" attempts have failed. Rather, she represents this plan as the result of a conscious choice made by two women at any stage of their adult lives. In turn, this couple may also choose their children from those who have been orphaned or abandoned and thus are also excessive to normal family structures. These couples would be exempt from the restrictions and legal inequities that determined conventional heterosexual marriages, since "the distinctive duty of obedience to man does not rest on women who do not enter the relations of married life. A woman who inherits property, or who earns her own livelihood, can institute the family state, adopt orphan children and employ suitable helpers in training them; and then to her will appertain the authority and rights that belong to man as the head of a family. And when every woman is trained to some self-supporting business, she will not be tempted to enter the family state as a subordinate, except by that love for which there is no need of law" (204).

Beecher's claims here seem quite stunning. She frees unmarried women from any duty of obedience to men in general, presuming that they can fulfill the requirements of owning land or property that traditionally entitle a man to citizenship. She claims that this sororal family is equal to other families but with the significant difference that women enter the alliance by choice and as equal partners. For this family Beecher claims the same economic, social, and spiritual endorsement as any other family. In some ways the most conservative of these four writers, Beecher thus demonstrated in her life the trajectory of initial acquiescence to normative domesticity and its interruption by crisis. Later, in her life and writings, which on their surface claim to adhere to normative domesticity, she enacts the most radical of remedies, advocating respectable occupations for single women, their freedom from patriarchal obedience, and their right to enter companionate marriages that would equal patriarchal alliances in legal and social respectability.

When Margaret Fuller was twenty-three years old and her contemporaries were marrying and/or beginning careers, her father moved the family to the isolated farming community of Groton. Because she had not yet married, she was expected to accompany them; her responsibilities would include helping with farm and house work and tutoring her siblings. Fuller thus sacrificed the stimulating intellectual and social life of Cambridge to assume duties that can best be described as those of the supernumerary spinster. Within eighteen months of moving to Groton, she found her obligations to her family intensified when Timothy Fuller died intestate. Because Margarett Crane Fuller was emotionally and intellectually unable to manage the family and because single women were legally unable to assume custody of dependent children and control inherited money, the Fuller family was thrown on the mercy of Timothy's eldest brother. Abraham Fuller dispensed his brother's small estate grudgingly, to the extent that he refused to give money to Margaret as a way of disciplining her errant and unwomanly intellectual pretensions (Capper, *Margaret Fuller* 218; Blanchard 94; Chevigny 379, 399, n. 19).

As a result, Fuller was forced to postpone a trip to Europe that she had conceived of as foundational to her career as a student of European romanticism and absolutely necessary to the biography of Goethe she had planned to write. Rather than prepare herself for a pioneering career as a professional intellectual, Fuller found herself forced to do feminized labor— teaching and tutoring—while assuming traditionally masculine responsibilities of financial planning, disciplining children and planning for their future welfare, and making decisions about the family's residences. The disjunction fueled her developing perceptions of the tenuous nature of socially prescribed gender roles, as is apparent in her letters from the period. In November 1835, she wrote: "I have often had reason to regret being of the softer sex, and never more than now. If I were an eldest son, I could be guardian to my brothers and sister, administer the estate, and really become the head of my family. As it is, I am very ignorant of the management and value of property, and of practical details" (*Letters* 1:237).

Emotional crisis, also precipitated by confusion over gender-appropriate behavior, followed economic upheaval. Within three years after her father's death, Fuller experienced a series of ill-resolved friendships that seem to have demonstrated to her, as did Beecher's bout with the inflexibility of Calvinism, the inability of conventional friendships—and especially of heterosexual pairings—to offer dependable emotional fulfillment. Following her father's death, Fuller formed an especially charged friendship with Samuel Ward, seven years her junior, and Anna Barker, four years younger than she. Her flirtation with Ward was fueled by their mutual intellectual passion for European art. While the difference in their ages initially led Fuller to treat Ward maternally, the affection soon took on overtones of heterosexual romance. At the same time Fuller was nurturing a passionate and probably homoerotic friendship with Barker. She shared Barker's confidence and even her bed,[6] dedicating poems to her "beloved" Anna, her "heart's sister and [her] fancy's love" (Capper, *Margaret Fuller* 280).

Needless to say, when Fuller learned in October 1839 that Ward and Barker planned to be married, it precipitated an extreme emotional crisis. Her aroused and confused passions were exacerbated by two other frustrated friendships. As she negotiated a new basis for her relationship to Barker and Ward, Fuller became emotionally entangled with Caroline Sturgis, a former student some nine years her junior. Sturgis, however, retreated from Fuller's demands for emotional reciprocity. At the same time, Fuller had begun the most intense period of her friendship with Ralph Waldo Emerson, whom she had first met in 1836. Four years of platonic and intellectual friendship had subtly changed into a more erotically charged series of exchanges; Emerson, scholars agree, apparently used the relationship as a test case on which to base his essay "Friendship" (Chevigny 76), while Fuller seems to have taken up a personal challenge to call forth Emerson's emotional commitment to her (regardless—or perhaps because of—his marital status). As a result of the difficulties precipitated by these heightened relationships Fuller reconstructed her ideas about friendship and conventional sexual relationships. According to Capper, her journal entries from this period "almost all focused on her bi-gender identity as the source of her plight" (*Margaret Fuller* 287). She became sure that she would never marry, having seen a number of her younger male friends choose marriage with less intimidating women and having failed to forge a heightened friendship

with Emerson. In her journal she writes "How can a woman of genius love
& marry? A man of genius will not love her; he wants repose" (qtd. in
Capper, *Margaret Fuller* 288). Even as she composed her letter terminating
her relationship with Ward, Fuller set about to fashion a life that did not
follow the "common womanly lot" (*Memoirs* 1:98).

Her first experiment in this new direction was to plan the Conversations,
a venue in which she could explore how women might combine intellectual
rigor with more conventional feminine qualities. Topics for discussion
were inflected by an interpersonal agenda and included issues such as
Intellectual Power, Practical Reason, and Love, whose abstract definitions
had complicated Fuller's own emotional relations. The conspicuous emotional, intellectual, and economic success—and threat—of this pedagogical
enterprise is epitomized by Emerson's retrospective remark that "the loveliest
and the highest endowed women were eager to lay their beauty, their grace,
the hospitalities of sumptuous homes, and their costly gifts, at her feet"
(*Memoirs* 1:281). In the Conversations, Fuller demonstrated the degree of
interest such open discussions of conventionalities—those Nancy Johnson
dismissed as irrelevant "religion or Philosophy"—might spark. They proved,
as well, that her pedagogical approach—which respected women's intellect,
challenged their conditioned shyness, and offered emotional support—
could succeed.

During the next several years, Fuller edited the *Dial* and found employment as a correspondent for the New York *Tribune*. In the aftermath of yet
another failed love affair—this time with James Nathan—Fuller left New
York in August 1846 to serve as the *Tribune*'s European correspondent. Here
she met many of Europe's leading revolutionaries and social theorists with
whom she discussed reforms that seemed impossible to enact in the United
States. Here, too, she became involved in the most important emotional
liaison of her life. From the written accounts, it is apparent that this
relationship was both an emotional and an intellectual experiment in how
such alliances might be managed.

Scholars bent on normalizing Fuller's life interpret her affair with Gio-
vanni Ossoli and the child she bore as the natural fulfillment of her long-
frustrated womanly impulses. For example, after her death, Emerson sorted
through the documents comprising the *Memoirs* in an attempt to establish
the chronology of her European trip, the probable date of her marriage,
and the birth of her son at least nine months later (Chevigny, rev. ed. 416).
Given Fuller's unease with such conventional arrangements, it is much more

probable that the Ossoli affair demonstrates her resistance to the economic and emotional abuses of traditional marriage. Her relationship with Ossoli reversed all the commonplaces of conventional domesticity: she was ten years older than he and by all accounts his intellectual superior, although this difference does not seem to have caused him the strain such inequities produced in American men. No convincing evidence has been found to document their marriage. According to Chevigny, "she lived apart from Ossoli until their last year, as much from choice as from the need of secrecy" (rev. ed. 374). Since Ossoli's financial status was always in doubt, she was the couple's main source of money (giving rise to rumors that he married her mistakenly thinking she was an American heiress); when they decided to return to the United States, she planned to continue to support Ossoli and their son by writing and teaching Italian history.

Nor does Fuller's relation to her child—conceived when she was thirty-seven years old—follow the conventional patterns for American motherhood. Despite having confided to her journal some years earlier her wish to have a child,7 she was dismayed to find herself pregnant, apparently because she dreaded the social stigma of an illegitimate pregnancy. To Caroline Sturgis Tappan she wrote "with this year, I enter upon a sphere of my destiny so difficult, that I, at present, see no way out, except through the gate of death. . . . I have no reason to hope I shall not reap what I have sown" (*Letters* 5:43). Notwithstanding the delight she took in her infant son, she did not hover over him, but left him in the care of a nurse so that she could return to Rome to support the revolutionary cause.

After the Revolution failed and Fuller had determined to return to the United States with Ossoli and their child, she confronted the enormity of the "social inquisition" her domestic arrangements would occasion at home among friends less convinced than she that conventional family structures ought to be resisted. To Emelyn Story she wrote:

> I am sure your affection for me will prompt you to add, that you feel confident whatever I have done has been in a good spirit and not contrary to *my* ideas of right; for the rest, you will not admit for me, as I do not for myself, the rights of the social inquisition of the U.S. to know all the details of my affairs. If my mother is content, if Ossoli and I are content, if our child when grown up is content, that is enough. You and I know enough of the U.S. to be sure that many persons there will blame whatever is peculiar, the lower persons everywhere, are sure to think that whatever is mysterious must be bad, but I think there will remain for me a sufficient number of friends to keep my heart warm

and help me to earn my bread; that is all that is of any consequence.
(*Letters* 5:285)

However, Fuller may have overestimated the degree of support she would
have from her friends, especially since she had informed them about Ossoli
and her child only belatedly and with a minimum of supporting detail. As a
result, rumors of her "Fourierist or socialist marriage, without the external
ceremony" (qtd. in Chevigny, rev. ed. 393) preceded her return. Sarah Clarke,
a close friend, wrote Fuller protesting that she knew no details with which
to counter the increasing gossip. Clarke's letter, however, is also a precise
measure of the degree of censure Fuller would encounter, even from close
friends: "to me it seemed that you were more afraid of being thought to have
submitted to the ceremony of marriage than to have omitted it" (Chevigny,
rev. ed. 394). Marcus and Rebecca Spring, with whom Fuller had traveled
in Europe, advised her not to return to the United States at all.

Although she apparently did not confide the details of her personal
choices to friends, Fuller did plan to publish the theoretical and philosophical speculations upon which those actions were premised. She was
particularly interested in European manifestations of Fourierism, writing to
Mary Rotch that she was "as great an Associationist as W. Channing himself,
that is to say as firm a believer that the next form society will take in remedy
of the dreadful ills that now consume it will be voluntary association in
small communities. The present forms are become unwieldy" (*Letters* 5:71).
Fuller's untimely death prevented both the full print explication of her
theories and the actual test of her earlier statement that "social wedlock is
ordinarily mere subterfuge and simulacrum: it could not check a powerful
woman or a powerful man" (qtd. in Capper, *Margaret Fuller* 288). Whether
American pressure to conform to "social wedlock" would have checked
Fuller remains an open question. It is clear, however, that a woman who
had originally expected to submit to it found, through a series of emotional
and economic crises, a location in which to begin a reasoned experiment
in resistance.

Unlike Beecher and Fuller, Sarah Josepha Hale found her expectations
of marriage, family, and children to be amply fulfilled—albeit tardily, since
she did not marry until age twenty-five—in a union with David Hale, a
lawyer five years older than she. This union, by her account, was idyllic.
However, Hale died unexpectedly, leaving his wife very little money with
which to support their five children. So closely did Sarah Hale control
the biographical information about herself that there is little primary or

supporting documentation to interpret her subsequent actions. But the pattern of Hale's fifty-seven-year widowhood offers the basis for a rereading of her motives, especially if it is seen as a public performance, complete with costume and script, that questions normative domesticity by extravagantly parodying its most cherished public forms.

Hale's account of her financial difficulties following her husband's death suggests the care with which she scripted the biographical information she released to the public. Rather than suggest that David Hale may have been spendthrift, his widow writes, "his business was large . . . but he had hardly reached that age when men of his profession begin to lay up property,—and he had spared no indulgence to his family. We had lived in comfort, but I was left poor" (*Wreath* 387). Such careful telling suggests that other parts of her autobiographical script are likewise open to other interpretations. Certainly this is the case with regard to her accounts of how she negotiated this financial crisis. Most narratives have it that Hale first tried to support herself by doing needlework but failed. She then "engaged in authorship as a profession" (Hart 93); her invitation to edit the *Ladies' Magazine* resulted from a providential happenstance. Hale's version of this sequence of events, written upon her retirement from *Godey's* in 1877 and admittedly a "brief" account, has as its goal to "trace with gratitude" the "leadings of Divine Providence" after her husband's demise: "In 1827 I received a letter . . . inviting me to come to Boston and take charge of a Ladies' Magazine which should be established for me in that city. This was not only unsolicited, but entirely unexpected. Attention had been probably attracted to me because I had gained a prize offered by a Boston paper for a poem; and my first novel, 'Northwood,' had just been published in that city. . . . My faith in God was so strong, that this change seemed to me to be the ordering of Divine Providence, and I accepted these new duties and responsibilities as appointed by His will" (95 [Dec. 1877]: 522).

While the substance of this account is accurate, Hale edited out several pertinent but distinctly nonprovidential details. Although she briefly undertook a millinery business, it is apparent that that was merely a stopgap measure until she could establish her literary reputation, an aim she may have had in mind even before her husband died. In earlier biographical accounts whose purpose was not to claim divine intervention, she admitted to having written "some poems, a few of which were published, previous to my marriage; and during my husband's lifetime, he occasionally sent an article of mine to the Journals" (*Wreath* 385). Following his death, even as she was trimming hats, she also actively submitted essays and poems for publication. Isabelle Entrikin names at least seven journals and papers to which Hale contributed during the years immediately following her husband's death. During this period, as well, she was writing the manuscript of her first novel, *Northwood*. Nor did she merely submit her work anonymously or through the mails. In 1826, she personally called on publishers in Boston and circulated chapters of the new manuscript.

It seems apparent, then, that Hale actively pursued a career path that offered her the best possibility of a steady and substantial income. In her autobiographical sketch in *The Ladies' Wreath* she declares, "The very few employments in which females can engage with any hope of profit and my own constitution and pursuits, made literature appear my best resource" (388). Thus, although the offer to edit the *Ladies' Magazine* may have been unexpected, it certainly was not illogical. The workings of Providence may be traced directly to Hale's own efforts, cloaked in a rhetoric of American womanhood that maintained she acted only "in the hope of gaining the means for [her children's] support and education" (*Godey's* 43 [Dec. 1850]: 326).

Like her more outspoken contemporary Margaret Fuller, Hale did not sacrifice herself to her young family or to the ideals of sentimental motherhood. Since the terms of her arrangement with the *Ladies' Magazine* required her to move to Boston, she left four of her five children with relatives or in boarding schools in Newport. Nor did she ever apparently consider remarrying. She wrote to Matthew Carey in 1834 that "she had then worn mourning 'almost twelve years'" (Entrikin 16), although custom proclaimed a mourning period of only a year or so. She continued to wear black clothing for the rest of her life. According to Sherbrooke Rogers, "her sincere devotion to David's memory is unquestionable, but she also found black becoming" (27). In the same fashion that she constructed for herself the identity of a Republican mother laboring for the support of her children "as their father would have done" (*Godey's* 95 [Dec. 1877]: 522), she also burnished the public image of herself as grieving widow, reminding her readers of her justification for an eminently successful public life—long after her obligations to support her children ceased.

Although on their surface Hale's actions are utterly representative of ideological preconceptions of how a widow might behave, they may also be read as italicizations of—and emphasis added to—those preconceptions. A comparatively young woman, and by all accounts attractive enough to have remarried, Hale chose the relative freedom of widowhood. Having married and given birth, she could draw on her experiential authority as the basis of her prescriptive writings on domesticity. She remained immune to the obligation to remarry by her display of protracted grief over the death of David Hale. After an initial period of financial distress, she found that her property and money were legally hers and that she could pursue a career. Beginning at age forty, she did so, writing actively for the remainder of her life. Although in later life she boarded with her daughter and son-in-law, she did not "retire" nor did she assume the position of household adjunct. Rather, she moved her offices into the upper floors of their home and made her family into adjuncts, employing them as unpaid receptionists, messengers, and copyists.

Other themes consonant with the concerns of an independent unmarried woman can be read in Hale's profession of normative domesticity. Her ongoing interest in women's education is not merely the logical extension of her ideological stake in Republican motherhood but also a self-interested call for women to prepare themselves for the eventuality of economic disaster. Her attention to the progress of married women's property legislation in the pages of *Godey's* suggests that she had a deep personal interest in the legal arrangements that would protect the rights of women. As opportunities for women's work expanded, Hale noted their proliferation, publicizing the activities of women in education, law, medicine, art, and civil service. Others of her columns even recognize that marriage is not the only or best way for a woman to live her life if there are other possibilities for support. For example, in an editorial promoting Beecher's AWEA, Hale writes, "That earlier marriages are productive of much of the unhappiness of married women, of many sorrows, sickness, and premature decay and death, there can be no doubt" (45 [Aug. 1852]: 193). Characteristically, Hale's intent is to promote a career that is consistent with womanly sensibilities; its italicized subtext, however, acknowledges that marriage is itself an economic system, a realization that the pattern of her own life had taught her, and from which her independent widowhood exempted her.

Fanny Fern responded to the public outrage over the increasing number of women giving public lectures by asking whether such employment were "less commendable than marrying somebody—anybody—for the sake of being supported, and finding out too late as many women do, that it is the toughest possible way of getting a living?" (*Ledger* 8 Dec. 1866). Certainly her response was inflected by her own experience in three marriages. Her marriage to Charles Eldredge was happy but short, and probably furnished the raw material for many of her early newspaper columns that glorify family, home, children, and domesticity. Those early columns, in turn, have been the main source of her literary reputation—until recently—as an unabashed sentimentalist, "the grandmother of all sob sisters" (Hart 97). Such a classification is far from the truth but illustrates how effectively Fern parodied the forms of normative domesticity.

Charles Eldredge, a successful but improvident businessman, died young, leaving his widow with no inheritance and several young children to care for. She remarried quickly "for the sake of being supported" because neither her own family nor the Eldredges would help her financially. Nor did they offer her emotional sustenance. Her marriage to Sam Farrington, a widower with two children of his own, exposed Fern to physical, psychic, and economic abuse and taught her that marriage was "the toughest possible way of getting a living." After two years, she separated from Farrington; two years later he divorced her for desertion.

At this period she began to support herself by writing, and not until she was relatively well established as an author with independent means did she again remarry. The choices Fern made after 1851, when she left Farrington, suggest that her subsequent observances of the outward forms of domesticity were undertaken with an eye to how a woman might avoid marriage's abuses. She challenged patriarchy not by resisting it but by exploring how it might be modified to give women broadened legal, emotional, and economic rights. When she married James Parton, she was forty-five years old; he was thirty-four. The couple signed a legal document securing to Fern the property she brought to the marriage as well as "all property which may hereafter arise or accrue to her by reason of any new works which may be prepared by her, as her separate Estate and *as if she were unmarried* with full power and authority to apply or dispose of the same" (qtd. in Warren *Fanny Fern* 153; emphasis added). Fern and Parton had no children of their own; their family was, in fact, of similar composition and intent to the "family state" Beecher would later propose: an amalgam of individuals—Fern's children from previous marriages, as well as a granddaughter who had been abandoned by her father—whose personal, legal and professional identities did not become subsumed to James Parton's.

Fern's writings after 1850 comprise a body of social theory consistent with her actions. She exposed the economic basis of marriage and the physical and emotional abuses it masked and even encouraged. She delineated the ideological underpinnings of the marital law, especially the de facto legal endorsement of a sexual double standard. And, as did these writers who were her contemporaries, Fern touted the respectability and even preferability of alternative living arrangements for women while giving serious consideration to how they might prepare themselves educationally and economically to enter such arrangements.

As the number of women in the workplace increased, and as the range of their occupations widened, so did the public outcry against their "unsexing" themselves through these purportedly demeaning activities. In a column entitled "Pay for Women" Fern responds to the public excoriation of women doctors who receive pay for skills thought to be the natural endowments of womanly charity. She emphasizes that both medicine and wifehood are implicated in capitalist exchange: "Does anybody object when women *marry for pay?*—without love, without respect, nay, with even aversion?" (*Ledger* 16 July 1870). Her frequent defenses of women workers, whether doctors or lecturers, seamstresses or prostitutes, demonstrate the centrality of women's labor to capitalist exchange. Fern advocated that the goods women bring to market be intellectual or physical skills rather than the erased or anonymous merchandise of domestic labor or sexual favor with or without sanction of marriage.

As did Fuller, Fern wrote about the inequities of intellect and power entailed in marriage, although unlike Fuller she tied them to the minutiae of everyday married life. Foregrounding the arbitrariness of ideological prescriptions of womanly retirement, self-effacement, self-sacrifice, and sexual passionlessness, she enjoins husbands not to let their wives lapse into mental stagnation, nor to cease treating them tenderly after marriage. "Women and Their Discontents," a chapter of *Folly as It Flies*, contains several columns Fern wrote on this issue. She warns men not to assume that wives have no pleasure in mental exertion and reminds them that as physical beauty fades, mental beauty becomes increasingly important. "It is pitiable to see a husband without a thought that he might and should occasionally, have given his wife a lift out of the petty, harrowing details of her woman's life, turn from her, in company, to address his conversation to some woman who, happier than she, has had time and opportunity for mental culture" (63). This chapter, with its emphasis on the need for women to maintain mental acuity by reading widely and writing privately in journals, by socializing, by attending church, and by actively seeking relief from the stultifying round of menial domestic tasks, demonstrates in specific terms the material bases of Fuller's more abstract question, "How can a woman of genius . . . marry?" (qtd. in Capper, *Margaret Fuller* 288).

Unequal economic, social, and physical power in marriage produced not only mental stagnation but physical abuse. Fern's address to this issue, unusual for a woman of her time, was sometimes less direct but frequently demonstrated that physical abuse was the logical outcome of illogical assumptions about woman's natural delicacy, sensitivity, and purity. For example, in her column on "Female Lecturers," Fern counters the assumption that public speaking would expose a woman to jeering and verbal abuse that would be fatal to her frail nature. She asks in return, "And what if a hiss should meet her sensitive ear from an adder in her audience? Does it sting more than would a brutal word at her own fireside, whither she was lured by promises of love until death?" (*Ledger* 8 Dec. 1866). Other columns insist that these presuppositions about women's delicacy not be used unthinkingly to explain the high proportion of women who died in childbirth or from exhaustion after years of hard domestic labor.

These assumptions about women's delicacy also perpetuated the sexual double standard that structured Victorian marriage and undergirded much of nineteenth-century domestic law. Assuming that women's purity and faithfulness, so central to their womanly character, must be maintained at all costs,[8] and assuming feminine passionlessness, as well, public opinion and legal statute alike held that men would "naturally" seek sexual gratification outside marriage. Fern exposes this frequently undiscussed inconsistency and gives it material referents by exposing its physical consequences: "And as to the 'soil and stain on woman's purity,' which timidity, and conservatism, and selfishness insists [sic] shall follow the act [of voting], it might be well, in answer, to draw aside the veil from many homes in New York, *not* in the vicinity of the Five Points either, where long-suffering, uncomplaining wives and mothers endure a defilement and brutality on legal compulsion, to which this, at the worst estimate ever made by its opponents, would be spotlessness itself." Fern's attention to such abuse is not mere sensationalism. Rather, her exposure makes public what men and women knew privately to be true, that ideologies of feminine frailty were essential to a system of marriage that ceded economic, physical, and political power to men. These presumptions produced abuses that transcended social class and that called for a similarly transcendent solution: woman suffrage. To give women the vote is to offer them a "lever of power" by which they might be "lifted out of their wretched condition, of low wages and starvation" (*Ledger* 5 Jan. 1867).

Fern had access to factual information with which to counter what she deemed as an erroneous public perception that marriage always protected a woman's best interests. That knowledge, as well as her own experience with abuse, led Fern to argue publicly that women had a right to seek divorce. "A Word on the Other Side" begins the debate by challenging the sexual double standard: "I have no patience with those who preach one code of morality for the wife, and another for the husband. If the marriage vow allows him to absent himself from his home under cover of the darkness, scorning to give account of himself, it also allows it in her." Her declaration that "there is no sex designated in the fifth commandment" echoes Nancy Johnson's dismissal of and Margaret Fuller's challenge to "religion and Philosophy." Characteristically, Fern's support for this outspoken contention is mainstream—the Christian proscription of adultery. Yet Fern does not assume that those who would break marriage vows would honor biblical commandments. Therefore, in the likely case that the abuse persist, women should "take their lives in their hands, and say to a dissolute husband, 'this you can never give, and this you shall not therefore take away.' . . . 'But the children?' Aye—the children—shame that the law should come between them and a good mother! Still—better let her leave them, than remain to bring into the world their puny brothers and sisters. Does she shrink from the toil of self support? What toil, let me ask, could be more hopeless, more endless, *more degrading* than that from which she turns away?"

Here Fern presumes that sexual infidelity is not a victimless crime, asserting that men who are unfaithful in marriage endanger the health of their wives and children. In addition to the then-shocking recommendation that women might seek divorce of their own volition, Fern advocates an even more unthinkable eventuality—that a woman might put her own well-being, health, and safety before that of her children. While mid-nineteenth-century law provided for divorce under extreme circumstances, it frequently sought to control the exit of women from unhappy marriages by awarding custody of children to the father. Fern's argument points to the extremes implied in the law, maintaining that within marriage, abuse might be so violent that to submit to it or to bring additional children under its aegis would be ethically reprehensible. Thus, she reasons, the best escape from a legally mandated solution is to parody the law's provisions. She continues: "There are aggravated cases for which the law provides no remedy—from which it affords no protection;. . . . In such cases, let a woman who *has the self-sustaining power* quietly take her fate in her own hands, and right herself.

Of course she will be misjudged and abused. *It is for her to choose whether she can better bear that at hands from which she has a rightful claim for love and protection, or from a nine-days-wonder-loving public.* These are bold words; but they are needed words—words whose full import I have well considered, and from the responsibility of which I do not shrink" (*Ledger* 24 Oct. 1857) The extent to which this was a radical statement is underscored by Fern's uncharacteristic final apologia and her extensive use of italics in the passage. She does not advocate that a woman leave a marriage without provocation and without the possibility of supporting herself. Further, her declaration is ambiguous, able to be read both as a caution against hasty action by women who cannot support themselves and as a warning to the husbands of those who can. Most significantly, Fern advocates that such action be taken "quietly" and individually, not as part of a public and organized movement. Such an approach may allow for more radical change on the individual level than reform pursued by organized groups.

As did Beecher and Fuller, Fern suggested that women might choose not to marry. Unlike the columns that expose abuse, these opinions are usually presented humorously and in the subjunctive. Aware that the variety of employment available to women had begun to expand and diversify, Fern argued that women might prefer to pursue a career rather than to marry, especially if marriage entailed sacrificing economic rights. She declares, "Still it remains that there are women, like men, who can *marry a cause.* Who can be happier and more useful in laboring for, and promoting it, than they could be as parents and heads of families" (*Ledger* 23 May 1863). The economic sense of this assertion is borne out and amplified in a second column, "Female Lecturers": " *They* can stand [the spiteful comments from lip and pen]!—with a good house over their independent heads, secured and paid for by their own honest industry. They can stand it!— with greenbacks and Treasury notes stowed away against a rainy day. *They* can stand it!—with any quantity of 'admirers' who, not having pluck or skill enough to earn their own living, would gladly share what these enterprising women have accumulated. May a good Providence multiply female lecturers, female sculptors, female artists of every sort, female authors, female astronomers, female book-keepers, female—anything that is honest, save female *sempstresses,* with their pale faces, hollow eyes and empty pockets, and a City Hospital or Almshouse in prospective" (*Ledger* 8 Dec. 1866). Thus, as do Hale, Fuller, and Beecher, Fern promotes women's access to occupations that would pay well. Such economic parity would enable them to reject alternatives—unhappy marriage, sewing, prostitution—that entailed inevitable disease, poverty, and intellectual or physical abuse.

Finally, as did her contemporaries, Fern wrote about alternatives for social and emotional fulfillment outside heterosexual reproduction. While Beecher advocated partnerships between women who might then adopt orphaned or abandoned children, and Fuller advanced ideas of association-ism, Fern openly supported women's living as single individuals, either as widows (like Sarah Josepha Hale) or as spinsters. "What Sort of Old Maid I Should Be" typifies Fern's approach to the issues. She begins by echoing the predominant cultural judgments of single women, condemning unmarried intellectual women as "not women." In the process, a readership who held such opinions is invited to assent to her argument. Such a woman, she suggests, is "an icicle—an ossification—a petrification—an abortion—a monster—." In the next paragraph, however, she reverses the assertion: "Pshaw—there are no such women; they are only making the best of what they can't help; they are eating their own hearts out and making no sign in dying. They ought all to be wives and mothers." Thus Fern counters one cultural misperception (that not to marry is unwomanly) with another, more predominant and undeniable one (that all women desire to marry and to have children). The logic proceeds one step further, however, denying one term of this proposition in support of the other more radical but undeniable proposition. If "no man had sense enough to endow me with the names of wife and mother . . . I would just adopt the first fat baby I could find, though I had to work my fingers to the bone to keep its little mouth filled" (*Ledger* 26 June 1858). Fern places the responsibility for effecting marriage where the culture says it belongs—with men. She simultaneously exposes the fact that the functions of wife and mother are not natural to women but linguistic positions under the sway of masculine prerogative. Finally, she turns to the ultimate masculine system of law to propose a parodic alternative to marriage and family: adoption, with economic support provided by the mother. In this proposal, then, Fern echoes Beecher's notion that the inequities and abuses of traditional marriage might best be countered by private emotional and economic arrangements between women, arrangements that claim for women the rights and responsibilities of patriarchy without subjecting them to its abuses.

Despite their outspoken public statements, Beecher, Hale, Fuller, and Fern have been seen as generally uninvolved with or ancillary to the concerns of first-wave feminism, retrogrades in an era dominated by such reformers as Elizabeth Cady Stanton. This misperception has a number of causes. Editorial and familial control over primary material; the misogyny of institutions of literary production, transmission and literary history; and the models through which historians and scholars have understood nineteenth-century women's history have tamed the parodic actions of these four writers and relegated their revisionist writings to a secondary status.

The misunderstanding and misclassification of these writers simply because they were women began during their own lifetimes. Following the Civil War, the literary establishment became far less tolerant of writings by women about women's issues; as a result, women's texts were routinely marginalized and trivialized—in some cases by the very publishers who had initially made them successful. Joan Hedrick, for example, has demonstrated how Harriet Beecher Stowe's *Atlantic* editors, a group of men whose judgments came to dominate national literary taste, engaged in a systematic campaign to masculinize American literature, claiming that philosophical, social, and intellectual writing about substantive issues was the province of men while denigrating as sentimental tripe writing that had to do with women's issues. As a case in point, Hedrick traces the fate of two volumes written by the Beecher sisters—Catharine's *Truth Stranger than Fiction* (1850) and Harriet's *Lady Byron Vindicated* (1870). Both women had enjoyed solid public reputations. Both had documented abuses suffered by real women—Catharine's friend Delia Bacon and Harriet's correspondent Lady Byron—at the hand of male-dominated institutions such as the church and university. Although both books were printed, each was subsequently publicly challenged, excoriated, and dismissed out of hand as unseemly, unwomanly, hysterical, and inappropriate (*Harriet Beecher Stowe* ch. 21).

Fuller's threat to normative heterosexuality and to the fiction that sociopolitical thought was a manly domain was countered through fictional portrayals of her penned by her contemporary, Nathaniel Hawthorne, and in the succeeding generation by Henry James, both of whom found the force of her ideas immensely threatening. Hawthorne, once Fuller's friend, wrote a gossipy, blatantly inaccurate, and mean-spirited journal account of her relationship with Ossoli that was published in 1884 by his son Julian and that has, according to Chevigny, "spawned scores of apocryphal tales as no image of Fuller's defenders has done" (rev. ed. 418). Hawthorne also used Fuller as the basis for the frustrated, if powerful, feminist Zenobia in *The Blithedale Romance*. Unrequited love for a fellow social reformer leads Zenobia to drown herself, while Hawthorne's ideal woman in the novel is the ethereal and vacillating Priscilla. Hawthorne's disciplinary gesture is echoed by Henry James in *The Bostonians*, where Fuller's attempts at social reform are embodied in Olive Chancellor. James's fictional solution to "the Margaret problem" is similar to Hawthorne's: Olive loses her companion and spokeswoman, Verena Tarrant, to a real man, Basil Ransome.

The literary trivialization and institutional effacement of these women's work was unwittingly aided by zealous friends and descendants who wished to protect the reputations of their writer-relatives and who posthumously edited their correspondence and/or issued statements attesting to their spotless domestic reputations. For example, Fern's daughter, Ellen W. Parton, acknowledged to a researcher that her mother had married a second time, but only upon his "promise of secrecy, which I know as a gentleman you will keep. . . . His [Farrington's] name is immaterial as you will not mention him or the marriage either in person or on paper" (28 Feb. 1899; Sophia Smith Collection). Working under such restricted access to factual information, scholars necessarily emphasized the publicly acceptable version of Fern's acts, an interpretation that, in turn, obscured the more radical undertones of her columns. Similarly, Margaret Fuller's brother, Arthur, prefaced her *Woman in the Nineteenth Century* with a claim that the book represented her own independent response to the issues of domestic and gender ideologies and that she was not affiliated with "any existing organization" (6). Although his claim is not incorrect, its intent in 1855, when it was penned, was to protect his sister's feminine reputation from any taint of suffragism. Moreover, Fuller devotes about one-fourth of his introduction to demonstrating his sister's devotion to "the domestic concerns of life" (6) and even more space to establishing her "Christian faith and hope" (8).

Fuller's friends compounded what her relatives had begun. Although her literary reputation suffered less than did Beecher's, Fern's, or Hale's, it is largely because she was persistently classified as a transcendental handmaiden, Emerson's muse, and a somewhat ridiculous and unattractive bluestocking whose friendships with women were feeble attempts to compensate for her failure to attract a man and marry. Her first biographers, well-intentioned personal friends, systematically and permanently excised passages that threatened to sully Fuller's womanly reputation, although the writings might have offered a more complex version of her social and economic thought. In the *Memoirs,* for example, Emerson coyly skirts the issue of her friendships with women, hinting that "Her friendships, as a girl with girls, as a woman with women, were not unmingled with passion, and had passages of romantic sacrifice and of ecstatic fusion, which I have heard with the ear, but could not trust my profane pen to report" (1:281–82). This suggestive allegation is substituted for such passages as the following, which Emerson excised as he prepared the *Memoirs:* "I loved Anna for a time with as much passion as I was then strong enough to feel—Her face was always gleaming before me; her voice was echoing in my ear, all poetic thoughts clustered round the dear image. . . . Then again that night when she leaned on me and her eyes were such a deep violet blue, so like night, . . . and we both felt such a strange mystic thrill and knew what we had never known before. Now well too can I now account for that desire which I often had to get away from her and be alone with nature, which displeased her so, for she wished to be with me all the time" (qtd. in Capper, *Margaret Fuller* 281). Such a blatant statement of Anna Barker Ward's early desire for Fuller not only threatened the masculinity of Sam Ward but also established Fuller as an independent thinker and actor, a woman whose desire could be fulfilled by women, a woman who did not find her destiny in marriage and motherhood.

The complexity of these writers' words and deeds has been obscured by the paradigms of literary, historical, and theoretical interpretation as well. Beecher's proposals for companionate marriage have been overlooked in part because she advanced them in the service of a conservative political agenda. In 1869, the same year in which *American Woman's Home* was first issued, Beecher countered proposals of suffragists in an essay entitled "Something for Women Better than the Ballot." Here she pointed out their failure to account for the needs of unmarried women who were forced to "[depend] chiefly on the labor of others till marriage is offered" (2). At this moment, when the adult white male population of the United States had been reduced by the Civil War, the economic fate of unmarried adult women was no small issue. Not surprisingly, Beecher proposed that such women needed access to honorable professions: "The grand difficulty, which those who are seeking the ballot would remedy, is, the want of honorable and remunerative employment for unmarried or widowed women. It is not clear how the ballot would secure this; while a long time must elapse before public opinion would arrive at this result" (7). Beecher proposes a more immediate solution that depends neither upon legislation nor on the vagaries of public opinion. In the manner of her contemporary Fanny Fern, she addresses already dominant public perceptions about women's abilities and exploits them in the service of a more radical idea, proposing that the public permanently endow institutions to train women in professions. As a result, their economic positions would improve and, because they need not marry or be subject to marital inequities, they would not need access to the franchise. "Then every woman would look forward to a cheerful home of her own, where she could train the children of her Heavenly Father for their eternal home. If not married, or if not blessed with children, she could gather the lost lambs of her Lord and Saviour, and lead them to the green pastures and still waters of eternal life" (12). While Beecher's argument that the franchise would come too slowly to solve immediate dilemmas seems short-sighted and retrograde to contemporary eyes, her claim that women need not marry to have children seems strikingly contemporary, as does her implicit claim that they might function as de facto pastors to their offspring and affiliates. Thus far, however, her ideas have been subsumed to the histories of more successful political movements and proposals.

It is possible, in fact, to argue that the reforms of marriage and domesticity advocated by Fern, Fuller, Beecher, and Hale effectively replicated the political goals of their more public and organized feminist contemporaries. Karlyn Kohrs Campbell, for example, classifies the grievances enumerated in Stanton's "Declaration of Sentiments" as protests against "(1) violations of natural rights; (2) disabilities of married women; (3) religious discrimination [including barring women from the ministry and endorsing a 'double standard of morality']; and (4) denials of opportunity for individual development" (53). Campbell's four categories also summarize the problems these writers sought to solve through their individual actions: Fern advocated the franchise; Beecher argued for social institutions that would effect a similar recognition of women's needs; Hale and Fuller argued in newspaper columns that women had identities, rights, and responsibilities as citizens. All four writers, as I have shown above, recognized and wrote about the legal, emotional, and physical disadvantages incurred by married women. All publicly decried a differential standard of morality; Beecher sought to claim a pastoral identity for single women. Finally, each pursued a professional career and celebrated the expanding opportunities for women to claim an economic identity through productive work.

The persistent image of these women as conservative, retiring, and apolitical has been fostered, as well, by a binary and reductive historical model of gendered separate spheres. Such a model placed women like Beecher, Hale, and Fern squarely within the private sphere, attributing to them all the characteristics taken to describe that realm and disregarding the details of their lives and writings that did not coincide with those characteristics. Thus, for example, Beecher's *Treatise on Domestic Economy* and *American Woman's Home* have been reprinted in several editions while texts such as *Letters to the People on the Difficulties of Religion* and "Something for Women Better than the Ballot" remain in archives and special collections. In a similar fashion, Hale has gained her sole notoriety to the contemporary literary audience as an editor of *Godey's Lady's Book*, within whose pages the ideals of "True Womanhood" supposedly received their definitive articulation. A careful reading of the full range of *Godey's*, however, necessarily complicates such a taxonomy, as Laura McCall's content analysis of the magazine has established. Fanny Fern was recalled to literary attention by Mary Kelley's important study of the "literary domestics," a book whose model included her as one of a dozen reluctant women writers whose fame was thrust upon them. Margaret Fuller, by contrast, was never included in the categories of "private woman," "True Womanhood," or "literary domestic." Instead she was given a sort of honorary manhood as a transcendentalist, a classification that both hides her connections to these women and to other women writers who were her contemporaries, and effects a hierarchy of literary value that prefers abstract thought to action and subtlety to polemic.

It goes without saying that extensive and valuable work has been done under the model of separate spheres. In fact, the solutions of each of these women to her own difficulties with patriarchal systems of marriage, emotional support, separation, and economic inheritance appear to honor such a trope, as do their fictional writings and some versions of their (auto)biographies. Beecher's and Hale's lives as unmarried women matched public preconceptions of how spinsters and widows ought to behave vis á vis domesticity. Thus Beecher's work on behalf of women's education was seen as a way to give unmarried women public respectability until they could marry. Sarah Josepha Hale, the model grieving widow, proceeded to make a career of prescribing the details of normative domesticity to married middle-class women. Fern's divorce from Sam Farrington initially sullied her reputation, but by publishing a number of conventionally sentimental columns Fern reestablished an image of herself as a woman rich in sympathy who had managed to maintain her domestic identity while (or in spite of) being economically successful. Fuller, who might have presented the most significant challenge to domestic presuppositions, died before she could enact the logical outcome of the social reform she had first pursued as an abstract possibility and then begun to experiment with in Italy. It remained for her relatives and friends to refurbish her image as a fulfilled woman.

But italicizing the trope of separate spheres opens to reinterpretation the acts and full range of writings of these four women. Attending to the full range of their writings—their nonfiction journalism, conduct books, letters, and journals—yields a more complex understanding of their importance within their cultural milieu, as well as their interest to our own day. These women, raised in traditional families, and educated by nontraditional women, sought as adults to respect their heritage and to refine its possibilities. They sought and found emotional fulfillment not necessarily related to heterosexual romance and argued that other women might do likewise. They dissociated nurture from motherhood and posited alternate configurations of family that included women and children whose single or orphaned status excluded them from the private sphere. They demonstrated that intellectual rigor in a woman was not foreclosed by the marriage vow and that economic viability need not be premised on sexual exchange. Accounting for such complexity thus requires that subsequent understandings of nineteenth-century domesticity be undertaken with a difference.

Notes

Introduction: Eccentric Domesticity

1. Armstrong studies this connection in British fiction. Gillian Brown studies the political/philosophical interplay between American individualism and domestic privacy, while Gossett and Bardes analyze the political agendas of fiction written by women in the nineteenth-century United States.

2. By professional, I mean two things: each of these women earned enough money by writing to be self-supporting, and each identified herself as an author. I make this distinction in contrast to earlier studies by Douglas and Kelley. In Douglas's tabular identification of writing women, she writes that she has "listed 'housewife' as an occupation for any woman, married or unmarried, who devoted significant time and energy to the management of a home" (403). But Hale and Beecher, especially in later life, either lived with relatives or in boardinghouses and took special care not to be burdened with household tasks. Fern also employed domestics, as did the Fuller family. As an adult, Fuller boarded with others and traveled broadly. The point that "management" is not the same as "housewife" is centrally related to the prolific written output of these four women.

Chapter One. Her Father's Best Boy: Catharine Beecher and Margaret Fuller

1. I use this attribution intentionally, since "Lyman Beecher's family" included the children born to three wives.

2. Litchfield Law School, the first formal school of law in the United States, opened in 1784. Its students included Noah Webster, Aaron Burr, John C. Calhoun, Horace Mann, and George Catlin (von Frank 62, n. 19). See also Brickley, "Sarah" for more information about the Law School and other intellectual institutions of Litchfield (20).

Chapter Two. Fatherless Daughters: Sarah Josepha Hale and Fanny Fern

1. To my knowledge, no such diploma exists. Entrikin notes that Horatio Buell "appears to have been valedictorian of his class" at Dartmouth but does not repeat this story.

2. Welter uses a "survey" of *Godey's* as a major source in establishing the characteristics of the "Cult of True Womanhood"; Douglas calls Hale "determinedly moderate [and the] chief exponent of the doctrine of the feminine sphere" (54).

3. While studies such as Gere's, Martin's, and Tucker's see coeducational groups as an anomaly, the existence of the Coterie and the Semi-Colon Club implies that such groups were relatively common. Hale's group, which began meeting about 1815, directly contradicts Louis Tucker's explanation that women's participation in Cincinnati's Semi-Colon Club was owing to "the more liberal attitude prevailing in the West" (17). The Litchfield gatherings of

Law School and Female Academy students, as well as Beecher's Hartford Female Seminary levées, also demonstrate that men and women frequently socialized in such literary gatherings.

4. Many, if not most, scholars who have studied Hale have characterized—even vilified—her as primarily responsible for the most repressive qualities of what has been somewhat misleadingly labeled a "doctrine" of "separate spheres." See particularly Welter, Conrad, and Douglas. But see also more recent work, notably Baym, who asserts, "Attempts to attach today's rhetorical labels of liberal, conservative, radical, or reactionary to Hale only call attention to differences between the ways in which various intellectual positions converged and intersected then and the ways they do now" ("Onward" 262 n. 13). See also McCall for an important first step at reconfiguring *Godey's* part in the construction of the discourse of separate spheres and Kerber "Separate" for the definitive deconstruction of the concept.

5. I refer to this writer both as Sara Willis and as Fanny Fern, according to whether I write of her preprofessional life or of the print identity that became synonymous with the biographical subject in later years.

6. The seminary's other paper, the *School Gazette*, "Published at Study Hall," was probably circulated within the school, as suggested by its contents—mostly jokes with local referents and essays whose intent is disciplinary. Additionally, since many of these pieces were composed by Catharine Beecher (they are duplicated in her ms. album of poems dedicated to her father), I assume that the main purpose of the *School Gazette* was to give students practice in penmanship. Neither paper has content that is identifiable, by signature or by style, as being written by Sara Willis.

Chapter Three. Patronymics, Property, and Proper Naming

1. "There is no support for later speculation by some critics that H. was Nathaniel Hawthorne" (Fuller *Letters* 1:228). The editor of the volume, Hudspeth, following Fuller, assumes that the respondent was a man; it is possible, although not probable, that "H" was a woman.

2. Calvin Stowe had toured Europe in 1836 to investigate the Prussian school system. "His Report on Elementary Instruction in Europe [was] circulated in every school district in Ohio and widely reprinted by the legislatures of other states" (Hedrick, *Harriet Beecher Stowe* 111).

3. The biographical evidence, in fact, suggests that she did depend on these connections to some extent. According to Patricia L. McGinnis, "Mason Brothers, who published Ruth Hall, were the sons of Lowell Mason . . . an old friend of the Willis family" (12).

4. For purposes of this argument, I assume that most *Godey's* readers were women. Yet evidence from the magazine itself indicates that men subscribed to and presumably read *Godey's* as well. For example, Civil War soldiers were said to have formed subscription clubs.

5. Beecher participated in a similar activity of hierarchical naming, specifically applied to domestic servitude. For details of her reasoning, see chapter 7, "The Difference Between Authors and Servants."

6. For a similar judgment, see an anonymous essay in *Godey's* entitled "A Few Words on Etiquette": "Never use the term genteel—it is only to be found in the mouths of those who have it nowhere else" (33 [Aug. 1846]: 87).

Chapter Four. Domestic Masquerade

1. Gunn recounts in his journal that both Fanny and her daughter Grace had cut their hair (Warren 184); Fern's version of the escapade into the city indicates only that she tucked her hair up into the cap she wore.

Chapter Five. The Domestic Manners of American Ladies

1. In this chapter, subsequent references to the *Treatise* are to the 1846 (third, revised) edition unless otherwise indicated.

2. Blumin and Warner suggest that consumer possessions—"wool carpeting, wallpaper, and all manner of furnishings" as well as private bedrooms and "indoor toilets"—differentiated the middle classes of the mid-nineteenth-century United States. (330). Each of the possessions that Blumin lists is mentioned, with instructions for its proper use and care, in the *Treatise*.

3. According to Laurie, "the proportion of self-employed craftsmen declined from 1-in-5 in 1840 to less than 1-in-10 in 1860." In Cincinnati, where nearly 33 percent of the mechanics had owned homes in 1820, "the proportion plummeted to 6% in 1838 and to under 5% in 1850" (58, 59).

4. Gillian Brown's reading of the *Treatise* argues that to define character as transcendent of class resulted in feminine "stability achieved through complete self-denial" (22). Aligning Catharine Beecher's conduct book with Harriet Beecher Stowe's and Nathaniel Hawthorne's fictions, Brown argues that "domestic ideology" denies and removes women from productive labor.

5. According to Fisher, such operations of homogeneity served to "[erase] letter by letter the accent, style of laughter, customs and costumes of [public and] family life, dress, and idiom of the old country so as to be, at last, simply American. In every American personality there exists a past history of erasure" (63). Fisher's dictum is only partly correct, however. *Erasure* implies a successful process that slights the possibility of resistance and overlooks how "old country" uses and customs modified American identities engrafted onto them, processes that this chapter recognizes but that are outside its scope of investigation. Here I adapt Fisher's structure but not his terminology, suggesting that the tropes of palimpsest or grafting better characterize the process.

Chapter Six. Domesticated Eloquence

1. Hale may have written fiction about women public speakers. An anonymous 1839 novel, *The Lecturess,* has been attributed to her by the L.H. Wright microfilm series, *American Fiction, 1774–1850*. The primary evidence for this attribution seems to be the title, which respects Hale's advocacy of the feminine noun. Beyond that, I have located no convincing proof that she wrote the novel.

2. Men attended the conversations for a brief interlude in March and April 1841.

Chapter Seven. The Difference between Authors and Servants

1. Throughout this chapter, I use the singular article, echoing the nineteenth-century usage, but aware of the diversity this signifier masks.

2. For purposes of this argument, I echo these authors' assumptions that servant women were unmarried. I will occasionally refer to married "help," as well, especially those who worked as occasional employees, such as washerwomen.

3. It is possible, even likely, that these confidences were textual constructs of Hale and Fern, not actual communication from biographically verifiable correspondents. Nevertheless, the trope of intimate feminine confidence prevails in writings on domesticity, particularly in the figural construct of women gossiping about "the servant problem."

4. Both G. Brown and Romero use Catharine Beecher's books of domestic practice primarily as a preliminary step to analyses of Harriet Beecher Stowe's *Uncle Tom's Cabin*.

And both Brown (219–20, nn. 9–11) and Romero (715–21) call Stowe's crisis of illness in
the 1840s "hysteria," although they understand its relation to domesticity in different ways.
Hedrick, however, does not read Stowe's symptoms during this decade as constituting hysteria.
Although she discusses Harriet and Calvin Stowe's awareness of George M. Beard's *American
Nervousness* (141), she attributes Stowe's physical disabilities to "the cumulative effects of
chronic mercury poisoning, cholera and miscarriages" (176). Hedrick cites neither Romero
nor Brown. None of these sources seems aware of Burbick's essay that establishes that worry
about hysteria or "nervousness" was not confined to women only. See also Herndl for a book-
length study of literary versions of "invalid women" and their relation to medical discourse.
    5. Indenture marked a middle ground between racial slavery and hired "help." The Beecher
family employed several "bound" servants whose lengthy terms of legal indebtedness led
Lyman Beecher to characterize them as "a part of the family" (*Autobiography* 1:87). It is likely
that Catharine had these legally stabilized loyalties in mind as she enjoined a similar loyalty
on waged servants.

Chapter Eight. Domesticating Pedagogy

    1. Neither of these anecdotes is persuasively documented. Both were written long after
the incidents purportedly took place. Higginson's account of Fuller is written at a fifty-year
remove, Stowe's some sixty years after Catharine's death. I use them here as illuminating and
suggestive possibilities, not for their factual content.
    2. As with much that Beecher wrote, this address cannot be taken as the literal truth.
Other accounts paint a different picture of these early days of the seminary. For example, in
her *Suggestions Respecting Improvements in Education*, written six years later for an audience of
the school's trustees, she implies that disciplinary disorder prevailed during the school's early
months: "The teachers spent their time in the following manner. Upon entering the school
they commenced in the first place the business of keeping in order and quietness an assembly
of youth, full of life and spirits, and many of them ready to evade every rule, were not the
eye of authority continually upon the watch. . . .
    "By the time the duties of the day were over, the care of governing, the vexations of
irregularities and mischief, the labour of hearing such a number and variety of lessons, and
the *sickness of heart* occasioned by feeling that *nothing was done well,* were sufficient to exhaust
the animal strength and spirits, and nothing more could be attempted, till the next day arose
to witness the same round of duties. While attempting to teach in this manner, the writer felt
that no single duty of a teacher could possibly be performed" (22–23).

Chapter Nine. Domesticity with a Difference

    1. I emphasize this point in contradistinction to Mary E. Wood's assertion that "a romantic
friendship between middle-class white women . . . was only acceptable as long as it did not
enter public discourse, in other words, as long as it did not threaten the heterosexuality
implicitly in the dominant genres of nineteenth-century America" (6–7). Several of these
women wrote publicly about same-sex alliances and sometimes did so as an explicit challenge
to heterosexual domination.
    2. Until recently, although overwhelming documentary evidence chronicles the passionate
attachment of women to other women, critics and biographers have been reluctant to call
these attachments lesbian, fearing, perhaps, the invidious overtones of such a classification.
I see both Beecher's and Fuller's relationships as lesbian, quite possibly in a physical sense,
and certainly in the political implications of the term as a system of feminine relations

opposed to patriarchy. Here I follow Sheila Jeffreys's definition of lesbianism as "a passionate commitment to women, a culture, a political alternative to the basic institution of male supremacy, a means through which women have always gained self-respect and pursued their own goals and achievements with the support of other women. It is more than likely to include a sensual component, which may or may not take a genital form" (24).

3. According to Brickley, "While she was a student . . . Matilda became engaged to . . . Loring Curtis Hubbell. . . . For unknown reasons, however, Matilda jilted Loring Hubbell in 1824 and married Abraham Dirck Brinkerhoff. . . . Catharine Beecher was extremely upset by Matilda's jilting of Hubbell" ("Female" 515–16). After Brinkerhoff's death in 1860 Matilda married Loring Hubbell (Brickley correspondence).

4. See, for example, Nancy Miller, Jacobus, and Irigaray. Each of these critics considers linguistic operations by which language, itself a masculine system, can be made to accommodate feminine perceptions. In this case, I am adapting Miller's concept of italicization to material acts and their consequences, as well as to the textual representations of those acts.

5. In this pattern, she was not unlike her teacher and mentor, Sarah Pierce, who explored in poetry the possibilities for women to form utopian alliances outside traditional family models. See von Frank's analysis of Pierce's poem, "Verses, written in the Winter of 1792, & addressed to Abigail Smith Jr."

6. See Fuller's journal entry for 30 October 1842: "Sam was away, and I slept with Anna the first time for two years. It was exquisitely painful to feel that I loved her less than when we before were thus together in confiding sleep, and she too is now so graceful and lovely, but the secret of my life is sealed to her forever. . . . I took pleasure in sleeping on Sam's pillow" (Habich 290). While I do not claim that Fuller's claim of "sleeping with" holds the same sexual connotations as it does in contemporary slang, I do read this passage as indicative of an erotic relationship between the two women.

7. In or around 1839, Fuller had written, "I have no child, and the woman in me has so craved this experience that it has seemed the want of it must paralyze me." This passage is frequently quoted omitting the two following sentences, which are essential to its correct interpretation: "But now as I look upon these lovely children of a human birth what slow and neutralizing cares they bring with them to the mother. The children of the muse come quicker with less pain and disgust, [and] rest more lightly on the bosom" (qtd. in Capper, *Margaret Fuller* 289).

8. Legal opinion reinforced this popular perception. According to Grossberg, law's relation to betrothal and marriage was based in this inconsistency. A man could be released without penalty from an engagement to a "soiled" woman on the basis of fraud (41); Victorian law also presumed "the passionlessness of normal women" (47). See his chapter 2 for details of this legal logic.

Bibliography

Archival Sources

Boston Public Library
Cincinnati Historical Society
    The Semi-Colon Collection
Connecticut Historical Society, Hartford
    Hoadly Collection
    David Johnson Papers
Newport Richards Free Library, Newport, N.H.
    Sarah Josepha Hale Collection
Arthur and Elizabeth Schlesinger Library on the History of Women in America, Cambridge, Mass.
    Beecher-Stowe Collection
Smith College, Northampton, Mass.
    Sophia Smith Collection
Stowe-Day Foundation, Hartford, Conn.
    Acquisitions
    Katharine S. Day Collection
    Foote Collection
    Memoranda Books
Vassar College Archives, Poughkeepsie, N.Y.
    Special Collections
Watkinson Library, Trinity College, Hartford, Conn.
    Ledger Collection

Primary Sources

The Annual Catalogue of the Hartford Female Seminary. Hartford, Conn.: George F. Olmsted, 1831.
Beecher, Catharine E. *The Duty of American Women to Their Country.* New York: Harper, 1845.
——. *Educational Reminiscences and Suggestions.* New York: J.B. Ford, 1874.
——. *The Elements of Mental and Moral Philosophy, Founded upon Experience, Reason, and the Bible.* Hartford, Conn., 1831.
——. "Essay on the Education of Female Teachers for the United States." 1835. Schlesinger Library.
——. *An Essay on Slavery and Abolitionism, with Reference to the Duty of American Females.* Philadelphia: Henry Perkins, 1837.
——. *The Evils Suffered by American Women and Children: The Causes and the Remedy.* New York: Harper, 1846.
——. "The Evils Suffered by American Women and Children: The Causes and the Remedy." Presented in an Address by Miss. C. E. Beecher to Meetings of Ladies in

Cincinnati, Washington, Baltimore, Philadelphia, New York and Other Cities. Also an
   Address to the Protestant Clergy of the United States." New York: Harper, 1846.
———. "Fanny Moreland; or, Use and Abuse of the Risibles." In *The Christian Keepsake and
   Missionary Annual for 1847*. Boston: Phillips and Sampson, 1847.
———. Introduction to *The May Flower and Miscellaneous Writings*, by Harriet Beecher
   Stowe. Boston: Phillips, Sampson, 1855.
———. *Letters to the People on Health and Happiness*. 1855. Reprint, New York: Arno, 1972.
———. *Letters to Persons Who Are Engaged in Domestic Service*. New York: Leavitt and Trow,
   1842.
———. *Miss Beecher's Domestic Receipt-Book; Designed as a Supplement to her Treatise on
   Domestic Economy, 3d. Edition*. New York: Harper, 1846.
———. *The New Housekeeper's Manual: Embracing a New Revised Edition of The American
   Woman's Home; or, Principles of Domestic Science. Being a Guide to Economical, Healthful,
   Beautiful, and Christian Homes. Etc.* New York: J.B. Ford, 1873.
———. "Something for Women Better than the Ballot." *Appleton's Journal* 23 (4 Sept. 1869):
   1–12.
———. *Suggestions Respecting Improvements in Education, Presented to the Trustees of the
   Hartford Female Seminary, and Published at their Request*. Hartford, Conn.: Packard and
   Butler, 1839.
———. *Treatise on Domestic Economy for the Use of Young Ladies at Home and at School*. 1841.
   Reprint, New York: Schocken, 1977.
———. *Treatise on Domestic Economy for the Use of Young Ladies at Home and at School*. Rev.
   ed. New York: Harpers, 1846.
———. *Treatise on Domestic Economy for the Use of Young Ladies at Home and at School*. Rev.
   ed. New York: Harpers, 1868.
———. *The True Remedy for the Wrongs of Woman: with a History of an Enterprise Having
   That for Its Object*. Boston: Philips, Samson, 1851.
———. *Woman Suffrage and Woman's Profession*. Hartford, Conn.: Brown and Gross, 1871.
Beecher, Catherine E., and Harriet Beecher Stowe. *The American Woman's Home*. 1869.
   Reprint, Hartford, Conn.: Stowe-Day Foundation, 1991.
Brickley, Lynne Templeton. Personal correspondence with author. 9 Sept. 1994.
Fern, Fanny. *Caper-Sauce*. New York: G.W. Carleton, 1872.
———. *Fern Leaves from Fanny's Portfolio*. Auburn and Buffalo, N.Y.: Miller, Orton, and
   Mulligan, 1854.
———. *Fern Leaves from Fanny's Portfolio*. Second Series. Auburn and Buffalo, N.Y.: Miller,
   Orton, and Mulligan, 1854.
———. *Folly as It Flies*. New York: G.W. Carleton, 1870.
———. *Fresh Leaves*. New York: Mason Brothers, 1857.
———. *Ginger-Snaps*. New York: G.W. Carleton, 1870.
———. *A New Story Book for Children*. New York: Mason Brothers, 1864.
———. *Ruth Hall*. 1855. In *Ruth Hall, and Other Writings*, edited by Joyce W. Warren. New
   Brunswick, N.J.: Rutgers University Press, 1986.
Fuller, Margaret. *The Letters of Margaret Fuller*. Edited by Robert N. Hudspeth. 6 vols. Ithaca:
   Cornell University Press, 1983–1988.
———. *Summer on the Lakes in 1843*. Facsimile ed. Neuwkoop: B. DeGraff, 1972.
———. *Woman in the Nineteenth Century*. New York: Norton, 1971.
———. *Woman in the Nineteenth Century and Kindred Papers Relating to the Sphere, Condition
   and Duties of Woman*, edited by Arthur B. Fuller. Boston: John P. Jewett, 1855.
Godey's Lady's Book. 1832–1877.

Hale, Sarah [Jane?]. *The Countries of Europe and the Manners and Customs of Its Various Nations.* N.p.: McLoughlin Brothers, N.d.

[————]. *The Genius of Oblivion and Other Original Poems.* Concord: Jacob B. Moore, 1823.

Hale, Sarah Josepha. *The Good Housekeeper; or, The Way to Live Well and to Be Well While We Live.* Boston: Weeks, Jordan, 1839.

————. *The Ladies' Wreath; A Selection from the Female Poetic Writers of England and America. With Original Notices and Notes: Prepared Especially for Young Ladies. A Gift-Book for All Seasons.* Boston: Marsh, Capen and Lyon, 1837.

————. *Manners; or, Happy Homes and Good Society All the Year Round.* 1867. Reprint, New York: Arno, 1972.

————. ed. *Modern Cookery, in All Its Branches,* by Eliza Acton. Revised by Mrs. S.J. Hale. Philadelphia: Lea and Blanchard, 1845.

————. *Mrs. Hale's New Cook Book.* Philadelphia: T.B. Peterson, 1857.

————. *Mrs. Hale's Receipts for the Million: Containing Four Thousand Five Hundred and Forty-Five Receipts, Facts, Directions, etc. in the Useful, Ornamental, and Domestic Arts, and in the Conduct of Life.* Philadelphia: T.B. Peterson, 1857.

————. *The New Household Receipt-Book.* New York: H. Long, 1853.

————. *Northwood: or, Life North and South.* 1852. Reprint, New York: Johnson Reprint, 1970.

————. *Sketches of American Character.* 6th ed. Boston: Benjamin Bradley, 1838.

————. *Woman's Record; or, Sketches of All Distinguished Women from the Creation to A.D. 1854, Arranged in four eras. With selections from female writers of every age.* 2nd ed. Rev. ed. New York: Harper, 1855.

Ladies' Magazine. 1828–1837.

New York Ledger. 1855–1872.

Secondary Sources

Adams, Florence Bannard. *Fanny Fern, or A Pair of Flaming Shoes.* West Trenton, N.J.: Hermitage Press, 1966.

Albert, Judith Strong. "Margaret Fuller's Row at the Greene Street School: Early Female Education in Providence, 1837–1839." *Rhode Island History* 42, no. 2 (May 1983): 43–55.

Alger, William Rounseville. *The Friendships of Women.* Boston: Roberts Brothers, 1868.

Anderson, Benedict R. *Imagined Communities: Reflections on the Origin and Spread of Nationalism.* London: Verso, 1983.

Apple, Michael W. "Teaching and 'Women's Work': A Comparative Historical and Ideological Analysis." In *Expressions of Power in Education: Studies of Class, Gender and Race,* edited by Edgar B. Gumbert. Atlanta: Center for Cross-Cultural Education, 1984.

Armstrong, Nancy. *Desire and Domestic Fiction: A Political History of the Novel.* New York: Oxford University Press, 1987.

————. "The Rise of the Domestic Woman." In *The Ideology of Conduct: Essays in Literature and the History of Sexuality,* edited by Nancy Armstrong and Leonard Tennenhouse. New York: Methuen, 1987.

————. Nancy, and Leonard Tennenhouse, eds. *The Ideology of Conduct: Essays in Literature and the History of Sexuality.* New York: Methuen, 1987.

Bardes, Suzanne, and Barbara Anne Gossett. *Declarations of Independence: Women and Political Power in Nineteenth-Century American Fiction.* New Brunswick, N.J.: Rutgers University Press, 1990.

Barthes, Roland. "Novels and Children." *Mythologies.* Trans. Annette Lavers. New York: Hill and Wang, 1982.

Baym, Nina. "Onward Christian Women: Sarah J. Hale's History of the World." *New England Quarterly* 63, no. 2 (June 1990): 249–70.

———. *Woman's Fiction: A Guide to Novels by and about Women in America, 1820–1870.* Ithaca: Cornell University Press, 1978.

Beecher, Lyman. *The Autobiography of Lyman Beecher.* Edited by Barbara M. Cross. 2 vols. Cambridge, Mass.: Harvard University Press, 1961.

Berkin, Carol Ruth, and Mary Beth Norton. *Women of America: A History.* Boston: Houghton Mifflin, 1979.

Berlant, Lauren. "The Female Woman: Fanny Fern and the Form of Sentiment." In *The Culture of Sentiment: Race, Gender, and Sentimentality in Nineteenth-Century America,* edited by Shirley Samuels. New York: Oxford University Press, 1992.

Birnbaum, Michelle. "Dark Dialects: Scientific and Literary Realism in 'Uncle Remus.'" *New Orleans Review* 18, no. 1 (1991): 36–45.

Blanchard, Paula. *Margaret Fuller: From Transcendentalism to Revolution.* New York: Delta/Seymour Lawrence, 1978.

Blumin, Stuart M. *The Emergence of the Middle Class: Social Experience in the American City, 1760–1900.* Cambridge: Cambridge University Press, 1989.

———. "The Hypothesis of Middle-Class Formation in Nineteenth-Century America: A Critique and Some Proposals." *American Historical Review* 90, no. 2 (Apr. 1985): 299–338.

Bobbit, Mary Reed. "A Bibliography of Etiquette Books Published in America Before 1900." *Bulletin of the New York Public Library* 51 (Dec. 1947): 687–720.

Boose, Lynda E. "The Father's House and the Daughter in It." In *Daughters and Fathers,* edited by Lynda E. Boose and Betty S. Flowers. Baltimore: Johns Hopkins University Press, 1989.

Boose, Lynda E., and Betty S. Flowers, eds. *Daughters and Fathers.* Baltimore: Johns Hopkins University Press, 1989.

Bourdieu, Pierre, and Jean-Claude Passeron. *Reproduction in Education, Society and Culture.* Trans. Richard Nice. London: Sage, 1977.

Boydston, Jeanne. *Home and Work: Housework, Wages, and the Ideology of Labor in the Early Republic.* New York: Oxford University Press, 1990.

Boydston, Jeanne, Mary Kelley, and Anne Margolis, eds. *The Limits of Sisterhood: The Beecher Sisters on Women's Rights and Woman's Sphere.* Chapel Hill: University of North Carolina Press, 1988.

Brickley, Lynne Templeton. "'Female Academies Are Everywhere Establishing': The Beginnings of Secondary Education for Women in the United States, 1790–1830." Unpublished qualifying paper, Harvard Graduate School of Education, 1982.

———. "Sarah Pierce's Female Academy." In *To Ornament Their Minds: Sarah Pierce's Litchfield Female Academy, 1792–1833,* edited by Catherine Keene Fields and Lisa C. Kightlinger. Litchfield, Conn.: Litchfield Historical Society, 1993.

Brodhead, Richard H. *The School of Hawthorne.* New York: Oxford University Press, 1986.

———. "Sparing the Rod: Discipline and Fiction in Antebellum America." In *Cultures of Letters: Scenes of Reading and Writing in Nineteenth-Century America.* Chicago: University of Chicago Press, 1993.

———. "Veiled Ladies: Toward a History of Antebellum Entertainment." *American Literary History* 1, no. 2 (Summer 1989): 273–94.

Brown, Gillian. *Domestic Individualism: Imagining Self in Nineteenth-Century America.* Berkeley and Los Angeles: University of California Press, 1990.

Brown, Richard D. *Knowledge Is Power: The Diffusion of Information in Early America, 1700–1865.* New York: Oxford University Press, 1989.

Burbick, Joan. " 'Intervals of Tranquillity': The Language of Health in Antebellum America."
    Prospects 12 (1987): 175–99.
Burstyn, Joan N. "Catharine Beecher and the Education of American Women." *New England
    Quarterly* 47 (1974): 386–403.
Burt, Olive. *First Woman Editor: Sarah J. Hale.* New York: Julian Messner, 1960.
Butcher, Patricia Smith. *Education for Equality: Women's Rights Periodicals and Women's Higher
    Education, 1849–1920.* New York: Greenwood Press, 1989.
Butler, Judith, and Joan W. Scott, eds. *Feminists Theorize the Political.* New York: Routledge,
    1992.
Butler, Judith. *Gender Trouble: Gender and the Subversion of Identity.* New York: Routledge,
    1990.
Campbell, Karlyn Kohrs. *Man Cannot Speak for Her.* Vol. 1 of *A Critical Study of Early Feminist
    Rhetoric.* New York: Praeger, 1989.
Campbell, SueEllen. "Feasting in the Wilderness: The Language of Food in American
    Wilderness Narratives." *American Literary History* 6, no. 1 (1994): 1–23.
Capper, Charles. *Margaret Fuller: An American Romantic Life.* Vol. 1, *The Private Years.* New
    York: Oxford University Press, 1992.
———. "Margaret Fuller as Cultural Reformer: The Conversations in Boston." *American
    Quarterly* 39 (1987): 509–28.
Carby, Hazel V. *Reconstructing Womanhood: The Emergence of the Afro-American Woman
    Novelist.* New York: Oxford University Press, 1987.
Carnes, Mark C., and Clyde Griffin, eds. *Meanings for Manhood: Constructions of Masculinity
    in Victorian America.* Chicago: University of Chicago Press, 1990.
Castle, Terry. *The Apparitional Lesbian: Female Homosexuality and Modern Culture.* New York:
    Columbia University Press, 1993.
Chevigny, Bell Gale. *The Woman and the Myth: Margaret Fuller's Life and Writings.* Old
    Westbury, N.Y.: Feminist Press, 1976.
———. *The Woman and the Myth: Margaret Fuller's Life and Writings.* Rev. ed. Boston:
    Northeastern University Press, 1994.
Clark, Gregory, and S. Michael Halloran, eds. *Oratorical Culture in Nineteenth-Century
    America: Transformations in the Theory and Practice of Rhetoric.* Carbondale: Southern
    Illinois University Press, 1993.
Cmiel, Kenneth. *Democratic Eloquence: The Fight over Popular Speech in Nineteenth-Century
    America.* New York: Morrow, 1990.
Conrad, Susan Phinney. *Perish the Thought: Intellectual Women in Romantic America, 1830–
    1860.* New York: Oxford University Press, 1976.
Cott, Nancy F. *"The Bonds of Womanhood": Woman's Sphere in New England, 1780–1835.* New
    Haven: Yale University Press, 1977.
Coultrap-McQuin, Susan. *Doing Literary Business: American Women Writers in the Nineteenth
    Century.* Chapel Hill: University of North Carolina Press, 1990.
Cross, Barbara M., ed. *The Educated Woman in America: Selected Writings of Catharine Beecher,
    Margaret Fuller, and M. Carey Thomas.* New York: Teachers College Press, 1965.
Davidson, Cathy N. *Revolution and the Word: The Rise of the Novel in America.* New York:
    Oxford University Press, 1986.
Dedmond, Francis B. "The Letters of Caroline Sturgis to Margaret Fuller." In *Studies in
    the American Renaissance,* edited by Joel Myerson. Charlottesville: University Press of
    Virginia, 1988.
Doane, Mary Ann. *The Desire to Desire: The Woman's Film of the 1940s.* Bloomington: Indiana
    University Press, 1987.

Donegan, Jane B. *"Hydropathic Highway to Health": Women and Water-Cure in Antebellum America*. New York: Greenwood Press, 1986.

Donzelot, Jacques. *The Policing of Families*. Trans. Robert Hurley. New York: Pantheon, 1979.

Douglas, Ann. *The Feminization of American Culture*. New York: Knopf, 1977.

Dublin, Thomas. *Transforming Women's Work: New England Lives in the Industrial Revolution*. Ithaca: Cornell University Press, 1994.

Dudden, Faye E. *Serving Women: Household Service in Nineteenth-Century America*. Middletown, Conn.: Wesleyan University Press, 1983.

Eisler, Benita, ed. *The Lowell Offering: Writings by New England Mill Women (1840–1845)*. New York: Harper and Row, 1977.

Ellison, Julie. *Delicate Subjects: Romanticism, Gender, and the Ethics of Understanding*. Ithaca: Cornell University Press, 1990.

Emerson, Ralph Waldo, W.H. Channing, and J.F. Clarke, eds. *Memoirs of Margaret Fuller Ossoli*. 2 vols. Boston: Roberts Brothers, 1884.

Entrikin, Isabelle Webb. *Sarah Josepha Hale and "Godey's Lady's Book."* Philadelphia: Lancaster Press, 1946.

Faderman, Lillian. *Surpassing the Love of Men: Romantic Friendship and Love Between Women from the Renaissance to the Present*. New York: Morrow, 1981.

Fergenson, Laraine R. "Margaret Fuller as a Teacher in Providence: The School Journal of Ann Brown." In *Studies in the American Renaissance*, edited by Joel Myerson. Charlottesville: University Press of Virginia, 1991.

Fetterley, Judith. "Commentary: Nineteenth-Century American Women Writers and the Politics of Recovery." *American Literary History* 6, no. 3 (Fall 1994): 600–611.

Finley, Ruth E. *The Lady of Godey's: Sarah Josepha Hale*. Philadelphia: Lippincott, 1932.

Fisher, Philip. "Appearing and Disappearing in Public: Social Space in Late-Nineteenth-Century Literature and Culture." In *Reconstructing American Literary History*, edited by Sacvan Bercovitch. Cambridge, Mass.: Harvard University Press, 1986.

————. "Democratic Social Space: Whitman, Melville, and the Promise of American Transparency." *Representations* 24 (Fall 1988): 60–101.

————. *Hard Facts: Setting and Form in the American Novel*. New York: Oxford University Press, 1985.

Flood, Lynn. "A Life of Angels: Margaret Fuller's World." *Ladder* 16, nos. 9–10 (June-July 1972): 28–34.

Foucault, Michel. *Discipline and Punish: The Birth of the Prison*. Trans. Alan Sheridan. New York: Pantheon, 1977.

————. *The History of Sexuality*. Vol. 1, *An Introduction*. Trans. Robert Hurley. New York: Vintage, 1980.

————. *Madness and Civilization: A History of Insanity in the Age of Reason*. Trans. Richard Howard. New York: Vintage, 1973.

————. "What Is an Author?" Trans. Josué V. Harari. In *The Foucault Reader*, edited by Paul Rabinow. New York: Pantheon, 1984.

Freedman, Estelle B., et al., eds. *The Lesbian Issue*. Chicago: University of Chicago Press, 1982.

Geary, Susan. "The Domestic Novel as a Commercial Commodity: Making a Best Seller in the 1850s." *Bibliographical Society of America Papers* 70 (1976): 365–93.

Gere, Anne Ruggles. *Writing Groups: History, Theory, and Implications*. Carbondale: Southern Illinois University Press, 1987.

Gilmore, William J. *Reading Becomes a Necessity of Life: Material and Cultural Life in Rural New England, 1780–1835*. Knoxville: University of Tennessee Press, 1989.

Godey, Louis Antoine. "Sarah Josepha Hale." *Godey's Lady's Book* 41 (Dec. 1850): 326.

Graff, Gerald. *Professing Literature: An Institutional History.* Chicago: University of Chicago Press, 1987.

Grossberg, Michael. *Governing the Hearth: Law and the Family in Nineteenth-Century America.* Chapel Hill: University of North Carolina Press, 1985.

Habich, Robert D. "Margaret Fuller's Journal for October 1842." *Harvard Library Bulletin* 33 (Summer 1985): 280–91.

Hall, David D. "The Uses of Literacy in New England, 1600–1850." In *Printing and Society in Early America,* edited by William L. Joyce, et al. Worcester, Mass.: American Antiquarian Society, 1983.

Haltunnen, Karen. *Confidence Men and Painted Women: A Study of Middle-Class Culture in America, 1839–1870.* New Haven: Yale University Press, 1982.

Harris, Susan K. *Nineteenth-Century American Women's Novels: Interpretative Strategies.* New York: Cambridge University Press, 1990.

Hart, James D. *The Popular Book: A History of America's Literary Taste.* New York: Oxford University Press, 1950.

Hart, John S. "Sarah J. Hale." *The Female Prose Writers of America.* 1852. Reprint, Ann Arbor: UMI, 1980.

Harveson, Mae Elizabeth. *Catharine Esther Beecher (Pioneer Educator).* New York: Arno Press, 1969.

Hayden, Dolores. *The Grand Domestic Revolution: A History of Feminist Designs for American Homes, Neighborhoods, and Cities.* Cambridge, Mass.: MIT Press, 1981.

Hedrick, Joan D. *Harriet Beecher Stowe: A Life.* New York: Oxford University Press, 1994.

———. "Parlor Literature: Harriet Beecher Stowe and the Question of 'Great Women Artists.'" *Signs* 17, no. 2 (1992): 275–303.

Helly, Dorothy O., and Susan M. Reverby. *Gendered Domains: Rethinking Public and Private in Women's History: Essays from the Seventh Berkshire Conference on the History of Women.* Ithaca: Cornell University Press, 1992.

Herndl, Diane Price. *Invalid Women: Figuring Feminine Illness in American Fiction and Culture, 1840–1940.* Chapel Hill: University of North Carolina Press, 1993.

Higginson, Thomas Wentworth. *Margaret Fuller Ossoli.* Boston: Houghton, Mifflin, 1884; Cambridge: Riverside Press, 1899.

Horowitz, Helen Lefkowitz. *Alma Mater: Design and Experience in the Women's Colleges from Their Nineteenth-Century Beginnings to the 1930s.* Boston: Beacon Press, 1984.

Horsman, Reginald. *Race and Manifest Destiny: The Origins of American Racial Anglo-Saxonism.* Cambridge, Mass.: Harvard University Press, 1981.

Irigaray, Luce. *This Sex Which Is Not One.* Trans. Catherine Porter, with Carolyn Burke. Ithaca: Cornell University Press, 1985.

Jacobus, Mary. "The Questions of Language: Men of Maxims and *The Mill on the Floss.*" *Critical Inquiry* 8 (1981): 207–22.

Jeffreys, Sheila. "Does It Matter If They Did It?" *Not a Passing Phase: Reclaiming Lesbians in History, 1840–1985.* London: Women's Press, 1989.

Johnson, Harriet Hall. "Margaret Fuller as Known by Her Scholars." In *Critical Essays on Margaret Fuller,* edited by Joel Myerson. Boston: G.K. Hall, 1980.

Johnson, Nan. "The Popularization of Nineteenth-Century Rhetoric: Elocution and the Private Learner." In *Oratorical Culture in Nineteenth-Century America: Transformations in the Theory and Practice of Rhetoric,* edited by Gregory Clark and S. Michael Halloran. Carbondale: Southern Illinois University Press, 1993.

Joyce, William L., et al., eds. *Printing and Society in Early America.* Worcester, Mass.: American Antiquarian Society, 1983.

Kaminer, Wendy. *I'm Dysfunctional, You're Dysfunctional: The Recovery Movement and Other Self-Help Fashions*. New York: Addison-Wesley, 1992.

Kasson, John F. *Rudeness and Civility: Manners in Nineteenth-Century Urban America*. New York: Hill and Wang, 1990.

Katz, Jonathan. *Gay American History: Lesbians and Gay Men in the U.S.A.: A Documentary.* New York: Thomas Y. Crowell, 1976.

Katz, Michael B. *The Irony of Early School Reform: Educational Innovation in Mid-Nineteenth Century Massachusetts.* Cambridge: Harvard University Press, 1968.

Katzman, David M. *Seven Days a Week: Women and Domestic Service in Industrializing America.* New York: Oxford University Press, 1978.

Kaufman, Polly Welts. *Women Teachers on the Frontier.* New Haven: Yale University Press, 1984.

Kelley, Mary. *Private Woman, Public Stage: Literary Domesticity in Nineteenth Century America.* New York: Oxford University Press, 1984.

Kennedy, George. *Classical Rhetoric and Its Christian and Secular Tradition from Ancient to Modern Times.* Chapel Hill: University of North Carolina Press, 1980.

Kerber, Linda. "The Paradox of Women's Citizenship in the Early Republic: The Case of *Martin vs. Massachusetts*, 1805." *American Historical Review* 97, no. 2 (1992): 349–78.

———. "Separate Spheres, Female Worlds, Woman's Place: The Rhetoric of Women's History." *Journal of American History* 75 (June 1988): 9–39.

———. "'Why Should Girls Be Learn'd and Wise?' Two Centuries of Higher Education for Women as Seen Through the Unfinished Work of Alice Mary Baldwin." In *Women and Higher Education in American History,* edited by John Mack Faragher and Florence Howe. New York: Norton, 1988.

———. *Women of the Republic: Intellect and Ideology in Revolutionary America.* New York: Norton, 1980.

Kerber, Linda, et al. "Beyond Roles, Beyond Spheres: Thinking about Gender in the Early Republic." *William and Mary Quarterly* 46 (1989): 565–85.

Kolodny, Annette. "Margaret Fuller: Recovering Our Mother's Garden." *The Land Before Her: Fantasy and Experience of the American Frontiers, 1639–1860.* Chapel Hill: University of North Carolina Press, 1984.

Kunciov, Robert, ed. *Mr. Godey's Ladies: Being a Mosaic of Fashions and Fancies.* Princeton: Pyne Press, 1971.

Lasser, Carol. "The Domestic Balance of Power: Relations Between Mistress and Maid in Nineteenth-Century New England." *Labor History* 28 (1987): 5–22.

Laurie, Bruce. *Artisans Into Workers: Labor in Nineteenth-Century America.* New York: Noonday Press, 1989.

Lemaire, Anika. *Jacques Lacan.* Trans. David Macey. London: Routledge, 1979.

Linner, Edward R. *Vassar: The Remarkable Growth of a Man and His College, 1855–1865.* Ed. Elizabeth A. Daniels. Poughkeepsie, N.Y.: Vassar College, 1984.

Lystra, Karen. *Searching the Heart: Women, Men, and Romantic Love in Nineteenth-Century America.* New York: Oxford University Press, 1989.

Martin, Lawrence. "The Genesis of Godey's Lady's Book." *New England Quarterly* 1 (1928): 41–70.

Martin, Theodora Penny. *The Sound of Our Own Voices: Women's Study Clubs, 1860–1910.* Boston: Beacon Press, 1987.

Matthews, Glenna. *"Just a Housewife": The Rise and Fall of Domesticity in America.* New York: Oxford University Press, 1987.

McCall, Laura. "'The Reign of Brute Force Is Now Over': A Content Analysis of *Godey's Lady's Book*, 1830–1860." *Journal of the Early Republic* 9 (Summer 1989): 217–36.

McGinnis, Patricia L. "Fanny Fern, American Novelist." *Biblion* 2 (1969): 2–37.

Melder, Keith. "Mask of Oppression: The Female Seminary Movement in the United States." *New York History* 55 (1974): 261–79.

Miller, Nancy K. "Emphasis Added: Plots and Plausibilities in Women's Fiction." In *The New Feminist Criticism: Essays on Women, Literature and Theory,* edited by Elaine Showalter. New York: Pantheon, 1985.

Miller, Perry. "'I Find No Intellect Comparable to My Own.'" *American Heritage* 8 (Feb. 1957): 22–25, 96–99.

———. ed. *Margaret Fuller: American Romantic. A Selection from Her Writings and Correspondence.* Ithaca: Cornell University Press, 1963.

Mitchell, Thomas R. "Julian Hawthorne and the 'Scandal' of Margaret Fuller." *American Literary History* 7, no. 2 (Summer 1995): 210–33.

Monaghan, A. Jennifer. "Literacy Instruction and Gender in Colonial New England." *American Quarterly* 40 (1988): 18–41.

Morison, Samuel Eliot. *Three Centuries of Harvard, 1636–1936.* Cambridge, Mass.: Harvard University Press, 1936.

Myerson, Joel, ed. *Critical Essays on Margaret Fuller.* Boston: G.K. Hall, 1980.

———. "Margaret Fuller's 1842 Journal: At Concord with the Emersons." *Harvard Library Bulletin* 21 (July 1973): 320–40.

Ong, Walter. "Latin Language Learning as a Renaissance Puberty Rite." In *Rhetoric, Romance, and Technology: Studies in the Interaction of Expression and Culture.* Ithaca: Cornell University Press, 1971.

Parker, E.P. "Harriet Beecher Stowe." *Eminent Women of the Age: Being Narratives of the Lives and Deeds of the Most Prominent Women of the Present Generation.* Ed. James Parton, et al. Hartford, Conn.: S.M. Betts, 1868.

Parmelee, Joseph W. "History of Newport." In *History of Cheshire and Sullivan Counties,* edited by D. Hamilton Hurd. Philadelphia: J.W. Lewis, 1886.

Parton, Ethel. "Fanny Fern at the Hartford Female Seminary." *New England Magazine* 24 (March 1901): 94–98.

Parton, James, ed. *Fanny Fern: A Memorial Volume, Containing her Select Writings and a Memoir.* New York: G.W. Carleton, 1873.

———. "Memoir of Fanny Fern." In *Fanny Fern: A Memorial Volume, Containing her Select Writings and a Memoir.* New York: G.W. Carleton, 1873.

Pascoe, Peggy. *Relations of Rescue: The Search for Female Moral Authority in the American West, 1874–1939.* New York: Oxford University Press, 1990.

Pattee, Fred Lewis. *The Feminine Fifties.* New York: D. Appleton-Century, 1940.

Pease, Jane H., and William H. Pease. *Ladies, Women, and Wenches: Choice and Constraint in Antebellum Charleston and Boston.* Chapel Hill: University of North Carolina Press, 1990.

Reid, Ronald F. "The Boylston Professorship of Rhetoric and Oratory, 1806–1904: A Case Study in Changing Concepts of Rhetoric and Pedagogy." *Quarterly Journal of Speech* 45 (1959): 239–57.

Reunion Hartford Female Seminary, June 9, 1892. Hartford, Conn.: Case, Lockwood and Brainard, 1892.

Ricciotti, Dominic. "Popular Art in *Godey's Lady's Book:* An Image of the American Woman, 1830–1860." *Historical New Hampshire* 27 (1972): 3–26.

Robbins, Bruce. *The Servant's Hand: English Fiction from Below.* New York: Columbia University Press, 1986.

Rogers, Sherbrooke. *Sarah Josepha Hale: A New England Pioneer, 1788–1879.* Grantham, N.H.: Tompson and Rutter, 1985.

Rollins, Judith. *Between Women: Domestics and Their Employers.* Philadelphia: Temple University Press, 1985.

Romero, Lora. "Bio-Political Resistance in Domestic Ideology and *Uncle Tom's Cabin.*" *American Literary History* 1, no. 4 (1989): 715–34.

Rosaldo, Michelle Zimbalist. "The Uses and Abuses of Anthropology: Reflections on Feminism and Cross-Cultural Understanding." *Signs* 5 (1980): 385–406.

218

BIBLIOGRAPHY

Rotundo, E. Anthony. "Romantic Friendship: Male Intimacy and Middle-Class Youth in the Northeastern U.S., 1800–1900." *Journal of Social History* 23 (Fall 1989): 1–25.

Rugoff, Milton. *The Beechers: An American Family in the Nineteenth Century.* New York: Harper and Row, 1981.

Ryan, Mary P. *Cradle of the Middle Class: The Family in Oneida County, New York, 1790–1865.* Cambridge: Cambridge University Press, 1981.

———. *Empire of the Mother: American Writing About Domesticity, 1830–1860.* New York: Haworth Press, 1982.

———. *Women in Public: Between Banners and Ballots, 1825–1880.* Baltimore: Johns Hopkins University Press, 1990.

Sahli, Nancy. "Smashing: Women's Relationships Before the Fall." *Chrysalis* 8 (1979): 17–27.

Salmon, Marylynn. *Women and the Law of Property in Early America.* Chapel Hill: University of North Carolina Press, 1986.

Samuels, Shirley, ed. *The Culture of Sentiment: Race, Gender, and Sentimentality in Nineteenth-Century America.* New York: Oxford University Press, 1992.

Sanchez-Eppler, Karen. "Bodily Bonds: The Intersecting Rhetorics of Feminism and Abolition." *Representations* 24 (1988): 28–59.

———. *Touching Liberty: Abolition, Feminism, and the Politics of the Body.* Berkeley and Los Angeles: University of California Press, 1993.

Schlesinger, Arthur M. *Learning How to Behave: A Historical Study of American Etiquette Books.* New York: Macmillan, 1946.

Scott, Anne Firor. "The Ever-Widening Circle: The Diffusion of Feminist Values from the Troy Female Seminary." *History of Education Quarterly* 19 (1979): 3–25.

Scott, Joan Wallach. "Experience." In *Feminists Theorize the Political,* edited by Judith Butler and Joan W. Scott. New York: Routledge, 1992.

———. *Gender and the Politics of History.* New York: Columbia University Press, 1988.

Showalter, Elaine. *Sisters' Choice: Tradition and Change in American Women's Writing.* Oxford: Clarendon Press, 1991.

Shuffelton, Frank. "Margaret Fuller at the Greene Street School: The Journal of Evelina Metcalf." In *Studies in the American Renaissance,* edited by Joel Myerson. Charlottesville: University Press of Virginia, 1985.

Silverman, Kaja. *The Subject of Semiotics.* New York: Oxford University Press, 1983.

Sklar, Kathryn Kish. *Catharine Beecher: A Study in American Domesticity.* New Haven: Yale University Press, 1973.

———. Introduction to *Treatise on Domestic Economy.* 1841. Reprint, New York: Schocken, 1977.

Smith, Sidonie. *A Poetics of Women's Autobiography: Marginality and the Fictions of Self-Representation.* Bloomington: Indiana University Press, 1987.

Smith-Rosenberg, Carroll. "The Female World of Love and Ritual: Relations Between Women in Nineteenth-Century America." *Signs* 1, no. 1 (1975): 19–27.

Spacks, Patricia Meyer. *Gossip.* New York: Knopf, 1985.

Stallybrass, Peter, and Allon White. *The Politics and Poetics of Transgression.* Ithaca: Cornell University Press, 1986.

Stansell, Christine. *City of Women: Sex and Class in New York, 1789–1860.* New York: Knopf, 1986.

Stanton, Elizabeth Cady, et al., eds. *History of Woman Suffrage.* Vol. 1, 1848–1861. New York: Arno Press, 1969.

Steele, Jeffrey, ed. Introduction to *The Essential Margaret Fuller.* New Brunswick, N.J.: Rutgers University Press, 1992.

Story, Ronald. *The Forging of an Aristocracy: Harvard and the Boston Upper Class, 1800–1870.* Middletown, Conn.: Wesleyan University Press, 1980.

Stowe, Charles Edward, and Lyman Beecher Stowe. *Harriet Beecher Stowe: The Story of Her Life.* Boston: Houghton Mifflin, 1911.

Stowe, Charles Edward. *Life of Harriet Beecher Stowe, Compiled from Her Letters and Journals.* Boston: Houghton, Mifflin, 1890.

Stowe, Harriet Beecher. "Catharine E. Beecher." In *Our Famous Women,* edited by Harriet Beecher Stowe, et al. Hartford, Conn.: A.D. Worthington, 1884.

———. *The Mayflower; or, Sketches of Scenes and Characters Among the Descendants of the Pilgrims.* New York: Harpers, 1844.

Stowe, Lyman Beecher. *Saints, Sinners, and Beechers.* Indianapolis: Bobbs-Merrill, 1934.

Takaki, Ronald. *Strangers from a Different Shore: A History of Asian Americans.* New York: Penguin, 1989.

Tonkovich, Nicole. "Advice Books." *Oxford Companion to Women's Writing in the United States.* New York: Oxford University Press, 1995.

———. "Rhetorical Power in the Victorian Parlor: *Godey's Lady's Book* and the Gendering of Nineteenth-Century Rhetoric." In *Oratorical Culture in Nineteenth-Century America: Transformations in the Theory and Practice of Rhetoric,* edited by Gregory Clark and S. Michael Halloran. Carbondale: Southern Illinois University Press, 1993.

———. "Traveling in the West, Writing in the Library: Margaret Fuller's *Summer on the Lakes.*" *Legacy* 10, no. 2 (1993): 79–102.

———. "Writing in Circles: Harriet Beecher Stowe, the Semi-Colon Club, and Women's Literary Culture." In *Nineteenth-Century Women Learn to Write,* edited by Catherine Hobbs. Charlottesville: University Press of Virginia, 1995.

Tucker, Louis L. "The Semicolon Club of Cincinnati." *Ohio History* 73, no. 1 (1964): 13–26, 57–58.

Vanderpoel, Emily Noyes. *Chronicles of a Pioneer School from 1792 to 1833, Being the History of Miss Sarah Pierce and Her Litchfield School.* Cambridge, Mass.: University Press, 1903.

———. *More Chronicles of a Pioneer School from 1792 to 1833, being Added History of the Litchfield Academy Kept by Miss Sarah Pierce and her Nephew, John Pierce Brace.* New York: Cadmus Book Shop, 1927.

van Why, Joseph S. "Introduction." *The American Woman's Home.* 1869. Reprint, Hartford: Stowe-Day Foundation, 1991.

Vicinus, Martha. "Distance and Desire: English Boarding-School Friendships." In *The Lesbian Issue,* edited by Estelle B. Freedman et al. Chicago: University of Chicago Press, 1982.

———. *Independent Women: Work and Community for Single Women, 1850–1920.* Chicago: University of Chicago Press, 1985.

Vinovskis, Maris A., and Richard M. Bernard. "Beyond Catharine Beecher: Female Education in the Antebellum Period." *Signs* 3 (1978): 856–69.

von Frank, Albert J. "Sarah Pierce and the Poetic Origins of Utopian Feminism in America." *Prospects* 14 (1989): 45–63.

Walker, Nancy A. *Fanny Fern.* New York: Twayne, 1993.

Warbasse, Elizabeth Bowles. *The Changing Legal Rights of Married Women, 1800–1861.* New York: Garland, 1987.

Warren, Joyce W. *Fanny Fern: An Independent Woman.* New Brunswick, N.J.: Rutgers University Press, 1992.

———. "Introduction." *Ruth Hall and Other Writings,* by Fanny Fern. New Brunswick, N.J.: Rutgers University Press, 1986.

Welter, Barbara. "The Cult of True Womanhood: 1820–1860." *American Quarterly* 18 (1966): 151–74.

——. *Dimity Convictions: The American Woman in the Nineteenth Century.* Athens: Ohio University Press, 1976.

White, Barbara A. "Pioneering Women and the New Hampshire Image: Sarah Josepha Hale, Marilla Ricker, and Grace Metalious." In *The New Hampshire Image: As We and Others See Us.* Concord: Friends of the Humanities in New Hampshire, 1985.

Williams, Raymond. *The Long Revolution.* New York: Columbia University Press, 1961.

Wishy, Bernard. *The Child and the Republic.* Philadelphia: University of Pennsylvania Press, 1968.

Wood, Mary E. " 'With Ready Eye': Margaret Fuller and Lesbianism in Nineteenth-Century American Literature." *American Literature* 65, no. 1 (Mar. 1993): 1–18.

Wright, Richardson. *Forgotten Ladies: Nine Portraits from the American Family Album.* Philadelphia: Lippincott, 1928.

Index

CPSIA information can be obtained at www.ICGtesting.com
Printed in the USA
LVOW12s0918090814

398051LV00001B/97/P